Food on Foot

The Food on the Go Series

Series Editor
Ken Albala, University of the Pacific, kalbala@pacific.edu

The volumes in this series explore the fascinating ways people eat while getting from one place to another and the adaptations they make in terms of food choices, cutlery and even manners. Whether it be crossing the Atlantic in grand style on a luxury steamship, wedged into an airplane seat with a tiny tray, or driving in your car with a Big Mac in hand and soda in the cup holder, food has adapted in remarkable ways to accommodate our peripatetic habits. Eating on the go may be elegant or fast, but it differs significantly from everyday eating and these books explain why in various cultures across the globe and through history. This is the first series to systematically examine how and why mobility influences our eating habits, for better and worse.

Books in the Series

Food on the Rails: The Golden Era of Railroad Dining, Jeri Quinzio (R&L, 2014)

Food at Sea: Shipboard Cuisine from Ancient to Modern Times, Simon Spalding (R&L, 2014)

Food in the Air and Space: The Surprising History of Food and Drink in the Skies, Richard Foss (R&L, 2014)

Food on Foot: A History of Eating on Trails and in the Wild, Demet Güzey (R&L, 2017)

Food on Foot

A History of Eating on Trails and in the Wild

DEMET GÜZEY

ROWMAN & LITTLEFIELD
Lanham • Boulder • New York • London

Published by Rowman & Littlefield
A wholly owned subsidiary of The Rowman & Littlefield Publishing Group, Inc.
4501 Forbes Boulevard, Suite 200, Lanham, Maryland 20706
www.rowman.com

Unit A, Whitacre Mews, 26-34 Stannary Street, London SE11 4AB

British Library Cataloguing in Publication Information Available

Library of Congress Cataloging-in-Publication Data
Names: Güzey, Demet, author.
Title: Food on foot : a history of eating on trails or in the wild / Demet Güzey.
Description: Lanham : Rowman & Littlefield, [2017] | Series: Food on the go |
Includes bibliographical references and index.
Identifiers: LCCN 2016041844 (print) | LCCN 2016051218 (ebook) |
ISBN 9781442255067 (cloth : alk. paper) | ISBN 9781442255074 (Electronic)
Subjects: LCSH: Wild foods. | Food habits—History. | Outdoor recreation—History. |
Survival—History.
Classification: LCC TX369 .G89 2017 (print) | LCC TX369 (ebook) | DDC
394.1/209—dc23
LC record available at https://lccn.loc.gov/2016041844

∞™ The paper used in this publication meets the minimum requirements of
American National Standard for Information Sciences—Permanence of Paper for
Printed Library Materials, ANSI/NISO Z39.48-1992.

Printed in the United States of America

Contents

Food on the Go, Series Foreword

How familiar is the lament? "No one sits down to eat any more! People just grab something on the street or at the drive through. That's not a proper meal; it's just noshing on the way from one place to another." Food on the move is nothing new. There has always been street food and fast food. People have always eaten in transit. Our tendency to dismiss such meals as quick and convenient but never of any real gastronomic distinction does injustice to the wide variety of foods available to people travelling, and sometimes these meals could be quite elegant indeed. Think of the great caravans trekking across the steppes of Western Asia, parking their camels and setting up tents for a sumptuous feast of dried fruits, nuts, flatbreads and freshly roasted kebabs. Or think of the great age of early air travel when airlines had their own specially designed dishware and served elegant, if seat-tray-sized, meals prepared by trained chefs. Meals served on trains in the nineteenth century were among the most celebrated of their day and of course luxury cruises pride themselves on fine dining as an indispensable feature of the entire experience. Food truck fare, offered to pedestrians, has now become the cutting edge in hip cuisine.

Travelling food need not be grand though. Sometimes it merely supplies sustenance – the hikers trail mix or high protein pemmican to sustain the intrepid hunter on the great plains. It can also be pretty rough if we think of the war time C-Rations or hard tack and rum given to sailors in the colonial era. It seems as if some modes of transport have their own repertoire of foods, without which the trip would not be complete. What's a road trip without chips and junk food? Is there anyone who doesn't miss the little packs of salty peanuts on domestic flights? Travelling food also poses its own unique set of challenges, both for food preparation and consumption. Imagine stoking a fire on a wooden ship! Or flipping an omelet while the train rumbles violently over the tracks. Hand held food, perhaps the way of the future, is the quintessential traveling format, but so too are special styrafoam containers and sporks, not to mention the leather bota, aluminum canteen or plastic water bottle. Traveling food has its own etiquette as well, looser than the dining table, but interestingly quite private, perhaps intentionally in considering the public setting.

When I first thought of this series I don't think I had ever thought through how many foods are specially designed for travel, or how complex and very culturally bound food eaten on trains, planes, cars, bikes, horseback, etc. can be. I will never forget a long train ride I took from Rome to the Tyrolean Alps. A young family sat across from me and they were well stocked with goods. Out came a salami, a loaf of bread, a hunk of cheese, a bottle of wine. They were making a mess, gesticulating wildly, chattering in Italian. It all looked delicious, and they savored every morsel. By the time we approached the German-speaking region, they had neatened themselves up, tidied the area, switched languages and every trace of their Italian repast was gone, and would have been completely unseemly, I think, that far north. That is, people do have explicit gastronomic traditions for travel that are as bound up with nationhood, class, gender and self as any other eating habit. So it is about time we thought of these kinds of meals as a separate genre, and this series I hope will fill the gap in our understanding of why we eat what we do on the move.

Ken Albala, University of the Pacific

Acknowledgments

The idea, or rather my idea, for this book started to shape while I was trekking in northern India, in the geographically isolated mountains of Ladakh, with our Everest guide friend Jamie McGuiness, six other like-minded travelers, more than twenty horses, two expedition cooks and their helpers, and a mobile kitchen. I wanted to write about the food culture in the mountain and trekking expeditions, as I was fascinated by the planning of food and the self-sufficiency of cooks, exceeding expectations to produce tasty food for everyone's wishes, despite difficulties of finding water and working in a kitchen tent. They provided more than sustenance; they cooked up joy and comfort day-in day-out, squeezed in a dining tent above 4,000 meters. I was also intrigued by the culture of planning, carrying, preparing, and sharing of food in other hikes and expeditions, because no matter where one went and how technical or leisurely the travel was, to the wilderness everyone brought his or her own food, eating habits, and judgments on what is good to eat.

As the idea expanded to food on foot and trails other than those in the mountains, I was challenged to trespass across geographies, histories, and inevitably the philosophies of walking and eating. Luckily, in the wilderness of culinary research, many people guided me with their help, suggestions, and discussions by recounting their own experiences and by connecting me to other adventurers, explorers, and experts. I am grateful to have tiptoed in this special world even as an observer.

First of all, I must thank the library archivists I talked to. My appreciation for their work has multiplied after researching for this book. I am especially grateful for The Alpine Club for allowing access to journals and books, and for the discussions with librarian Tadeusz Hudowski and honorary archivist Glynn Hughes. The Royal Geographical Society Archives department helped me tremendously in finding relevant books, journals, and images, and for allowing me to see (but not touch) the astonishing artifacts from historical polar and Everest expeditions.

For the images used throughout the book, I am thankful to Susan Hare from the Alpine Club, Jamie Owen from the Royal Geographical Society, Emily Dean from the Imperial War Museum, Jacquelyn Wilson from the University of West Florida Historic Trust, Jasmine Rodgers from the Science and Society Picture Library, Becky Fullerton from the Appalachian Mountain Club, Keith Muir from the Colong Foundation for Wilderness, Philip Grover from the Pitts Rivers Museum, Jennifer Neal from the Brooklyn Museum, Gary Cohen and Maritza Chacacanta from PEAK destination management company, Paul Ward of Cool Antartica, Kenneth Koh, Jamling Bhote, Tom Ward, Hyun-Jung Kim, and Engin Özendes.

Many people gave me insights into old and new practices and shared with me their expertise in eating on their feet: Sierra Club Executive Deputy Director Bruce Hamilton; mountaineer Kenneth Koh; trekking guide Sherpa Gelbu Pemba Chawa; ultramarathon runners Marco Olmo, Raffaele Brattoli, and Alberto Tagliabue; food historian Silvano Serventi; desert explorer Michael Asher; and a walking library on Shikoku pilgrimage trail, Professor David Moreton.

I am in debt to the series editor Ken Albala; without his vision for the series and trust in me, I would not have started the book, and without his positive attitude and guidance, I would not have finished it. I would also like to thank Rowman & Littlefield editor Suzanne Staszak-Silva for her invaluable help in bringing the manuscript to publication.

Finally, I would like to thank Luca, my patient partner, for enjoying our endless discussions on trail foods and for sharing a passion for good food and a good laugh no matter under which conditions we eat.

Writing a book is like climbing a mountain. As you go up higher, you lose sight of the summit and there seems so much more to go. Yet you climb it little by little by putting one foot after the other. And once you get to the summit, you become dizzy from the thin air and the breathtaking view. Then, you come down, have a good meal, and plan another climb.

Introduction

"In the beginning was the foot," said the American anthropologist Marvin Harris.[1]

Humans stood erect and walked before they had consciousness or speech, about four million years ago. Walking is an elemental human movement. It is one of our infant development milestones, like eating solid foods. What sets us apart from other terrestrial mammals is that we have two hands and two feet with which we stand up and make, use, and carry tools and food. Walking enables us to take ourselves to places and bring things back to other people.

Historically, humans walked out of necessity, of social status and class. They then walked to explore landscapes, to discover the earth. Later people walked to discover their own limits, whether it was physical, moral, or spiritual. Food has always been the greatest companion of walks, out of necessity first and foremost, but also out of comfort and pleasure.

This book is about eating on foot during walks: big, small, daily, weekly, vertical, desert, military, and everyday walks. Walking in snow, on sand, on trail, walking to discover geographical boundaries as well as personal boundaries, walking to experience what is around us, and walking to arrive to a new place.

In this book, I aimed to look at what food means in our walks and how the meaning of walks are represented in our food. In my research and interviews, I was looking for a common thread, a food or a cooking tool that we always used, no matter where we walked. I read and listened to the stories of explorers, mountaineers, athletes, pilgrims, soldiers, and anyone who walks and eats. What I found was more profound than a common tool or a recipe. Tracing the common history of eating and walking on different geographies, I saw that what we eat changes the way we walk and why we walk changes what we eat on those walks. I found that people brought their food culture to where they went, especially when they wanted to control the environment, and some others instead took away the food culture of where they have been, especially when they wanted to be absorbed by their environment. It turned out to be just as interesting to ask *why* we eat while we are in transition on foot, as *what* we eat and *how*.

Only in the last hundred years of evolution do we see that in our daily lives we can get away without walking at all. In today's lifestyle in many developed countries, the function of walking has changed. We developed transportation tools that carry us. With this came the limitation of the need for walking. The transportation revolution has changed the way we use our body and mind while we are in transit. Walking for pleasure, to be able to drive but to choose to walk, has become a declaration of class. Today most of us walk when we feel like exercising, or when our step-counting bracelets remind us that we need to walk a bit more, despite our computer chair– and car seat–bound lifestyles.

As the way we view walking has changed, what we wear, eat, and do while we walk have all received a different meaning. Similarly, when we see walking as an activity to display resistance and optimize performance, food has a different meaning than when we walk to discover wilderness with no inhabitants but penguins and whales or when we visit a place with local people living in it.

Walking seems to be the most obscure thing in the world, something obvious and banal, unless it is attached to something bigger, like arriving somewhere for the first time. Walking can be ordinary but also extraordinary, depending on why, where, and when we walk, for the reward is measured by distance, conditions, obstacles, and rarity. Walking outdoors is also access to open space that is public and not owned. In this sense we are not only in movement away from home when we walk, but we are also walking away from private and from owning. For the sole walker, this brings a sense of adventure. For the organized walker (for example, in a club), this also means political empowerment of owning the public space. In either case, walking is and remains a statement, an act of culture, just as eating is.

CHAPTER 1

Food on Trails

When we travel on foot, we inevitably get hungry. We need to take or buy and replenish food to keep going. The food (and water) supply determines where and how far we go, how long we stay, and if and how we come back. Eating is elemental this way. Eating is also cultural, because we make choices of what we take and how we prepare it. No matter where we walk and how far, we take our food identity with us.

Going outside brings with it the need for convenient food. Before the invention of canning in the nineteenth century, food taken on trails was often food preserved usually for the winter months (e.g., dried or salted meat, which was light, ready to eat, and lasted a journey). Throughout the history of walking, we come across these convenience foods. The Chinese more than two thousand years ago used dried snake for their trips, while Indians took with them dried rice and dried bummelo fish known as Bombay Duck. For mountain journeys, Tibetans took a mixture of yak butter and tea leaves in a bamboo stick slung over the shoulder; when they stopped, they mixed the concoction and drank it. Pemmican was the preserved meat of American Indians. *Charqui* was the South American version of preserving meat, which was slaughtered after hunting. The meat was boned and defatted, cut into slices, and dipped in brine or rubbed with salt. It was then kept in the animal's hide for ten to twelve hours to absorb the salt and release its juices, and then hung in the sun to dry. It could be eaten like that or pounded and boiled. Homemade bread, cheese, and potted meat were rather fresher luxuries that could be taken along on a trail. American travelers took cornbread, which was called johnnycake, probably derived from journey cake.[1]

Nomads and people of native tribes, unlike travelers, were on trails constantly and had to find other food strategies such as hunting for birds and fishing, and foraging for fruits and plants. They hunted when they could, preserved it if they had enough, and supplemented this with foods that they collected. Outside of the subarctic, most foragers subsisted mainly on nuts, vegetables, fruits, and even protein-rich insects, because animals would be less likely to get. People of the Andes had coca leaves, which reduced fatigue and hunger, sharpened the mind, and helped against the altitude. Similarly, in West Africa locals were chewing on bitter and astringent cola nuts. Its caffeine helped digestion and kolanin was an invigorating stimulant. In India, chewing *paan* reduced hunger, anaesthetized the mouth, and sweetened the breath. This was a package of leaves from the betel nut, powdered lime, and *catechu* (a highly astringent, high tannin, red-brown substance from an infusion of acacia wood chips).[2] In anthropology, foraging on food is called pedestrian foraging, justifiably so, as pedestrian means a person traveling on foot. Australian Aborigines are one of the most well-known pedestrian foragers.

Agricultural societies instead had grains and animals from which they could produce and preserve a wide range of foods. For travelers from these societies, sustenance during a walk meant taking food along for the travel, mostly from home, and sometimes from the locals and nomads at the destination. Distance of travel on foot was determined by how much food could be carried and where the next village was to buy food from.

From a picnic to a hike, to backpacking, to expeditions packing food and cooking tools defined the journey. The decisions of which food to take and how much defied the limits to our indoor living and defined our wildest intentions.

Let us start with the picnic.

Taking Dining Rooms Outdoors

The picnic might be at the threshold of eating while walking, as it involves much of the former and too little of the latter. In forests, in parks, besides a lake, at the beach, picnic is the art of selecting a scenic spot for sharing a meal on a cloth laid down.

In general, picnics do not require cooking, although cooked and chilled foods are often taken as a picnic only lasts a few hours. M. F. K. Fisher describes in her *Pleasures of Picnics* (1957) that "a picnic must be outdoors and away from home," "it must be a simple feast, and the food, the best obtainable, should be prepared to be eaten with fingers."[3] Her favorite picnic food was a flat sandwich, "the railroad." The recipe was simply to split a sourdough baguette and hollow it, spread butter, fill it with slices of ham, wrap it in a cloth, and then sit on it until flat. This sitting around might have caused picnics to be considered no serious matter, because "it's no picnic" has become a colloquial term to define tougher situations, such as expeditions, military trips, and mountain climbs.

Although the name seems have come from French *pique-nique* from the seventeenth century, likely a name given to a gourmandise meal indoors, it was the British who turned the word into picnic and took it outside. In other names and forms, eating outside had already existed longer, such as in Spanish *merienda* and the Italian *merenda*. Picnic, as we know it, made its first appearance in arts in the late eighteenth century.[4] Paintings and literature of eating al fresco contributed to the romanticism of the Victorian era in the nineteenth century: enjoying the outdoors, playing some games, and perhaps playing music, only if desired. They all fed into the easy social code of picnic.

Picnickers in the Countryside Near Halifax. Halifax, c. 1910.
Science Museum London.

Simplicity was not in the vocabulary of the Victorian idea of a picnic. One of the earliest picnic foods, Scotch eggs, were invented in the 1730s. They were named after the word "scotched," meaning processed. People would take these on long-distance carriage journeys as well as to picnics. They are prepared by wrapping a hard-boiled egg in sausage meat and coating in bread crumbs and baking or deep-frying. Scotch eggs were also called "picnic eggs" as they are one of the favorite picnic foods in England, along with pork pies and pasta salads.

In the early nineteenth century, painters like Caspar David Friedrich painted landscapes that conveyed an emotional response in viewers toward nature. Typically, he set a person in a landscape in scale such as in the *Wanderer Above the Sea of Fog* and directed the viewer to the gaze of this person. His paintings proposed a romantic contemplation of nature, giving two messages at once, that the nature was powerful and exhilarating, and that humans could take a part in it with self-reflection and a potential for grandeur. The Romantic Movement was a reaction to the Industrial Revolution, which had started half a century earlier in England. As scientists rationalized nature, artists now romanticized it. This examination of nature in art fed into the romantic impetus to walk in nature in the first half of the nineteenth century.

Around the same time in literature, the beauty of the Lake District in the northeast of England inspired some of England's best-known writers. The Romantic poets William Wordsworth, Samuel Taylor Coleridge, and Robert Southey were known as the Lake Poets. The second generation of Romantic poets such as Shelley and John Keats were also attracted to the Lake District. Their work inspired their readers to visit the Lake District, which came to represent isolation and solitude. Although Byron was not fond of the Lake District per se, he had common characteristics with the other poets: individuality, aspiration, and escape from society. Wordsworth, who wrote a prose poem guide to the Lake District ("Guide to the Lakes") and embarked on an extended tour of France, Switzerland, and Germany, romanticized walking for pleasure and as a way to self-discovery.

Picnics were associated with abundant food and drinks (sandwiches, finger foods, fresh fruit, salads, hard-boiled eggs, cold meats, soft drinks, wine or champagne), relaxed attitude, and no restraint on time or place or the presence of a physical activity. Picnics were also for everybody, as they were for the animals in the children's novel *The Wind in the Willows* by Kenneth Grahame, first published in 1908. It celebrated the nature of pastoral England with the adventures and camaraderie of its characters[5]:

"Hold hard a minute, then!" said the Rat. He looped the painter through a ring in his landing-stage, climbed up into his hole above, and after a short interval reappeared staggering under a fat, wicker luncheon-basket. "Shove that under your feet," he observed to the Mole, as he passed it down into the boat. Then he untied the painter and took the sculls again. "What's inside it?" asked the Mole, wriggling with curiosity. "There's cold chicken inside it," replied the Rat briefly; "coldtonguecoldhamcoldbeefpickledgherkinssaladfrenchrollscresssandwiches-pottedmeatgingerbeerlemonadesodawater—" "O stop, stop," cried the Mole in ecstasies: "This is too much!" "Do you really think so?" enquired the Rat seriously. "It's only what I always take on these little excursions; and the other animals are always telling me that I'm a mean beast and cut it VERY fine!"

Traveler's Boswell

In 1773, English writer Samuel Johnson traveled through Scotland in eighty-three days and wrote a travel memoir about it. His travel companion James Boswell instead wrote about Samuel Johnson, which would later become his biography. They toured the Highlands and islands together, by boat, by carriage, on horses, and on foot. Their trip added to the romantic notion of traveling on unspoiled land. Johnson likened the desire of wandering to an "epidemic."

In his travel book, Johnson noted similarities of Scottish food to that of England and contemplated on what is good to eat: "It is not very easy to fix the principles upon which mankind have agreed to eat some animals, and reject others; and as the principle is not evident, it is not uniform. That which is selected as delicate in one country, is by its neighbours abhorred as loathsome."[6] For an example, in the islands there were eels but the locals did not find them wholesome to eat. He also wondered why locals did not transplant other spices and tea. As a keen observer, in Roasay he noted that the ground was fitter for cattle than for corn and that as there are no foxes they could have hares and rabbits. In Ulinish, he suggested that fishing could end the famine if only it could be done in stormy seas in the winter. His notes were scientific, critical, and moral. He described men swallowing a glass of whiskey (*skalk*) in the morning without being drunken and praises the Scottish breakfast: "a meal in which the Scots, whether of the lowlands or mountains, must be confessed to excel us. The tea and coffee are accompanied not only with butter, but with honey, conserves, and marmalades. If an epicure could remove by a wish, in quest of sensual gratifications, wherever he had supped he would breakfast in Scotland." Yet he is quick to bash them right after: "In the islands however, they do what I found it not very easy to endure. They pollute the tea-table by plates piled with large slices of cheshire cheese, which mingles its less grateful odours with the fragrance of the tea."[7]

"His Boswell" instead was impressed by Johnson; he was the perfect companion, a good friend, so much that his name entered the English language as Boswell, Boswellian, or Boswellism to refer to someone who is the ultimate companion, a devoted admirer, biographer. It is in the selfless observation of the journey, as in Boswell's accounts, that we find how Johnson the traveler ate. At the time, this way of writing a biography was considered very personal and unusual[8]:

> On Friday, April 14, being Good-Friday, I repaired to him in the morning, according to my usual custom on that day, and breakfasted with him. I observed that he fasted so very strictly, that he did not even taste bread, and took no milk with his tea; I suppose because it is a kind of animal food.

Seeding Conservation

In walking and eating, picnic was merely a point of departure. Leaving parks, lakes, and forests for a day and longer for motivations of admiring the nature farther away and longer or for seeking solitude brought people from picnicking to hiking. Leaving the conveniences behind meant either accepting conditions ahead or preparing with greater control. Naturalists and conservationists were of the opinion to enjoy nature in the simplest way without trying to control it.

Walking and conservation was the mission of a nurseryman who became a folk hero in America. This was Johnny Appleseed. He was often depicted barefoot, dressed in rough pants and a coffee sack with holes cut out for his head and arms, spreading apple seeds everywhere he went. His story became such a myth that one could nearly forget that he was a real man, John Chapman. Johnny represented wilderness at the start of the nineteenth century. He traveled with a horse-load full of apple seeds in leather bags in Pennsylvania, Ohio, and Indiana (known as the West at the time) and distributed apple seeds and built nurseries. He was against grafting (inserting tissues of one plant inside another to create more resistant and profitable cultivars). For this reason, journalist Michael Pollan claimed that his apples were not edible but instead good for cider and that he was raising the spirit of farmers, as "the American Dionysus."[9] To add to his pilgrim-like modest existence, Johnny was a Christian missionary. As he traveled to give away his seeds, he never took money but accepted old clothing or other items, such as the tin pot he wore as a cap. At homes that he visited, he never took place at a table and instead ate his bread with a bowl of milk outside. As legislator and writer John Hough James wrote about him in 1862, "In the use of food he was very abstemious, and one of my informants think that he used only vegetable diet."[10] Chapman's diet reflected his primitive Christian image. He ate honey, berries, fruit, cornmeal for mush, and milk, which recalls the locust and wild honey diet of John the Baptist.

According to an anecdote, a preacher was once holding a speech on a public square in Mansfield and exclaimed, "Where is the bare-footed Christian, travelling to heaven." Johnny raised his feet in the air and shouted: "Here he is!"[11]

Johnny Appleseed continued planting seeds until his death in 1845. He has become a patron saint for American horticulture and a loved personage in literature, poems, and songs, after the publication of a romantic account of his life posthumously in 1871.[12]

Around this time, another American naturalist walking on a lean diet became known as the advocate of nature preservation. This was John Muir.

John Muir—One Man's Search for Solitude in the Wild

Traveling alone into the backcountry of Yosemite, carrying "only a tin cup, a handful of tea, a loaf of bread, and a copy of Emerson,"[13] John Muir was fascinated by the grandiosity of nature as much as he was amazed by our limitations to survive in it with our needs for food. In his memoir *My First Summer in the Sierra*, based on Muir's original journals and sketches of his 1869 stay in the Sierras, he writes:

> We have been out of bread a few days, and begin to miss it more than seems reasonable, for we have plenty of meat and sugar and tea. Strange we should feel food-poor in so rich a wilderness. The Indians put us to shame, so do the squirrels,—starchy roots and seeds and ark in abundance, yet the failure of the meal sack disturbs our bodily balance, and threatens our best enjoyments.[14]

Muir was hired to supervise a San Joaquin sheep owner's flock at the headwaters of the Merced and Tulomne Rivers. He was in the mountains from June to September. In his journal, he described the flora and fauna of the mountains, his visits to Yosemite, his climbs to mountains. He was analytical and reflective about our needs and how they made us detached from nature. "Man seems to be the only animal whose food soils him, making necessary much washing and shield-like bibs and napkins."[15]

Muir admired the shepherds and mountain men for being easily satisfied with food. He described their food as being far from delicate: "beans, bread, bacon, mutton, dried peaches, and sometimes potatoes and onions." Potatoes and onions were "luxury on account of their weight as compared to their nourishment." However beans, he noted, are portable, wholesome, and capable of going far. He praised the Indians for being able to live on whatever comes their way in case of food scarcity: berries, roots, birds' eggs, grasshoppers, ants, wasps, bumblebee larvae.

John Muir got married at the age of forty-one in 1880 and took care of a fruit farm with his wife Louie Wanda Strentzel. In his biography, Miller and Morrison explain that despite the Spartan eating habits Muir displayed on trails and treks, privately he consumed a lot. His friend Mary Keith was amazed by Muir's diet of oatmeal, crackers, tea, and sugar in the roughest country for weeks. Keith wrote that Muir had a cultivated taste and interest in American and European food. He wrote that Muir would survive on little food during treks because of his gorging for several weeks when he returned to the restaurants of refined civilization.[16] Isn't this only revealing how we might possess many layers of food cultures within us, displaying different attitudes depending on where we are and why we eat?

Muir emphasized that his true home remained in the wilderness. "Home is the most dangerous place I ever go to," he once said. "As long as I camp out in the mountains, without tent or blankets, I get along very well; but the minute I get into a house and have a warm bed and begin to live on fine food, I get into a draft and the first thing I know I am coughing and sneezing and threatened with pneumonia, and all together miserable. Outdoors is the natural place for a man."[17] In the end, it was pneumonia that took the naturalist of the Sierras, "John of the mountains," away from the solitude he enjoyed in wilderness. He would surely prefer the forest floor to a hospital bed any day: "Gladly, if I could, I would live forever on pine buds, however full of turpentine and pitch, for the sake of this grand independence."[18]

In 1892, John Muir established the Sierra Club and gave his name and legacy to the John Muir Trail and the preservation of wildlife.

Supply and Resupply of Food on Hiking Trails

The John Muir trail, which runs in conjunction with the Pacific Crest trail in the western United States, is one of the most popular backpacking trails almost entirely on backcountry and wilderness. More than a thousand people hike its 215 miles each year, completing it in about three weeks. Another longer trail is the 2,168.1-mile Appalachian trail, which requires between five and seven months to complete; 80 percent of hikers who start do not complete it. Most of the people who complete it do it in pieces over years.

Some complete it in one go. The ones who complete it in one go are called "thru-hikers." To be a thru-hiker means perseverance, determination, discipline, and good planning. Good planning naturally means thorough food planning.

Food planning on the Appalachian trail includes organizing supplies packed in daily provisions and resupplies packed and shipped to resupply points in the hike. Planning the amount, variety, and choosing foods that are easy to prepare and clean up is key. Most hikers pack dehydrated dinners in sealable plastic freezer bags; they pour boiling water right into these bags, wait for the food to hydrate, and eat straight out of the bag. Dreaming about indulgent and unavailable food like pizza and beer yet fully enjoying the warming rehydrated meal and the simple idea that one can take care of oneself in the wilderness is the reward.

Breakfast favorites are oatmeal or grits, powdered milk, and breakfast cereals. A typical lunch may include crackers and cheese, or canned tuna with tortilla or pita bread. For dinner, the idea is to transform boiled water into a meal as quickly as possible. Some hikers take freeze-dried meals, some prepare their own pre-cooked and dehydrated meals, and most simply take instant meals such as soups and ramen noodles to eat every evening, despite what this means in the long run: boredom from food and desperation for variety in taste.

The biggest challenge of planning food for so many days is weight: the weight of food, its packaging, and the weight of fuel to boil water and to cook meals. For this reason, hikers prepare one-pot meals and take plenty of energy bars. This adds to the dullness. Hikers can purchase groceries and other supplies in towns along the trail, but the opportunity to resupply is limited. Many thru-hikers set up a series of mail drops, sending packages to themselves in predetermined towns along the route. These packages, on average, contain about a week's worth of food and supplies to last until the next town where one can resupply. Packages are delivered to towns or sometimes trailheads, where it is not uncommon nowadays to see bins of unwanted food free to take for other hikers. Because hikers get very sick of the food they take with them, they sometimes do not want the resupply pack of the same thing, another seven days of granola bars for breakfast, for example. When they can, they exchange supplies to break the routine. This regime of food planning, resupply, and exchange of information and food of hikers creates a certain food culture among the thru-hikers. There are many online forums and blogs where hikers exchange recipes for dehydrating their own food and tips on packing, portioning, and preserving food. Food is more than a practical necessity. It is a crucial part of the experience, as a representation of the hiker's identity, where he or she can showcase a sophistication of taste or planning or efficiency.

Packaging is another side of the story, not only for weight but also for waste. When trails are used by so many people, "leave no trace" is a philosophy that all hikers must abide. "People don't necessarily plan ahead and think about the full life cycle of the things they are carrying," says Bruce Hamilton, executive deputy director of the Sierra Club. "If you are responsible to carry out your garbage with you, then you are much more conscious of how much weight in excessive packaging you are taking." For backpacking trips, he prepares his own dehydrated meals and dehydrated sauces and salsa that he can easily mix into pasta or rice. He also takes chili peppers to spice up a meal. To have some trail comfort, every hiker has a different trick: "I have my little flask of whiskey that I take with me," says Hamilton. "I mix it with glacier water."

Hikers pack a lot of snacks to eat during their walk. Nibbling on nuts and dried fruits while walking is a typical pastime of a hiker. This calls for an investigation into the name trail mix.

Trail mix is considered an ideal snack food for hikes because it is lightweight, easy to store, and nutritious, providing a quick boost from the carbohydrates in the dried fruit and/or granola, and sustained energy from the mono- and polyunsaturated fats in nuts. Before trail mix was called trail mix, many nomad cultures were preparing their own versions. As they collected berries, nuts, and seeds, they mixed them with other high caloric food like dried meats. This was the basis of preservation and snacking on trails and in the wild. For example, pemmican is one of the first trail mixes, made by Native Americans.

An earlier version of the "Appalachian trail mix" was mentioned in *Hiking the Appalachian Trail* in 1975, although the preparation was completely different. The recipe called to mix two parts whole rice with one part barley and one part lentils, and to cook it for a full hour. For "pleasing results," it recommended to mix it with a half can of Spam.[19] Clearly this savory concoction was not as pleasing to pass the test of time, as today all trail mixes are sweet and made with nuts and dried fruits instead.

The name "original trail mix" was first claimed by the company Hadley Fruit Orchards in a US trademark, claiming its first use was in 1968, and commercialized in 1977. This trademark described trail mix as: "Snack food mix consisting primarily of raisins, processed sunflower seeds, processed pumpkin seeds, processed peanuts, processed cashews, processed almonds, soybean oil and/or cottonseed oil and/or canola oil and/or almond oil and salt."[20] Despite the commercial use in 1977, the term trail mix was used in various publications before that.

Gorp is another name for trail mix. The *Encyclopedia of American Food and Drink* defines gorp as "a mixture of dried fruit, seeds, nuts, and chocolate chips used as high-energy food for athletes, particularly hikers and mountain climbers, a meaning known in print since 1968."[21] Gorp is believed to stand for "good old raisins and peanuts." It can also stand for "granola, oats, raisins, and peanuts." The *Oxford English Dictionary* cites a possibility that gorp might refer to "to eat greedily" as a 1913 reference to the verb *gawp up*.[22]

In Canada, trail mix is known as Pink Buggie, which has its origins from a brand of trail mix made by the Kyle Hancock franchise, which only uses pink smarties. In New Zealand and Australia, it is known as *scroggin*, which may be an acronym, taken from the first letter of eight ingredients: sultanas, chocolate, raisins, orange peel, ginger, glucose (sugar), improvisation or imagination (i.e., the chef is supposed to add a favorite ingredient), and nuts. Scroggin was taken as a snack by Australian bushwalkers (which we will see later). Although there is an ongoing battle between New Zealand and Australia on who used the term first, Australians claim the word since early 1980s, but the New Zealanders have evidence for it from 1940.[23]

Making scroggin can be tricky because it is no ordinary trail mix. Here is a recipe for this mostly sweet trail treat.[24]

Scroggin
Ingredients (for 4 cups):
½ cup sultanas
½ cup chocolate chips
½ cup raisins
½ cup candied orange rind
½ cup crystallized ginger
½ cup roasted unsalted nuts
½ cup liquid glucose
½ any other seed or dried fruit
Directions:
Mix together all ingredients.
Add other ingredients you like, as long as they are in lesser amounts.

Campsite Classics

One of the first guides for camping was written by John M. Gould, an infantryman with the Union Army. As a soldier, he knew all about camping. He wrote down all that he knew in a book, where he gave practical tips on how to organize the camp, what to wear, and what to eat and how to eat it. Gould started by saying that in open air the appetite is so good and to make your own meals is so pleasurable that one finds that whatever may be cooked is excellent. According to him, the essentials of a camp cook were a frying pan and a coffeepot, "even if you had to carry it on your back."[25] He was ahead of his time, seeing an era when people would hike and camp for fun.

In fact, the first recreational camp started in the 1860s with The Gunnery Boarding School, followed by the Young Women's Christian Association and the Young Men's Christian Association in the late nineteenth century. The Boy's Club, Boy Scouts, and Girl Scouts built camps in the early twentieth century. In the 1930s, the National Park Service developed recreational areas and campgrounds, which dramatically increased the popularity of camping. Still, for most people, camping was defined within the boundaries of a club or an organization, and done in a settled camp.

Gould recounted how in the army he was baking meat in an iron pot under ashes overnight to get even the toughest meat to soften. In his pages, we find a recipe for baked beans.

> The beans are first parboiled in one or two waters until the outside skin begins to crack. They are then put into the baking-pot, and salt pork at the rate of a pound to a quart and a half of dry beans is placed just under the surface of the beans. The rind of the pork should be gashed so that it will cut easily after baking. Two or three tablespoonful of molasses are put in, and a little salt, unless the pork is considerably lean. Water enough is added to cover the beans.
>
> A hole three feet or more deep is dug in the ground, and heated for an hour by a good hot fire. The coals are then shoveled out, and the pot put in the hole, and immediately buried by throwing back the coals, and covering all with dry earth. In this condition they are left to bake all night.[26]

Girl Scouts had also made many recommendations about which foods to take along and how to prepare them in their larder (supply) in the booklet *Tramping and Trailing with the Girl Scouts*. Although many of their recipes had catchy names such as galloping guinea pig, spotted dog, and *ring tum diddy*, one simple recipe caught attention: some more. It was a dessert consisting usually of toasted marshmallow and pieces of chocolate bar sandwiched between two graham crackers.[27] This was a quick fix with cookies, which became an iconic campfire food known as s'mores, instantly popular in the United States and Canada.

This recipe truly reflects the cheerful attitude and the joyous feeling Girl Scouts had on having the soft turf under foot and smelling the fragrant wood fire.

Some More

Ingredients (for 8 sandwiches):

16 graham crackers

8 bars of plain chocolate

16 marshmallows

Directions:

Toast two marshmallows over the coals to a crisp gooey state and then put them each inside a graham cracker and make a sandwich with the chocolate in the middle. Wait until the heat of the marshmallow melts the chocolate a bit, then enjoy. You would want some more, although the Girl Scouts suggest that one is really enough.[28]

A group from the AMC's Cold River Camp in North Chatham, New Hampshire. 1930s. Appalachian Mountain Club.

In the early 1900s, when hiking and camping were combined in one activity, a new term was coined for it: backpacking. A backpacker had to spend nights sleeping outdoors and used what he or she carried in his or her backpack. The official history of backpacking in the United States began in 1920 with Lloyd F. Nelson's invention of the camping backpack. Nelson fashioned a rigid *pack board*, which gave structure to the backpack and made it easier to carry for a long time. Before this time, army soldiers and hikers alike were using a rucksack, which was a loose sack with shoulder straps. After two world wars, people started to go into nature for the sole purpose of enjoyment. The National Scenic Trail Act in the United States proposed by President Lyndon Johnson in 1965 made trails more accessible. At the end of the 1960s, when the National Trail System was created, the interest in trekking boomed. As part of the national trail system, huts were built along trails where backpackers could sleep and later also eat.

Nowadays, backpackers can camp out but also stay in huts. Huts have a fairly standardized weekly menu; most of the dry goods for the season are flown in via helicopter in the spring, and planning for the amount of fresh foods to be carried in by the hut crews are tied to reservations for any given day with some estimation of potential changes in the number of people staying at the huts on any given night. The supply of food to the huts in the Alps is rather similar. It was not always the case.

In the nineteenth century, Alpine huts were reserved for "serious" mountain expeditions. They were mostly simple and ranged from lean-tos and shelters to a structure with a stove and a table. They were owned and operated by various alpine clubs. Over time, huts added kitchens and separate rooms. They started becoming attractive for tourists as well as mountaineers as they provided an escape from city life and had the looks of a countryside cottage with the amenities. Before World War I, the alpine huts were open to all visitors, offering limited food and primitive lodging. As more and more tourists arrived, the menu expanded, alcoholic drinks were served, and individual rooms could be rented. After World War I, new alpine club policies attempted to limit non-mountaineers by charging them higher fees. New huts, which were constructed after, were more spartan, and sleeping was on mattresses in communal rooms; the hut experience has become more primitive once more. What has not turned back, however, is the type of food they served. Meals of typical mountain dishes based on pasta, polenta, cheese, local cold cuts, and sausages have stayed as part of the nourishing menu, as well as beers and wines. Thousands of huts today make even the more difficult mountaineering in the Alps a day trip, supporting the alpine style for its speed and simplicity. The price of hut food and drink is very expensive, as they are often carried into these huts by helicopters or trekked up by the hut owners.

When the notion of carrying a camp stove, food, and utensils became something of the past, food on alpine climbs became an object of habits and comfort, as hut meals are supplemented with energy bars, nuts, chocolate, or some mountain cheese, whatever the mountaineer is used to eating at altitude with appetite. In the next chapter, we will see the fate of walks into new lands with no huts and food drop points.

CHAPTER 2

Walking in a New Continent

When people started walking in a new continent with no trails to follow, the real adventure began, and so did the stories of starvation and suffering. Any walk that was heroic included the possibility to die while trying, especially in hindsight.

The American South

In late May 1539, Hernando de Soto landed on what is now the west coast of Florida in the southeastern United States, with six hundred men, troops, servants, and staff, two hundred horses, and a pack of dogs. He was sent by the king of Spain to explore and settle the new continent. The king wanted him to start a Spanish colony. De Soto instead wanted to find a rich kingdom of native people, as he previously did while exploring Peru. They would spend the next four years traveling over 4,000 miles.

By the first spring, most of their supplies were consumed. De Soto ill-treated and enslaved the natives he encountered and seized any valuables and food they had. In October 1540, however, the tables were turned when a confederation of Indians attacked the Spaniards in present-day Alabama. All the Indians and twenty of De Soto's men were killed. Several hundred Spaniards were wounded. At this point, De Soto had the option to march south to meet with his ships along the Gulf Coast, but instead he continued northwestward in search of America's riches. In May 1541, his army reached and crossed the Mississippi River, probably the first Europeans ever to do so. From there, they traveled through Arkansas and Louisiana, still with few material gains to show for their efforts. Turning back to the Mississippi, De Soto died of a fever on its banks on May 21, 1542. The Spaniards, now under the command of Luis de Moscoso, traveled west again, crossing into north Texas before returning to the Mississippi.

De Soto and his men never found the gold and silver they desired, but only a collection of pearls in the present-day state of Georgia. Their journey was very important, however, for the exchange of other goods. Many of the things they brought from Spain did not exist in North America at the time. Horses, dogs, and pigs were new to the continent, as were European diseases. In exchange for this, they had found themselves in a new continent with unrecognizable plants. After they ran out of food, they started chewing on what they could find, catch, or steal. The race for gold turned into a race for food. Their journey map was convoluted and took turns depending on which tribes they found and where these tribes sent them next, with the promise of more food and supplies. In their travel notes, we see what they ate and what they learned to eat, such as "roots roasted and others boiled with salt," which could have been the arrowhead or swamp potatoes, or it may have been the roots of the American lotus. In July 1539, they came across cabbage palms and ate their hearts. They also ate young corn stalks and corn on the cob. There was the product of the *coonti* (also called Florida arrowroot), which the Indians alone knew how to prepare. When a Spaniard had eaten one of the raw roots, he died. In August as they traveled northwards, they had beans grown by the Indians. They ate chestnuts from trees that grew only two palms high. They ate maize, kidney beans, plums, and pumpkins (which were more savory than European ones). They also gathered and ate grain coarse millet, but their main starchy food was corn, either roasted green in the husk, boiled on the cob, pounded green for a porridge, or boiled with beans for *frijoles*. They drank a beverage made from the leaves of a tree they called *sassafras* (main ingredient of root beer). By the next spring, they found mulberries, strawberries, blackberries, and even romance. They enjoyed seeing countless roses at the sides of the trails. Coming into what is now east Tennessee, they entered a land of milk and honey. There was hickory nut milk, honey, and calabash gourd. They made oil for cooking from hickory nuts and bear fat. When they bore south again, they found grapes. In the winter of 1540 in today's Mississippi, there were small and sour plums, wild sweet potatoes, and sunflower seeds, acorns, and walnuts. Next fall, they found salt, Jerusalem artichokes, and persimmons.[1]

After they reached Mississippi for the second time, with nearly half of the original expedition dead, the Spaniards built rafts and traveled down the river to the sea, and then made their way down the Texas coast to New Spain, finally reaching Veracruz, Mexico, in late 1543. All in all, they had spent four years on the early American diet, which was then mostly vegetarian.

Donner Party

In the height of immigration to the American west, in 1846, two families with their children and servants, thirty-two people in total, left Springfield, Ohio, with caravans and great hopes. The distance was 2,500 miles and would take four months. That season, seven thousand wagons left with the same goal. However, only a few families like George Donner and James F. Reed were guided by a book *The Emigrant's Guide to Oregon and California* by Lansford Hastings. Hastings's book not only painted California as a second Eden but also gave a cutoff for caravans to follow, which should shorten the time of travel and ensure that the party could get to California before the winter. Their plan sounded too good to be true, as unknown to the party was the fact that Hastings had not taken his route himself with wagons. They would make one of the most bizarre tragedies in American migration history.

Their journey began with plenty of flour for bread, meat, and water. They took 150 pounds of flour and 75 pounds of meat for each person. There was rice, beans, and cornmeal. They had cattle for butter and milk. Early on, they joined another group of wagons, and several other families joined them along the way. The party became eighty-seven people as they approached Hastings's cutoff. Soon after, the terrain became rugged, water they found on the way was foul, and their cattle could not find green grass to eat. They continued on foot to relieve animals from their load. This route was slower and more difficult than hoped, and there was tension in the large group. In October, when Reed killed a party member during a fight, he was sent away as a punishment. By November, the settlers reached the Sierra Nevada but became trapped by a snowfall high in the mountains. Families settled in cabins they found from the previous year's pioneers. As their food supplies finished, they ate the carcasses of dead cattle, which did not last long. Desperation grew; life was miserable. Soon, they started eating a jelly made by boiling strips of oxhide that was used on their roof and as rugs for the winter. They also made a soup from boiled ox and horse bones.[2]

The party formed various small groups to attempt crossing the mountain on foot but most of them failed; they turned around, got lost, or died. Some of the survivors stumbled into a *Miwok* Native American camp. The *Miwoks* gave them acorns, grass, and pine nuts to eat. Back in the cabins, the only food that could still be found was mice. At this point, something contro-versial happened. Something that the group would not admit to years after. They began eating the flesh of those who died. When rescuers from Califor-nia were able to reach the party, it was February of the following year. At the camp, they only found a disheveled man, Lewis Keseberg. Although all other survivors denied having taken part in cannibalism, Keseberg admitted eating human flesh when he was confronted with death by starvation. "When my provisions gave out, I remained four days before I could taste human flesh. There was no other resort—it was that or death. . . . I cannot describe the unutterable repugnance with which I tasted the first mouthful of flesh."[3]

In the four months of entrapment and the fight to survive, thirty-nine people perished. Emigration to the American West decreased in the follow-ing years, mainly because of the Mexican-American War rather than the disastrous end of the Donner party. Nonetheless, their story became a man-ifestation of the boundaries of the human condition and food. It has been long accepted that cannibalism occurred at what is now called Donner Lake, but the descendants of the Donner family denied having had to eat human flesh before they left the lake to start their life in the fertile California land.[4]

Nardoo—Rewards and Dangers of Botany

George Bouchier Worgan, the naval surgeon that accompanied the first fleet in 1788, was the first settler who entered the Australian wilderness for discovery; he kept a journal of the first years of the colonization. He sent his experiences in letters to his brother Dick back in England. Historian Melissa Harper argued that even though Worgan's purpose was not leisure but work, because he had to look for productive and fertile land to settle, like all the British who came to Australia, he brought with himself the cultural heritage to walk for leisure.[5] In the 1780s, walking had become a mode of relaxation, as the romantic taste for scenery started to take over the image of walking because of being poor. Walking became a time for thinking, observing, reflection, and philosophy.

When crossing the continent became the objective of walking, rather than leisure, walking to find food changed to bringing food to support the walk. As Australia had no native animals that could carry a human, coloni-zation required settlers to walk into the bush. In 1838, only six horses landed on the island with the first fleet. Explorers did not use camels until 1846. Going on foot was the main type of transport, a mode of discovery. The exploration on foot severely limited the quantity of supplies that could be taken over the rough country.

Long before the British came to Australia, Aboriginal people crossed the country on foot as a way of living, forging tracks and going where the food was according to the season. Also as teenagers they went walkabout as a rite of passage, where they walked across the land to survive and to learn self-sufficiency to enter adulthood. They could recognize and forage for plants, preparing them in the right way, unlike the colonialists who entered the land on foot, high on hopes and low on experience.

In the mid-nineteenth century, the interior of Australia was a ghastly blank, an empty space to fill in maps. After the gold rush, Victoria in New South Wales had become the richest colony in Australia. They were looking for projects to fund, such as a south to north crossing of Australia. With support from the Royal Society of Victoria, Robert O'Hara Burke, an Irishman (who was a captain in the Austrian army, and after immigrating to Australia, an inspector in the Victoria police force) led an expedition with nineteen men on a journey out of Melbourne with the aim to be the first people to cross the continent from south to north. It was August 1860. They would investigate a 2,000-mile (around 3,250 kilometers) distance to find a route for a railway line or a route that would connect the newly invented telegraph line to Europe, via Java. At first, his second in command was G. J. Landells, who came to Australia in charge of the camels imported from India. Long before they set off on their journey, Burke and Landells quarreled, after which Landells resigned and returned to Melbourne. William John Wills (a surveyor) was then appointed second by Burke, and William Wright, who was supposed to be acquainted with the locality they were approaching, was engaged as third, another most unfortunate selection. Next to them there were Dr. Hermann Beckler, medical officer and botanist, and Dr. Ludwig Becker, artist, naturalist, and geologist, ten assistants, and three camel drivers.[6] What they went through has become an Australian outback legend.

They left Melbourne in winter, with twenty-six camels, twenty-three horses, six wagons, and supplies to last two years. Instead of taking cattle to be slaughtered during the trip, the expedition committee decided to take dried meat. The provisions included pemmican, salted pork, bacon, meat biscuits, potted meats, mutton, vegetables, flour, rice, sugar, salt, pepper, tea, coffee, chocolate, ghee, butter, captain's biscuits, lime juice, vinegar, mustard, ginger, dried apples, raisins, currants, and dates.[7]

Due to bad weather and this additional weight, the progress was slow. The party arrived at Menindee on the Darling River, where Wright joined them. Here Burke decided to split the party to advance faster and on October 19, 1860, he took Wills, six men, five horses, and sixteen camels and left Menindee for Cooper's Creek. Wright took charge of the main body waiting

at Menindee. They arrived at Cooper's Creek on November 11 and established a depot camp to wait for the rest of the party. Burke was too anxious
to wait and divided the party once more and took Wills and two other men,
Charles Gray and John King, and pushed on to the north coast on December
16 with six camels and a horse. He instructed the rest of the party to wait for
them at Cooper's Creek for three months. All this party splitting left them
with no botanist, geologist, naturalist, experience in bushcraft, or any of the
equipment purchased for the trip. Nonetheless, Burke pushed forward with
the other three men. When they arrived at a swampland, this stopped them
from reaching the northern coastline. By this stage, they were desperately
short of supplies, and they decided to turn around to meet the rest of the
party in Cooper's Creek.

On the return journey, lack of food and luck made them desperate. When
Gray became ill and took some extra flour to make a little gruel (a thin porridge), he was blamed and they had a big argument. A few days afterward,
Wills wrote in his diary that they had to halt and send back for Gray, who
was "gammoning" that he could not walk. Nine days afterwards, the unfortunate man died.

The story got even gloomier when they reached the depot at Cooper's
Creek on April 21, 1861, after the date they promised to be there, and found
it had been abandoned. The word "DIG" was carved on a tree. Dig they did,
and found a welcome store of provisions and a letter stating that the party
had left just on that day. Unable to move fast, they decided to not follow the
path where they came from but to follow the creek down to Mount Hopeless
in South Australia. They left a note on the dig tree and covered it well.
On their journey down south when they lost both of their camels, all they
could do was dry their meat and eat it. Giving up hope in arriving at Mount
Hopeless, they had to backtrack to Cooper's Creek. Wills visited the depot
to check if anyone had arrived but saw no sign. However, in the meantime,
Brahe and Wright had visited the place and found no sign of their return, as
Burke had covered the note too well, and had ridden away concluding that
they had not yet come back.

The three men were lost in flat country among sand hills with little
johnnycake (flat corn bread) and dried meat to survive on. By this time, all
of them suffered from symptoms of scurvy, sore gums, swollen ankles, and
were feeling weak. They tried to live like the Aborigines but found it very
hard. They tried hunting, often unsuccessfully. Once they were offered fish
and nardoo cakes by the Yantruwanta Aborigines, and they gladly accepted it.
This plant could help them survive. Nardoo was a desert clover fern. Its seeds
inside the spore case were like watermelon seeds and satisfied their hunger.

They searched for the plant themselves and began preparing their own *nardoo*, as they had seen the local people do: collecting its seeds and grinding and mixing them with water to make a thin paste like porridge. Despite eating up to "four or five pounds a day between us," as Wills noted in his journal, the two explorers grew weaker and thinner and developed symptoms such as shaking legs and a gradually slowing pulse. On Wednesday, June 12, 1861, Wills wrote, "King out collecting *nardoo*. Mr. Bourke and I at home, pounding and cleaning. I still feel myself, if anything, weaker in the legs, although the *nardoo* appears to be more thoroughly digested." Wills couldn't understand why he seemed to be starving, despite eating so much *nardoo*.

What Wills didn't know was that *nardoo* contained an enzyme called thiaminase that broke down thiamine (vitamin B1), making it unavailable to the body. Thiamine, although needed in only tiny amounts, is essential for energy metabolism and nerve and brain function. Day by day, they experienced the signs of beriberi disease, tremors of the hands, feet, and legs, and an incredible weakness, all despite seemingly eating enough. Day by day, the men slowly starved to death.

Nardoo, however, was an important food source to Aboriginal people. What Burke and Wills had not seen is that the Aboriginals would roast the spore cases (sporocarps) before grinding them. This simple step of heating would break down the thiaminase, making it harmless. Perhaps if Burke and Wills had watched the locals more carefully, they might have survived to become the first white men to cross the continent from south to north. *Nardoo* plant, which resembles a four-leaf clover, did not bring luck to the expedition.

At last, Burke and King decided to go up the creek to find the main camp of the natives and obtain food from them on June 26. Wills, who was now too weak to move, was left lying under some boughs, with an eight-day supply of *nardoo* and water, the others trusting that within that period they would have returned to him. In his last journal entry, four days before he died, Wills wrote: "Mr. Burke suffers greatly from cold and is getting extremely weak. Nothing now but the greatest good luck can save any of us. Starvation on *nardoo* is by no means very unpleasant but for the weakness one feels, and the utter inability to move one's self, for as far as appetite is concerned, it gives me the greatest satisfaction, certainly fat and sugar would be more to one's taste, in fact those seem to me to be the great stand by for one in this extraordinary continent, not that I mean to depreciate the farinaceous food, but the want of sugar and fat in all substances obtainable here is so great that they can become almost valueless to us as articles of food, without the addition of something else."

Burke and King did not make it far either. After Burke died, King continued and found deserted campgrounds of the natives and buried *nardoo*. He shot crows and managed to not starve. Then he returned to the spot where they had left Wills and found him dead. He left to search for the natives, who they had not seen for three weeks. Fortunately, he found them, and they helped him to live. "They appeared to feel great compassion for me when they understood that I was alone on the creek, and gave me plenty to eat."[8] He stayed with them by proving to be good at shooting crows or hawks, and in exchange received fish and *nardoo* cakes, until on September 15 he was rescued by Howitt's party sent from Melbourne in search of the missing men. Although several relief expeditions were sent out before that, none were successful in locating him. Seven men lost their lives. John King was the only one from the expedition who returned alive to Melbourne. However, he could not survive the neuropathy caused by vitamin B deficiency and soon after he returned, he died at the age of thirty-one.

Since then, *nardoo* got a lot of attention from Australian botanists and historians. It was discussed in length whether *nardoo* was a good food source. What is clear is that, for the Burke party, the local knowledge of how to use it was lost in translation. Aboriginals were considered to be part of nature, rather than culture. This is why their skills in using the resources of the land were overlooked. One of the mistakes of the trip was not to use a local guide, which was not uncommon at that time.

All drama aside, thanks to this trip and the six rescue trips that followed it, the continent was crossed on foot and the picture of inland Australia was completed.

Swagman—Walking as a Way of Living

By the 1950s on the Australian continent, walking was becoming a way of living. A "Wallaby," "Swagman," or "Swaggie" traveled around South Australia carrying all his possessions with him and living off the land. He would walk along country roads from farm to farm and look for jobs along the way. In exchange, he would get food and accommodation. In Britain, the term "tramp" was widely used to refer to vagrants in the early Victorian period. Tramp was derived from the Middle English as a verb meaning to "walk with heavy footsteps." In the United States, the word became frequently used during the American Civil War to describe long marches, often with heavy packs. The swagman was the Australian equivalent of the English tramp and the American hobo, used for migratory workers.

Swagmen on the wallaby track, 1910.
National Library of Australia, Power House Museum.

The swagman carried a swag, which was a bundle with his personal belongings, containing his rolled blanket and his few belongings such as spare clothes, needle and thread, and maybe a photograph or a book. A tomahawk was carried in the straps and a tucker bag, usually an old sugar bag, hung from the top of the swag with food, tobacco, a tin mug, and bowl for mixing damper. In his right hand, a swaggie carried his water-filled billy, sometimes wrapped in a bag to stop the campfire soot from rubbing off on his trousers. It was an art to balance the weight of the swag. After rolling, it was secured tightly with leather straps, rope, or greenhide, and carried over the swagman's shoulder with a leather strap or loop of rope. The swag had various names, which made it in swagman songs and literature, such as "bluey" or a "Matilda" so that when a swaggie took to the road he was said to be "humping the bluey" or "waltzing Matilda."

Swaggies often had nicknames prefaced by the name of their hometown such as "Dubbo Slim" or "Greta Blue." How the swag was rolled and carried gave away where the swaggie came from. Those from Victoria had long, neat, swags worn over the right shoulder and under the left arm. Queenslanders carried short, plump swags perpendicular between the shoulder blades, while New South Wales swaggies carried them on a slant from the right shoulder to the left hip. Swaggies usually had a beard and wore faded and patched clothes and a hat with corks or a net attached to repel the flies. Swagmen were independent and mostly survived on their bush skills. Sometimes they got lifts from drivers, but usually preferred to travel alone. Occasionally, they camped in groups at specific locations such as under bridges. Some traveled with a dog, as this was a tested method to create a trustworthy image for the housewives to hand them some food.

Visiting swagmen were a familiar part of country life on Australian farms. Some called so often they were "regulars" and would chop wood, milk the cows, pull thistles, or cut timber in return for meals and accommodation on an army stretcher in the harness shed. On some farms, only "regulars" were allowed to sleep over while others had to be content with their handout of sandwiches, hard-boiled eggs, and a billy of tea.

Women swaggies were also seen on the roads. Some were on the road to find work and most were prompted by their love of adventure. Still women were a rarity and therefore some examples made it to the news describing them like extraordinary beings. One of them was a tall, striking lady about forty years of age. She was known by the name "Her Ladyship" and wore white moleskin trousers and a blue linen overall. Her swag was neatly rolled and her billy and cooking utensils were polished like silver. She was a capable worker and could take any type of work. She would set her camp in a secluded spot and never spoke to a man or was seen traveling with one.[9]

Sundowners differed from swagmen in that they arrived at a farm at sundown asking for work when it was too late and left early in the morning. Another type of wanderer, who also preferred not to work, was the Murrumbidgee whaler who camped for long periods on the Murrumbidgee or Darling Rivers catching fish and begged food from the stations up and down the rivers.

Perhaps the best text that captures the genuine roughness and lack of home ties of the swagman life is the bush ballads of Andrew Barton "Banjo" Paterson. He was an Australian "bush poet" who wrote many ballads and poems about Australian rural and outback life.

Paterson is best known for a poem he wrote in 1895 called "Waltzing Matilda." It told the story of a swagman, an itinerant worker, making a drink of tea at a bush camp and capturing a sheep to eat. When the sheep's owner arrives with three police officers to arrest the worker for the theft, the swagman completes suicide by drowning himself in a nearby watering hole, after which his ghost haunts the site.[10] This song, however, had various versions and making a drink of tea was the version sponsored by the Billy Tea company, as the original song instead mentioned a water bag.

Another one of his ballads reflects the daily hardship of a swagman with humor and wit, and with no product placement.[11]

Oh, my name is Bob the Swagman, before you all I stand,
And I've had many ups and downs while travelling through the land.
I once was well-to-do, my boys, but now I am stumped up,
And I'm forced to go on rations in an old bark hut.
. . .

Ten pounds of flour, ten pounds of beef, some sugar and some tea,
That's all they give to a hungry man, until the Seventh Day.
If you don't be moighty sparing, you'll go with a hungry gut-
For that's one of the great misfortunates in an old bark hut.
. . .

The bucket you boil your beef in has to carry water, too,
And they'll say you're getting mighty flash if you should ask for two.
I've a billy, and a pit pot, and a broken-handled cup,
And they all adorn the table in the old bark hut.

The swagmen of the Depression years of the 1930s were different from the earlier swaggies. Out of work and food, more swagmen were walking the Australian roads. Thousands more were on the road at this time looking for food and work rather than the wandering lifestyle of earlier swagmen. Even though economic reasons might have steered some laborers to become swagmen, they were mostly people who enjoyed the bush and the freedom they had on the road. They illegally rode in goods trains or on the couplings of passenger trains because they could not afford the ticket for a seat. Near stations, it was common to see small stacks of stones on boundary walls or fences to indicate to other swagmen whether this house would give you a meal. At this time, they were often collectively referred to as bagmen, hobos, or just "bo's" and sometimes committed petty crimes. There was a swagman's language around the countryside. Signs and codes were left on the front gates of stations advising others of the likelihood of getting work or food. Local policemen in country towns distributed food vouchers. Food and light work were also given at special aid centers, the most famous being the Eagles Nest Swaggie's Camp near Toowoomba in Queensland.[12] Once the economic conditions improved by the 1950s, fewer swagmen were visible.

Although Australia had swagmen frequenting the bushes long before, bushwalking as a word was only invented in the 1920s. It meant hiking on- and off-trail. In the United States, bushwhacking is used for going off-trail while hiking, through dense undergrowth, bushes, or trees. Bushwalking as a concept started with the bush brotherhood.

Bush Brotherhood

In 1914, when two men started a journey on foot crossing the wilderness of the southern Blue Mountains in New South Wales, Australia, it became an adventure that would symbolize Australia's love of bushwalking. It also became an act of conservation. Over twenty-one days, Myles Dunphy and Bert Gallop traced Katoomba to Picton in the state's east, through thick scrub and across the Kowmung River.

Dunphy defined bushwalking as a romantic activity. For him, the wilderness was the true human experience. It was good for the mind, the soul, and the country. He built the romantic and esthetic values into conservation much like John Muir did on the other side of the world half a century earlier. It is possible to say that Myles Dunphy was for Australia what John Muir was for North America. The Blue Mountains were to Dunphy what the Sierras Nevada was for Muir.

After the walk, Dunphy and his friends founded the Mountain Trails Club in Sydney in New South Wales. This was not the first walking club in New South Wales. The Warragambe walking club was already active since 1895, but it was organizing commercial trips on roads and not on rough country. Dunphy instead wanted to organize treks and camping trips in the wild, to experience self-reliance and resourcefulness in nature. This was the first *bush*walking club and the start of the state's voluntary bushwalking and conservation movements.

Much adventure of the period, the early 1900s, was militaristic and imperialist, carrying the same values of bravery and national pride in the face of hardship to achieve superiority over the nature and other nations. As Dunphy was growing up, Australia was becoming a nation with a recovering economy. Shorter working weeks and attention to recreation and health created demand for activities outdoors. It defined the Australian character. Athletic qualities were part of the national pride. Different than explorers of his time elsewhere in the world, what motivated Myles Dunphy was a sense of adventure he shared with his mates.

What made Dunphy different than Muir was the fact that he did not like wilderness for its solitude and spirituality. He instead embodied the

Myles Dunphy and his gear, 1915.
The Colong Foundation Collection.

Australian sense of mateship on his walks, toward his trip mates and the farmers he came across. In a way, the bush was the idea of the unique Australian culture, where nature and mateship were blended. The new movement was called "bush brotherhood." In this sense, bushwalking could be seen as a nationalistic activity, on a very philosophical level.

The comparison between Muir and Dunphy is also interesting when it comes to food and supplies. Muir traveled with very little food and sometimes had to find food on his way on trails; sometimes, he nearly starved. Myles and his friends initially did not travel light. But eventually they approached the issue of weight and comfort like sportsmen. By trial and error, they learned what was good to pack and eventually made contributions to a generation of bushwalkers that followed. In the early walks, he and his friends used a swag and a tent that they patched up with an Australian flag. Later, they thought it was necessary to develop lightweight gear for overnight recreational bushwalking to be possible. For a walk down the Kowmung River valley in 1914, Dunphy developed two lightweight articles. These were the "dungal" swag and a waterproof cotton tent made from *japara*, a finely woven cotton cloth manufactured in India. This contributed to recreational bushwalking significantly. Basic lightweight equipment was the catalyst that enabled the community to explore and enjoy their local environment. In probably the oldest gear list Dunphy ever kept, a list he wrote to his friend Johannes Clement Charles Marie de Mol in 1916, he wrote in great detail what had to be in the swag. The swag had two bundles. One was called the swag and consisted of his blanket, straps, extra clothing in case it rained, toothbrush, underpants, boots, and small items such as a mirror, a comb, and a towel. The other one was his gunny bag with some food, utensils, soap, candles, and clean cloth for washing dishes. He remarked that food would be purchased at the Blackheath where they would depart but he mentioned to bring half a butter in tin and a sugar bag. On top of the page, he warned in capital letters that all articles listed must not exceed 35 pounds. To emphasize the weight limitation, he also added the things not to bring, which remarkably included a tie, hairbrush, and books.[13]

Women were also welcomed in the bush brotherhood, despite the non-inclusive name. In fact as early as 1909, Ethel Luth and her two other female friends were the first women to bushwalk through wilderness. They walked 250 kilometers in a week and had their dresses shipped to them at the end of the trail in a dress basket. It was so rare for women sleeping out that villages who heard about them came out to meet and greet them on their way.[14] Not all news about female swaggers was positive, however. The newspaper *Northern Standard* called the sighting of a woman swagger rather a sight of poverty. "Women in their swags tramping the bush, might be deemed a picturesque sight by decadent esthetes, but people of healthy tastes would prefer to describe it as a painful one—Sydney 'worker.'"[15]

In the early 1930s, hiking in Australia became a mainstream activity for people to get fresh air and exercise. People started taking public transportation to go to nature reserves and walking tracks. Hotels offered evening meals and accommodation for the walkers. The "real bushwalkers," however, were unhappy. They defined their activity as a wilderness experience, which required carrying a pack and camping out over several days. They wanted to create a boundary between themselves and mass hikers. They went to great lengths to defend their identity, for example by not publishing any guidebooks for twenty years and by park rangers removing information from maps.[16] This presents a very interesting discussion on the right to nature. Whose bush was it? Was the bush for bushwalkers, hikers, or the native title-holders? This is the eternal conflict between democracy and preservation, not only between pedestrians and vehicles but also between backpackers and guided treks, between adventure walking and excursions on trails.[17]

Historian Michael Symons described Australian settlers as "a modern army" and claimed that peasants are the origin of a national cuisine that Australia never had. The Australian national cuisine was therefore army food and camp food, with tinned jam, condensed milk, camp pie, and beer. Only since about three decades ago did Australian cuisine and interest in fresh produce develop.[18] An example of Australian leadership is in not settling as a single cuisine society.

The argument that Australian early settlers' food resembled camping food brings to mind the history of screw caps for wine bottles. The first screw cap technology was developed in 1858 by John Landis Mason for the now famous *mason* jar. It had a zinc twist cap and was used for canning. In 1889 in England, Dan Rynalds brought the application of screw cap to wine. It was not successful because the acid of the wine would corrode the metal of the cap. Only when the French company called Le Bouchage Mechanique invented an aluminum twist cap with a plastic liner inside in the 1960s was this technology suitable for wine bottles. In the late 1960s, this company was sold to Amcor, a Melbourne-based packaging company. In Australia, there was no insistence on the use of cork. One can argue that the nation was accepting the conveniences of using a screw cap versus the traditional cork, much more than in European countries where tradition dominated. From there, screw caps have spread to the rest of the world and have become more and more acceptable.

CHAPTER 3

Polar Explorations

The knowledge that the planet was a sphere started the challenge to reach the two poles. Due to harsh weather conditions, it took explorers centuries before they could travel the polar regions of the Earth—the Arctic region and Antarctica. When the poles were finally in reach, explorers made arduous travels on ship and then on foot or by sled to be the first to ever set foot on the North Pole and the South Pole.

The heroic age of Antarctic exploration started at the beginning of the nineteenth century and lasted for half a century. During this period, the Antarctica became the focus of an international effort. There was the race to be the first to the geographical and magnetic poles. Furthermore, these efforts brought with them the interest to explore the landscape and do scientific research. Each expedition became an epic story because of the feat of endurance that its members were exposed to. The explorers were deemed heroic as they had to overcome tragedies of the life-threatening environment. There was a romanticism associated with polar explorations, but the poles were isolated, deserted, cold, and alien to our imagination of landscape.

The limitations in these expeditions of the available technologies made them even more challenging. Developments in transport, communication, and provisions after World War II would revolutionize explorations. Until then, much suffering was endured as the explorers were working at the edge of their capabilities, in new geographies, temperatures, and distances, and with food that was rationed, rationalized, and lacking sufficient nutrition and often also taste.

In expeditions that became successful, which meant to make it back alive as much as reaching the poles, food planning and management was a major point of success. Controlling food supplies saved lives. But in the book of heroic expeditions to the Arctic and to Antarctica there were more pages dedicated to death than to success, especially in the chapters that took place on foot.

Arctic Lichen, Old Boots, and Cannibalism

Indigenous people of North America had many ways to survive in nature to prevent starvation. They passed on some of these to the early explorers, which created an appreciation of the necessity of foraged food that lasted over the years and was transferred to other geographies. One of these was *tripe-de-roche*, rock tripe.

In the archive rooms of the Royal Geographical Society in London rests a tiny little box wrapped in archival paper, next to tea and salt bags with red wax seals, a broken piece of an army biscuit, a block of chocolate covered with white bloom, and an unopened box of Bovril. This box is the size of a matchbox, and it is made of hard cardboard with some barely legible text on it which reads Goldsmiths Dublin. Inside lies what once was something edible, to the trained eye at least. It is a lichen, which has the color of cork

Trip-de-roche.
© Eugene Rae/Royal Geographical Society (with IBG).

or bark, partly light brown partly dark, and the roughness of the geography it comes from. It looks like dried leather or dried leaves, edges curled up and crumbled. This little lichen is *tripe-de-roche*, on which Captain Sir William Edward Parry's sailors lived during the voyage for the discovery of a north-west passage to the Pacific in 1824 to 1825.

Rock tripe is a lichen that thrives in the harshest arctic climates. It is an organism that consists of a fungus and algae that live in symbiosis. Rock tripe has long served as a source of emergency food because it survives through the winter. The French name *tripe-de-roche* precedes the translation into the English rock tripe; the term was coined by a Canadian. The Inuit peoples of the Canadian arctic regions considered rock tripe to be a food of last resort, to be eaten only in times of starvation, because it was thought to be danger-ous to eat continuously. Other Native Americans found it less dangerous and made it part of their regular food gathering and preparation. For example, the Cree used it as an additive to fish broth to make a thick soup that was not only eaten for nutrition but was considered to be somewhat medicinal, affording nourishment to the sick.

In another journey, this thin strip of lichen was the difference between life and death when John Franklin was on his first expedition to map out the Northwest Passage from Europe to Asia in 1822.

Sir John Franklin was a British Royal Navy officer and Artic explorer. When their birch bark canoes got damaged, the group of twenty men had to return back to their ship. Due to scarcity of their provisions and the length of the journey, Franklin decided to go back on a different route than before and started a journey in the cold, quickly using up their provisions and leading to a disaster. Two days after they started their journey back, Franklin wrote, "Our pemmican was now reduced so low that we could only issue a few mouthfuls to each person." In fact, these were the good days.

They went off-track and start taking a new course carrying their canoes on land. This was when their story of suffering, which would last over two months, began. After ten days of return journey, they ran out of meat. "We sat down to breakfast at 10.30 on September 4," wrote Franklin in his jour-nal, "and this, finished the remainder of our meat." They started depending on what they could find on their way, and they did not find much. They saw reindeer but could not get them. Winter started hitting hard, their tents and bedclothes froze, and they had no means of making a fire. They had to cross swamplands and foot-deep snow. When they decided to burn a damaged canoe to cook the rest of their portable soup and arrowroot, it brought wel-come (but temporary) relief after three days of fasting.

Their condition turned south when winter arrived early and their food stores were exhausted, and the men were ultimately reduced to eating lichen. When the lichen ran out, they boiled the leather soles of their spare boots and ate those. Franklin recorded this part of the journey, in his journal, where he described the starvation vividly: "Previous to setting out, the whole party ate the remains of their old shoes, and whatever scraps of leather they had, to strengthen their stomachs for the fatigue of the day's journey. . . . The *tripe-de-roche*, even where we got enough, only serving to allay the pangs of hunger for a short time."[1]

On one occasion, a Canadian voyageur shared with everyone meat he was saving for himself, which Franklin found touching. In the coming days, they went between starvation and finding some meat or lichen to eat. In his memoir, Franklin described the difficulty of walking more than a few miles a day without enough food and sometimes losing their way. He often described himself lucky they had a supper of *tripe-de-roche* with tea or *tripe-de-roche* with partridge they shot. At some point, some of the members of his party ate what they scavenged along the way: "They had halted among some willows where they had picked up some pieces of skin and a few bones of deer that had been devoured by the wolves last spring. They had rendered the bones friable by burning and eaten them as well as the skin; and several of them had added their old shoes to the repast."[2] The amount of energy that *tripe-de-roche* gave was so little that the men in the party sometimes refused to collect it, not convinced that the exertion was worth it. The extreme misery of the whole party was quite evident. And when there was no *trip-de-roche*, "we drank tea and ate some of our shoes for supper."[3] Or they boiled some bones they found with *tripe-de-roche* to make soup, masking the otherwise acrid taste of the bones. By this time, they had all lost a lot of weight and had body pain that prevented them from walking.

When they found themselves yet again on the banks of a river, threatened by death from starvation and cold and with no way to cross, the party split into three groups. Ahead of the main party was George Back in search of food and supplies. Franklin and the rest of the party followed at a slower pace. Robert Hood was too ill to travel any farther, and John Hepburn and John Richardson stayed behind to care for Hood. Four of the voyageurs traveling with Franklin decided to return to Hood, Richardson, and Hepburn. When among them only one, Michel Teroahauté, arrived carrying fresh wolf meat, the group suspected that Teroahauté had in fact killed the missing three, and the meat he had arrived with was the missing men. On that day, Richardson went to gather lichen and left Hood and Teroahauté alone. Hepburn was cutting firewood in the near distance. He heard a gunshot and hastened to the camp to find Hood dead. Teroahauté claimed that Hood shot himself, but the bullet hole at the back of his head was telling otherwise. Everyone was suspicious but did not say a word to Teroahauté. Teroahauté became increasingly erratic, and Richardson began to worry that Teroahauté would try to kill them as well. Eventually, one day Teroahauté remained behind to collect *tripe-de-roche*; he later caught up with the group without any lichen in his hands. This added to the suspicion of the group that Teroahauté was planning to kill them all. Richardson shot and killed Teroahauté in a pre-emptive strike. Richardson and Hepburn eventually reached Fort Enterprise to find Franklin with his men. There was no food or help Franklin had set out to find. The men managed to survive long enough for George Back to return with help and supplies.[4]

By the end of this trip, nine officers and fifteen men perished. Franklin survived this disaster of starvation and cannibalism, and he became a national hero (for his perseverance) upon his return to England. However, he eventually disappeared on his last naval expedition, attempting to chart and navigate a section of the Northwest Passage in the Canadian Arctic. He perished with 134 officers and sailors on his two ships, the *Erebus* and the *Terror*, on his fourth quest for the Northwest Passage in 1845. His entire crew perished from starvation, hypothermia, tuberculosis, lead poisoning, and scurvy. Tinned food has been suggested as the source of lead poisoning. Since then, research in the found bones of the crew members has proven that it was rather the unique water system fitted to the expedition's ships that produced drinking water very high in lead.

The nutritional and medicinal value of rock tripe fungi has been investigated to evaluate its viability as a survival food. A lichen supplementation was given to female mice for three weeks to measure its effects on growth, metabolism, and immune function in comparison to a control group fed a standard diet. The lichen-fed mice had a higher growth rate and ate more than the control group. The study tested the effect of this diet on vital organs and concluded that rock tripe was not only a good source of nutrition in survival situations but that it acted to stimulate the immune system (as manifest in an increase in the production spleen B-lymphocytes).[5]

It is no wonder then that rock tripe is also used as a medicine in China. Moreover, a type of rock tripe indigenous to Asia, *U. esculenta*, called *Iwatake* (literally meaning rock mushroom) is considered a delicacy in modern-day

Japan. It is so sought after that harvesters repel down steep slopes to collect it, favoring wet weather to reduce the risk of crumbling of the delicate lichen.

Pemmican—Bread of the Wilderness

Food for a polar expedition had to be organized into two parts. Food needed in the ship for going and (hopefully) returning, and food on sledge and in the field. All historical polar expeditions had many things in common: cold weather, damp clothing, men in confined space for what felt like eternity . . . and they had pemmican.

Fur traders and travelers referred to pemmican as "the bread of the wilderness."[6] Pemmican was a nutritious food because it was a concentrated mixture of fat and meat fur traders learned from the Cree people of North American Indians. The word pemmican comes from the Cree word pimîhkân, meaning "he makes grease," which itself is derived from the word pimî, "fat, grease."[7] The Cree processed hunted meat to keep it for a long time in a paste called pemmican. When they killed large numbers of animals, such as a herd of buffalos, this was their way of preserving food for their feast-or-famine living. This way, during harsh winter months, they thrived on this dried meat and grease.

Pemmican was mentioned by the Scottish explorer Sir Alexander Mackenzie on a journey from Canada to the Pacific in 1793. This was the first east to west crossing of North America north of Mexico (predating the Lewis and Clarck expedition by ten years).

> The provision called pemmican, on which the Chepewyans, as well as the other savages of this country, chiefly subsist in their journeys, is prepared in the following manner: The lean parts of the flesh of the larger animals are cut in thin slices, and are placed on a wooden grate over a slow fire, or exposed to the sun, and sometimes to the frost. These operations dry it, and in that state it is pounded between two stones; it will then keep with care for several years. If, however, it is kept in large quantities, it is disposed to ferment in the spring of the year, when it must be exposed to the air, or it will soon decay. The inside fat, and that of the rump, which is much thicker in these wild than our domestic animals, is melted down and mixed, in a boiling state with the pounded meat, in equal proportions: it is then put in baskets or bags for the convenience of carrying it. Thus it becomes a nutritious food, and is eaten, without any further preparation, or the addition of spice, salt, or any vegetable or farinaceous substance. A little time reconciles it to the palate. There is another sort made with the addition of marrow and dried berries, which is of a superior quality.[8]

In his legendary book *The Oregon Trail* on the expansion of America to the west, Francis Parkman describes pemmican (next to his regular dry bread and salt ration), offered by the Indians, as a nutritious food but does not make any personal comments on taste. "A wooden bowl was soon set before me, filled with the nutritious preparation of dried meat called pemmican by the northern voyagers and *wasna* by the Dakota."[9]

Pemmican for polar expeditions was prepared mainly from the lean meat of game animals such as elk, bison, or deer. The meat was cut into thin slices and dried until brittle. It was then pounded into a powder and mixed with melted fat. Dried and powdered cranberries were sometimes added. The mixture was stored in pouches made of animal skin, and it lasted for a very long time.[10] British polar expeditions also fed a type of pemmican to their dogs as "sledging rations." This was called "dog pemmican"; it was a beef product consisting of two-thirds protein and one-third fat, without a carbohydrate. It was later ascertained that although the dogs survived on it, this was not a nutritious and healthy diet for them, being too high in protein.

Over the years, pemmican would get more attention for its composition and taste. It would become a great help in polar success and a subject for recipe development, as it was mostly tasting bad.

Polarizing Achievement—Peary and the North Pole

North Pole explorer Robert Peary took pemmican on all of his expeditions from 1886 to 1909 for both his men and his dogs. In his 1917 book *Secrets of Polar Travel*, he devoted several pages to this food, stating, "Too much cannot be said of the importance of pemmican to a polar expedition. It is an absolute '*sine qua non*.' Without it a sledge-party cannot compact its supplies within a limit of weight to make a serious polar journey successful."[11]

In his book *With Peary near the Pole*, Eivind Astrup described the food of arctic exploration when traveling northward on Greenland: "Monday Morning, May 16th, 1892 - . . . Camped at seven o'clock this morning, having advanced six miles. Before turning into sleeping-bags we had a pleasant supper, or rather breakfast, consisting, besides the usual cup of pea-soup, of a piece of pemmican, and a large cup of scalding chocolate, famous food which I can safely recommend to any one." As indulgent as this sounds, the stocks were precious and as provisions decreased he had to find alternatives. "On May 28 we shot our first dog. Making the sledge lighter, we could afford to reduce their number, thus saving provisions and providing fresh food for the other dogs."[12]

Peary described the importance of food planning in his book that he wrote after the seventh and finally successful expedition:

> Supplies for sledge work are of special character, and have to be prepared and packed in such a way as to secure the maximum of nourishment with the minimum of weight, of bulk, and of tare (that is, the weight of the packaging). The essentials, and the only essentials, needed in a serious arctic sledge journey, no matter what the season, the temperature, or the duration of the journey—whether one month or six—are four: pemmican, tea, ship's biscuit, condensed milk. Pemmican is prepared and condensed food, made from beef, fat and dried fruits. It may be regarded as the most concentrated and satisfying of all meat foods, and is absolutely indispensible in protracted arctic sledge journeys.[13]

As listed by Peary, the ship supplies were standard food supplies: flour, 16,000 pounds; coffee, 100 pounds; tea, 800 pounds; sugar, 10,000 pounds; kerosene, 3,500 gallons; bacon, 7,000 pounds; biscuit, 10,000 pounds; condensed milk, 100 cases; pemmican, 30,000 pounds; dried fish, 3,000 pounds; and smoking tobacco, 1,000 pounds. For twenty-two men, these supplies lasted from July to December of 1909. Besides the stock, Peary mentioned walruses, whales, and seal as natural food supplies hunted for the dogs. Peary's ship arrived at Cape Sheridan. Supplies for the winter were unloaded and 246 dogs were brought ashore, smelly and noisy after eighteen days of sea journey. Twenty-three sledges were built for the northward journey. All supplies were landed over several days for the winter quarters. This way, in case the ship was lost or crushed by ice, the crew could spend the winter at Cape Sheridan and go to the pole in the spring, then walk 350 miles to Cape Sabine, cross the Smith Sound ice to Etah, and wait for a ship. All the supplies were packed in boxes for the purpose that once empty they would be used to build a house.

Peary described the cooking kit taken to sledge journeys in great detail[14]:

> The kitchen box for our sledge journey is simply a wooden box containing two double-burner oil stoves, with four inch wicks. The two cooking pots are at the bottoms of five-gallon coal-oil tins, fitted with covers. When packed they are turned bottom side up over each stove, and the hinged cover of the wooden box is closed. On reaching camp, whether tent or snow igloo, the kitchen box is set down inside, the top of the box is turned up and keeps the heat of the stove from melting the wall of the igloo or burning the tent; the hinged front of the box is turned down and forms a table. The two cooking pots are filled with pounded ice and put on the stoves; when the ice melts one pot is used for tea, and the other may be used to warm beans, or to boil meat if there is any.

Ship's biscuit left at Port Leopold by Sir James Ross in 1849.
© Royal Geographical Society (with IBG).

Each man had a hunting knife, which served many purposes like helping himself from the pot by sticking in his knife and fishing out a piece of meat. They did not carry "anything so polite as a fork," and one teaspoon was considered quite enough for a party of four.

The theory of fieldwork is that there shall be two meals a day, one in the morning and one at night. As the days grow short, the meals are taken before light and after dark, leaving the period of light entirely for work. Sometimes it is necessary to travel for twenty-four hours without stopping for food.

With regards to his previous failure to reach the pole, Peary acknowledged the important of food supplies like no other:

My body has always been able thus far to follow my will no matter what the demands might be, and my winter's work was largely a matter of refinement of equipment, and of mathematical calculations of pounds of supplies and miles of distance. It was the lack of food which had forced us to turn back at 87° 6'. Hunger, not cold, is the dragon which guards the Rhinegold of the Arctic.

The standard daily ration for work on the final sledge journey toward the Pole was the following: 1 pound of pemmican; 1 pound of ship's biscuit; 4 ounces of condensed milk; ½ ounce of compressed tea; and 6 ounces of liquid fuel, alcohol, or petroleum. This meant a total of 2 pounds, 4.5 ounces of solids per man per day.[15] Peary believed that no other food was needed for either heat or muscle building. The sledge dogs were also eating 1 pound of pemmican per day, but they could eat less under scarcity. Each sledge was loaded with food such that it could survive for fifty days. If needed, a few dogs would be sacrificed to feed to other dogs, and this could extend the time to sixty days.

Peary had difficulties in crossing the ragged ice of the Arctic with loaded sledges, the terrific wind, and the intense cold. It took a lot of strength to drag enough pemmican, biscuit, tea, condensed milk, and liquid fuel to keep sufficient strength. He writes that it was so cold on this last journey that sometimes the bottle of brandy he carried was frozen solid.

> I am often asked if we were hungry on that journey. I hardly know whether we were hungry or not. Morning and night we had pemmican, biscuit and tea, and the pioneer or leading party had tea and lunch in the middle of the day's march. Had we eaten more, our food supply would have fallen short. I myself dropped twenty-five pounds of flesh between my departure from the shop and my return to it.

Whether Peary reached the North Pole was a topic of controversy for more than seventy years (he had said he had to have been as close as 5 miles of the pole but not reached it fully); after much debate and expert analysis, in 1989, it was concluded by the National Geographic Society that he had reached the Pole in 1909.

It was much later for the first men to reach the North Pole solely on foot and with the aid of dog teams and airdrops. Wally Herbert and companions Allan Gill, Roy Koerner, and Kenneth Hedges of the British Trans-Arctic Expedition arrived to the North Pole on April 6, 1969, and continued on to complete the first surface crossing of the Arctic Ocean—and by its longest axis, Barrow, Alaska, to Svalbard. In 1986, Will Steger with seven teammates became the first man to be confirmed as reaching the pole by dogsled and without resupply.

In 2005, British explorer Tom Avery and four companions recreated the outward portion of Peary's journey, using replica wooden sleds and Canadian Eskimo Dog teams. By repeating Peary's trip, their objective was to prove that Peary reached the North Pole. They ensured their sled weights were the same as Peary's sleds throughout their journey. They reached the North Pole in thirty-six days and twenty-two hours—nearly five hours faster than Peary. As for food, Avery had the option to replicate Peary's pemmican, chocolate, and cookie diet, but he chose to match the calorie intake and stick to a modern expedition diet with which they were more familiar: freeze-dried evening meals and salami sticks. However, some other provisions were unchanged since Peary's times: breakfast muesli, chocolate, biscuits, tea, coffee, and powdered milk.[16]

In an interview, Avery stressed the importance of food provisions:

We were burning up to 10,000 calories a day, but we were probably consuming 6,500 to 7,000 calories a day, so you're effectively starving yourself. In the morning, we had granola with powdered milk, lots of sugar, hot chocolate, and tea. And then during the trail, we would have things like dried fruit, salami, nuts, cheese, high-energy foods, chocolate, fudge, biscuits, and flapjacks. And then in the evening we'd have a soup, and then a boil-in-the-bag freeze-dried meal. But then we would supplement everything with butter. We'd put it into our cups of tea in the evening. We were eating it raw by the end just because it has more calories per gram than any other food—it's got eight calories per gram. Olive oil has nine. The Norwegians just drink olive oil. And then one step further, lard is 10 calories per gram. Our daily butter fix got us through.[17]

South Pole—Plan or Perish

When the news flashed all over the world "The North Pole is reached!" and that it was Peary who had done so, another voyageur had to change his plans. It was September 1909, and Roald Amundsen was getting ready to explore the North Polar basin when the news broke. He announced that his expedition to the North Pole was still to be held and of scientific purpose, nothing to do with record-breaking. This he did to convince his financial contributors to keep supporting him. Amundsen was already heavily in debt, and he did not find that it would be wise to reveal his secret plan, which was heading to "the last great problem to solve," the South Pole. He delayed his original plan of departure by two years and collected enough funds to lead the expedition of his life.

Victory awaits him, who has everything in order—luck people call it. Defeat is certain for him who has neglected to take the necessary precautions in time; this is called bad luck.[18]

Roald Amundsen

Amundsen's plan was to depart from Norway before the middle of August, first to Madeira and southward through the Atlantic, and then to the east, passing to the south of the Cape of Good Hope and Australia, and finally pushing through the pack and into Ross Sea about New Year 1911. As a base of operations, he had chosen the Bay of Whales in the great Antarctic Barrier, the most southerly point he could reach with his ship *Fram*. Once on the shore, the plan was, as soon as the hut was built and provisions landed, to carry supplies into the field, and lay down depots as far to the south as possible. He was hoping to get the provisions to latitude 80 degrees south and start the sledge journey from there to the pole.

All groceries were packed in tin boxes inside wooden cases. He was proud to provide sufficient nutrition to his crew. For this journey, he consulted a nutrition expert, Professor Sophus Torup. He knew that his men needed high-energy, low-volume, concentrated food, high in fat and calories. According to his diary of the 1911 expedition, 4,590 kcal was provided to each man per day with the supplies of biscuits, pemmican, butter, cheese, sugar, and cocoa. Most of the energy came from carbohydrates at 4,427 kcal.

He procured half of the tinned foods required from a firm at Moss. The manager of this firm also prepared the pemmican for the men and dogs. The pemmican was essentially different from that which former expeditions had used. Previously, the pemmican had contained nothing but the mixture of dried meat and lard. However, for this expedition, vegetables and oatmeal were added. This improved flavor and, according to the account of Amundsen, also made the pemmican easier to digest. He wrote with self-satisfaction: "A more stimulating, nourishing, and appetizing food, it would be impossible to find."

For the dogs, he bought two kinds of pemmican, one made with fish and the other with meat. Both kinds contained, besides dried fish (or meat) and lard, a certain proportion of dried milk and middlings. The pemmican was divided into rations of 1 pound and 1.5 ounces, and could be served out to the dogs as it was.

Of course, the five months' ship voyage required a different food planning. For the dogs, he looked for a reliable supply of dried fish and some barrels of lard. He also kept pigs, fowls, and sheep on board. They had a full kitchen in the ship but on sledge journey they took a cooking instrument from Stock-holm called Primus. It used oil and was said to take up less space than other options such as the Nansen cooker, which Amundsen used before.

Sledging provisions were simple and nourishing, and according to Amundsen that a "rich and varied menu is for people who have no work to do."

Besides the pemmican, we had biscuits, milk-powder, and chocolate. The biscuits were a present from a well-known Norwegian factory, and did all honour to their origin. They were specially baked for us, and were made of oatmeal with the addition of dried milk and a little sugar; they were extremely nourishing and pleasant to the taste. Thanks to efficient packing, they kept fresh and crisp all the time. These biscuits formed a great part of our daily diet, and undoubtedly contributed in no small degree to the successful result. Milk-powder is a comparatively new commodity with us, but it deserves to be better known. It came from the district of Jæderen. Neither heat nor cold, dryness nor wet, could hurt it; we had large quantities of it lying out in small, thin linen bags in every possible state of the weather: the powder was as good the last day as the first. We also took dried milk from a firm in Wisconsin; this milk had an addition of malt and sugar, and was, in my opinion, excellent; it also kept good the whole time. The chocolate came from a world-renowned firm, and was beyond all praise. The whole supply was a very acceptable gift.[19]

Amundsen was lucky with the task of repacking. All his supplies came in a form that he could count them to divide rather than to weigh. Pemmican was already in half-kilogram portions. The chocolate was divided in small pieces. Milk powder was put in bags of 10.5 ounces, just enough for one meal. The biscuits could also be counted, but this was the most tedious work as each man would get forty pieces per day and there were thousands of biscuits to ration, six thousand to be exact. However, Amundsen was extremely happy with the biscuits consisting of oatmeal, sugar, and dried milk. This provision of a few things worked very well for him. The team did not suffer from a craving for fat and sugar, as is usually the case in these environments. Amundsen was happy that he left other foods such as sweetmeats, jam, fruit, and cheese in the ship before setting off on foot.[20]

Amundsen describes how the slaughtering of the dogs was crucial. This provided a feast for the remaining dogs as well as the men. "We found that dog cutlets made a delicious dinner. It was excellent—not quite as tender as one could have wished, if an appetite had been lacking, but to us perfectly delicious. I ate five cutlets and would have been glad if there had been more in the pot."[21] The cutlets were not fried, as the team had neither a frying pan nor butter. It was instead easier and quicker to boil them; adding some of the pemmican with vegetables into the soup made it nearly a meat soup with vegetables. After this feast, the men counted all remaining provisions of pemmican, biscuits, chocolate, and milk powder, and divided them carefully among the remaining sleds. This meant that every single biscuit was again taken out and counted, at which point there still was several thousands of them. From this point on, Amundsen was confident that he could continue with the eighteen dogs to reach the South Pole and come back with sixteen. As he later wrote in his notes, these extra feeds had no small share in his remarkable success.

Captain Robert Falcon Scott, a British Royal Navy officer, was Amundsen's rival to first reach the South Pole with his *Discovery* expedition. Scott led his first *Discovery* expedition to the South Pole with Ernest Shackleton and Edward Wilson in 1901. However, after two months and reaching eighty-two degrees south, they were forced to turn back because they were suffering from snow blindness and scurvy. In 1907 to 1909, Ernest Shackleton led another expedition to within 156 kilometers of the South Pole. He turned back after supplies were exhausted. When Scott and his four men finally reached the South Pole on January 17, 1912, they were one year later than Amundsen. What they would be remembered for was the unfortunate return journey. They failed to meet with supporting dog teams from the base camp. At 50 degrees Celsius below zero and 18 kilometers away from the next food depot, they were so tired and undernourished that they could not manage to walk more. Toward the end of the trip, Scott and his team only managed to walk 2 kilometers a day. Only 11 miles from the next depot, Scott and his companions died from a combination of exhaustion, starvation, and extreme cold. If they had make it to the provisions, they would have been able to cook, sleep, and spend the whole winter there.

Planning was the main difference between the trips of Amundsen and Scott. Amundsen took fifty-two huskies, five men, and three tons of supplies, whereas Scott relied on men hauling instead of sled dogs and took seventeen men and one ton of supplies. This ultimately resulted in the death of him and his companions, whereas Amundsen led the expedition that eventually reached the South Pole successfully on December 14, 1911.

Amundsen chose his provisions with great care. He took pride in that in his former expeditions no case of scurvy was seen. To beat scurvy, Amundsen carried fresh meat by hunting enough seals, until the trek started in the spring when tinned meat was used. By then, the men were fit and healthy to start a journey on rationed tinned food.

Sledging ration for one man for one day from Scott's Terra Nova Expedition in 1912.
© Royal Geographical Society (with IBG).

Scurvy—The Worst Enemy of Polar Expeditions

Early explorers had learned the impact of cold climate by trial and error. They experienced that in a cold climate more energy is needed to burn up for producing heat for the body and energy for physical activity. Most explorers were underprepared for these conditions, which limited their expeditions' success. However, their biggest enemy was neither cold nor hunger, it was scurvy. Amundsen called it his "worst enemy of polar expeditions." Scurvy was a grave problem, and it was somehow linked to the tinned expedition food they were eating, but how the two were linked remained a mystery for a long time.

Cases of scurvy were recorded for decades when polar explorers such as Scott and Shackleton were suffering from it in 1901. In their 1877 publication of the Scurvy Report on Mare's 1875–1876 expedition, Dr. Donnet and Dr. Fraser described the symptoms of scurvy. [22]

Change of face colour to a leaden hue, a heavy expression in the eye, apathy, feebleness in the knees and ankles, and pains, swelling of joints, swelling of gums, teeth falling, tightness of the chest and sometimes night blindness.

The end of the scurvy path was imminent: "In many instances sudden death occurs." As for the causes, they noted "the want of fresh vegetable food, or of some of the constituents which compose fresh vegetables, and probably also fresh animal." These foods are said to contain "antiscorbutic" properties, meaning having the effect of preventing scurvy. What made these foods antiscorbutic is today's common knowledge: ascorbic acid, also known as vitamin C. Scurvy was not seen in animals like the ones in arctic treks because they synthesize their own vitamin C.

The nutritional value of lemons and limes to prevent scurvy was already known from pragmatic studies in the eighteenth century, but it was not universally accepted. In 1753, Scottish physician James Lind conducted controlled trials at sea after which he recommended that orange and lemon juice be evaporated down to a concentrate. Similarly, in the 1780s court physician Gilbert Blane argued that scurvy might be prevented or cured by vegetables and fruit, particularly oranges, lemons, or limes. He was successful in convincing the admiralty to order 1.6 million gallons of lemon juice on board of British vessels. Yet Captain Robert Scott advised not to take lemon juice since its acidity could have adverse effects. In retrospect, the distrust in lemon juice might be because the vitamin C deteriorated in the processing and by copper vessels in which it was stored.[23]

In 1883, Benjamin Alvord wrote a letter in *Science* magazine noting his surprise for the lack of precautions taken against scurvy in an 1877 expedition to the North Pole by Nare and Stephenson. He recounted the *London Quarterly Review* report in January 1877: "of seventeen of the finest men of the navy, who composed the original party, but five were (on return) able to walk alongside. One was dead, and the remainder in the last extremity of illness." The *Science* letter claimed that all this was because the parties had no lime juice. It cited the words of Captain Nares as taking responsibility for the failed judgment as "up to the middle of May the lime juice remains as solid as rock. No sledge party employed in the arctic regions in the cold month of April has ever been able to issue a regular ration of lime-juice. In addition to the extra weight to be dragged, that its carriage would entail, there is the even more serious consideration of the time necessary in order to melt sufficient snow." After this, he called to action: "of course, hereafter, lime-juice in some shape or other must be carried in all sledging journeys; and we earnestly trust that some means will be found to make it in a lozenge, for, as liquid, there is, and will always be, extreme difficulty in using it in cold weather, unless arctic travelling is considerably curtailed." Based on this, the letter announced that even if lozenges of lime juice were not available for arctic expeditions, they can be found at the drugstores in a shape to be used as troches for colds. The main point of the article was to argue a more efficient way to include lime juice in an arctic exploration diet, and that was to add it in pemmican. The letter claimed that in 1880, General P. S. Wales already had the answer to the practical problem of carrying lemon juice in his report of the surgeon-general of the navy:

> The indispensible necessity of lime-juice in the sledging parties, and the difficulties of carrying it, and preparing it for use, induced me to suggests the propriety of combining the juice and pemmican in the proportion of one ounce to the pound of the latter. The pemmican is greatly improved in taste and flavor, and will, I believe, be more assimilable. This is an important modification, as there are persons who cannot eat the ordinary article.[24]

Direct evidence of vitamin C and scurvy, however, was only established in the 1930s. In 1933, working with Edmund Hirst's research team, Walter Norman Haworth was the first scientist to correctly deduce the structure of vitamin C, and in 1934 he reported the first synthesis of the vitamin. This compound had antiscorbutic properties, therefore the "a-scorbic acid" name was proposed for the compound. Haworth received the Nobel Prize for chemistry in 1937, sharing the prize with Swiss chemist Paul Karrer for his work on other vitamins. The first vitamin C tablet was used in polar expeditions in 1934.[25] But it would take a few more years before vitamin C became a regular supplement for those who go on long journeys with no fresh fruits and vegetables. This is because vitamins were not yet isolated, synthesized, or concentrated. Their effects were only known in their fresh host foods. After the 1930s, lemon juice concentrate was supplied for vitamin C. In 1934, Dr. Zilva of the Lister Institute in London suggested vitamin C as synthetic ascorbic acid tablets would be a valuable addition to an arctic exploration. In the same year, Dr. Coman provided synthetic vitamin C for the Ellsworth Antarctic expedition, and this was the first time a synthetic vitamin was used in an arctic expedition.

The Most Optimum Antarctic Diet

In 1939, American naval officer Admiral E. Byrd organized an expedition to the Antarctic on behalf of the US Antarctic Service. The expedition aimed to design the optimum ration for an Antarctic expedition, one that provides a concentrated, stable, and well-balanced nutrition that could be consumed daily.[26] It was recognized that the food must be easy to prepare and require a limited amount of heating before eating. In order to develop the most optimum diet, they considered the calories needed for a man to survive in Antarctica: the amount of protein, fat, and carbohydrate required, as well as mineral and vitamins. Assuming that a normal person of 5 feet 6 inches requires 2,000 calories per day for basal metabolism, they aimed for 5,000 calories for a polar expedition based on other experience and reports. They also defined an ideal ratio of protein to fat to carbohydrates for optimum digestion and caloric benefits. For example, although fat gives the highest caloric value per weight, it can be more difficult to digest in the absence of any carbohydrates. They felt that a ratio of 1:2:4 would be suitable for a man in Antarctica. As the amount of iron, calcium, and phosphorous were often reported to be short of required levels, they set a target of 10 milligrams, 800 milligrams, and 800 milligrams, respectively. They also acknowledged the preventive effect of vitamin C on scurvy, which had been recently understood, and proposed that in the absence of fresh fruit and vegetables, vitamin C needs to be supplemented in the arctic diet. In Byrd's expedition, a complete mix of synthesized vitamins were taken on board for the first time, as one oil-soluble tablet containing vitamin D, A, and E, and another water-soluble tablet containing vitamin C, B1, B2, and iron. Although the exact daily requirements were not certainly known for these vitamins then, this expedition was the first to carry an artificial source of vitamins covering completely the daily requirements of its members. This study also had the ambition to tackle pemmican.

Although it was no secret that polar explorers desired something tastier than pemmican, it was the only way to include a concentrated, high-caloric food into their diet; therefore, it was included in all sledge expeditions. In this most optimum Antarctic diet study, researchers wanted to develop a new pemmican that was sufficiently stable, inexpensive, nutritious, and pleasant to eat. They considered other staple foods such as milk powder, butter, sugar, and chocolate, and it was in pemmican that they could make the biggest difference. In collaboration with biologist Dr. Paul Siple, who is known to have defined the wind chill factor and coined the term "degrees Siple," they settled on a ration that weighed 32 ounces and provided 5,000 calories. Compared to previous rations, they took away some items such as pepper, dried vegetables, and onion powder, and placed them into the pemmican. There were two types of pemmican developed: one by Dr. Dana Coman of the John Hopkins Medical School and the other by Drs. Robert S. Harris and E. Lockhart of the Massachusetts Institute of Technology.

The Coman pemmican had beef marrow in the recipe. But the beef marrow was very sensitive and got spoiled, and there was no time to procure a new batch. So it was produced with beef suet. No testing of palatability was done with this new formula. Around 500 pounds of pemmican was produced with this recipe and packed in waxed cardboard containers. The ingredients of this pemmican were either cooked or already edible as they were; only the addition of water to the desired consistency was needed to make it ready for consumption.

Coman's pemmican recipe
Pure rendered beef suet 32%
Dessicated fine ground beef liver 12%
Soy bean flour 4%
Whole milk powder (Klim) 30%
Dehydrated pea and lima bean soup 5%
Dehydrated mashed potatoes 7%
Derbetain vegetable concentrate 8%
Iodized table salt 0.8%
Fresh ground spices (black pepper, cayenne pepper, Jamaica ginger, thyme)
    1.625%
Dried brewer's yeast 0.0375%

The palatability of the Harris formula pemmican was tested with taste enhancers such as peanut butter, coconut oil, powdered whole milk, vigex, and glutamic acid, but these failed to improve flavor; a very simple recipe was used instead. This pemmican required no cooking and contained a hardened vegetable fat, which prevented rancidity. About 3,000 pounds of this pemmican was prepared.

Harris's pemmican recipe
Prepared cereal 25%
Dehydrated beef liver (pre-cooked) 5%
Dehydrated beef (pre-cooked) 30%
Vegetable concentrate (Patten's) 10%
Hydrogenated vegetable oil (spray) 30%

Most items in the ration were purchasable, but chocolate and biscuits were specially formulated. The Loose-Wiles Baking Company prepared a double-thick graham cracker as part of the biscuit ration. Mrs. Anna E. Schneider of the Eugenia Mills Ccompany prepared a special trail biscuit that would be called "Eugenia Biscuit." Anna Eugenia Emma Schneider (b. 1889) was known as the first woman miller in the United States. Her Baltimore business produced Eugenia Whole Wheat Flour and supplied several hundred tins of biscuits for Admiral Byrd's 1939 expedition to the Antarctic.

Anna Schneider was no ordinary woman. She was an inventor of new foods of her time. She was involved in a whole grain nutrition campaign against white bread. One of the doctors and scientists supporting her work suggested she contact the planners of Byrd's expedition to the South Pole. This was Dr. Paul Siple. He asked Anna Schneider to develop a trail biscuit with the following requirements: they must taste good, and they must keep extremely well in the tropical heat on the way to the Antarctic and sub-zero temperatures after arrival. Her original idea of encapsulating honey into the biscuits was rejected. She then created a recipe that was tested by four laboratories and approved as the Eugenia biscuits. Their keeping qualities as well as their taste was right on target. The biscuits traveled to the Antarctic; the men on the expedition found them very tasty, and twenty-five years later some tins were opened and they were still delicious.[27]

Eugenia biscuit recipe, from Eugenia flour
Whole wheat flour 16 ounces
Honey 7.5 ounces
Coconut oil 2 ounces
Salt 1 ounce
Baking powder ½ ounce
Water 2 ounces

Anna Schneider created Eugenia's Eskimo Biscuits during the Second World War as a military survival food. In this recipe, she included even more honey. She marketed these cookies in the United States after the war as Eugenia Honey Biscuits. To this day, she is credited for raising awareness of the nutritional value of whole wheat in the diet.[28]

To provide variety, Eugenia Biscuits were supplemented with navy pilot biscuits and whole wheat crackers. Three types of chocolate were used. Nestlé sweet milk chocolate, Nestlé semi-sweet chocolate, and the Army Emergency ration; exact proportions were to be decided after some trials. In the end, six complete rations sufficient for three men for two months were prepared. Next to this, a supply of vitamin capsules, toilet paper, matches, and meta tablets (metaldehyde used as camping fuel) were included. The total ration had the following thirteen items of foodstuff: bacon, biscuits, butter, cocoa, cereal, dried fruit, lemon powder, chocolate, milk powder, mixed nuts, pemmican, salt, and sugar.

In order to save weight, all foods that came in tin containers were transferred into paper bags. During the experiment, it was found that paper bags caused a great problem because bags would break and powdered items would spill. Bacon, which was wrapped in a tar and paper–covered cloth bag, spoiled entirely with mold; perhaps a cellophane wrapping would have been a better choice. Also the nuts did not taste fresh after repacking, and they were rancid and unpleasant to eat. These packaging difficulties are solved today by lightweight multilayered plastic and aluminum portion packages, Ziploc bags, and vacuum packs. Another important field lesson was the psychological factors. Food in the field for every day over a long period of time had to offer not only quantity but also variety. For example, the sweetened chocolate was too sweet and therefore too difficult to eat in quantities assigned.

In the end, which pemmican won the taste test? Neither. The new pemmican created a problem, as people were not familiar with this food. It was found to be strange and too rich. Harris's recipe lacked the flavor. Coman's recipe had too much flavor and became monotonous. Harris's recipe had a better psychological effect from an appearance point of view. Coman's recipe appeared greasy upon preparation. The conclusion of the study on pemmican was that it required further development for taste. The final recommendation was that more variety in food was desired. The "perfect pemmican" had to remain as an oxymoron.

Hoosh and Seals on Elephant Island

Sir Ernest Shackleton, the British explorer of the heroic age of Antarctic exploration, went to the Arctic three times. The first time he was part of Captain Scott's *Discovery* expedition team. The second time, he was leading the *Nimrod* expedition to the South Pole. In his third attempt in 1914, he aimed to cross Antarctica from sea to sea via the pole with his ship *Endurance*. It was in this trip that he displayed a heroic survival story after his ship became trapped in pack ice and was slowly crushed before the shore parties could be landed. The crew escaped by camping on the sea ice until it disintegrated, then by launching the lifeboats to reach Elephant Island.

The island has no permanent settlement and has no flora or fauna to allow it. Shackleton's captain, Frank Horsey, wrote in his account of the event that the men pronounced the island's name with a silent "t" and the "H" prefixed, as "Hell-of-an-Island."[29] In season, Gentoo penguins, chinstrap penguins, and seals are the only creatures that frequent its shores. This island became famous as the desolate refuge of Ernest Shackleton and his crew in 1916, after the loss of their ship *Endurance*. After struggling with drifting ice, his ship landed on this island with twenty-eight men. When Shackleton sailed with five other men in an open lifeboat to a whaling station in South Georgia 800 miles away, he left his second-in-command, Frank Wild, in charge of the

The first drink and hot food for three and a half days. Weddell Sea Party crew arrival on Elephant Island, 1916.
© Royal Geographical Society (with IBG).

men on Elephant Island. The remaining men were to spend months living in two boats, overturned and reinforced with stones and lit by blubber lamps. They waited for Shackleton's return with a rescue ship for what became to be four or five months. The men hunted for penguins and seals, with very low success in autumn and winter. Many of them became ill and frostbitten, and in danger of starvation.

Frank Wild had the problem of obtaining and rationing of food. He couldn't be sure when Shackleton would come back with help. On one hand, he had to ensure that his men had just enough food to maintain their well-being and strength, and on the other hand, he didn't want to stock too much food, giving them the impression that the hope for rescue was too small. One account of those days of hardship comes from Thomas Orde Lees, who kept a diary on Elephant Island. Lees was put in charge of the food. He wrote his diary in a couple of bank checkbooks. Although he was not liked by many on the boat journey, once ashore when he started swapping and selling food, he became even less popular. Eventually, Frank Wild stopped all exchanges. However, Lees remained despised for his attitude and his snoring. In his later years, he said that he would be the first one to go in the party, if it had been reduced to cannibalism.

At first, their hut was in darkness. Lees made a blubber lamp as a night lamp. In this light he could read one of the few books, which also included Marston's penny cookery book. One of the first tasks for the men to tackle was making a stove. They installed a small stove that burned penguin skins. From a biscuit tin, they made a chimney, which became blocked at times but cleaned with a brush they made from penguin skins.

For the most part, they combined the rations with what they could kill: sea elephants, crabeaters, Weddell seals, cape pigeons, paddies, petrels, rock cod, thousands of limpets, and seaweed. From these animals, they ate steaks but also heart, liver, tongue, kidneys, and brains. In June, Lees's journal mentions having eaten too much steak; in July, he made an inventory of all the food stocks, which still contain biscuits and rations of vegetables, meat, fish, beetroot, cauliflower, parsnips, cabbage, carrots, green beans, onions, spinach, turnips, soup, suet, haddock, herring, tinned food, fish, veal and ham pate, corned beef, fish stew, calf head, mutton cutlets, roast mutton, duck and peas, jugged hare, lamb and peas, ham, petit pois, dry peas, dry milk powder, coffee, cocoa, jam, and steak.[30] They also invented their own recipes, such as blubber and *Virol* (bone marrow supplement in a jar), biscuit fried or made into a pudding. Hoosh was porridge of meat, fat, and melted snow, often thickened with crushed biscuit. This they made into other recipes, blubber fried in hoosh, hoosh with hot milk, and seal hoosh with sugar.[31]

The party was tired of the meat diet and had a craving for sugars. They missed the taste of onions and tomatoes. Even so, they were looking forward to their meal times as the main events of the day. By the time August arrived, food and fuel were running short. For some of the men, the greatest difficulty was the shortage of tobacco. When it ran out in mid-June, they became depressed. Lees wrote with jittery handwriting: "Men all out of tobacco makes them very irritable and impertinent. They sit about mopping and cursing." In his notes, his entries reflect the changing mood and food supplies. "The bright weather does us a lot of good by way of cheering us up. The dull wet days are correspondingly depressing." When they had to lie in their sleeping bags, life was dull, but when they were out gathering food, the days passed quickly. Lees recorded each day how many penguins and Weddell seals came by and if they killed any of them. On August 14, he wrote: "an enormous pregnant female Weddell came up onto the shore under ice foot close to hut and was killed. It had extra thick blubber. Hurley tries baking *dulse* (a red algea) all day + produces quite a passable jelly from it. Estimated 800lbs of seal. The steward fished if we were dissatisfied with the food."

Lees was again jolly on August 24 when he remarked that it was the most beautiful day. On August 30, he recorded that they still had food (biscuit, mutton broth with salt, mutton cutlets and potato, thinned peaches, and coffee) but no one had enough appetite to eat.

Shackleton's three attempts to rescue turned back due to heavy ice pack surrounding the island. They were finally rescued on the fourth attempt. The *New York Times* wrote that the men had just sat down to a lunch of seaweed and limpet when they were saved.[32] In Lees's diary, we find instead that a lunch of boiled seal carcass was interrupted when one of the men, Marston, calls the magic words: "A ship!"[33]

After the rescue, on September 11, 1916, the *New York Times* published accounts of an interview with Shackleton and Wild in which they described how sometimes the conditions did not allow any seals to land on the island and made their diet very scarce. When they had seal meat, it was a great joy among the men, even more when they found undigested fish in the stomach of a seal. Other times, their breakfast consisted of penguin fried in blubber, lunch was biscuits with raw blubber, and dinner fare was penguin breast and Bovril. When the summer months came, the ice started to melt and they found some seaweed on the rocks and they collected limpets, aquatic conical snails.[34]

Shackleton had known from his previous journeys that good feeding was important and eating fresh meat was a way to avoid scurvy. For this, he took vitamin pills with him. He also took along lime juice capsules, but these were never used. On Elephant Island, they ended up eating all the fresh meat they could hope for. For his part in the expedition, Lees would receive the Silver Polar Medal. Remarkably, when the rescue came, the men were in better condition than when they landed on Elephant Island. As Lees called it, "their full menu" kept them free from scurvy.

Today's Antarctic Trail Diet

Much of the exploration to the South Pole was about exploring the limits of the human condition as well as reaching extreme geographies. In more recent history in 1989, explorer Arved Fuchs set off to the South Pole with his partner Reinhold Messner, on his way to complete the Antarctic crossing over the South Pole on foot. The trip was the first to the pole with neither animal nor motorized help, but on skis and with parasail. His sled weighed more than a hundred kilos. He knew that it would be extremely cold and prepared with enough fuel and food. The total trip was 2,800 miles long. Sometimes, they could go 45 kilometers a day, but sometimes only 4 to 5 kilometers. They set off in November and reached the South Pole on New Year's Eve. Fuchs became the first man to reach both poles in the same year

A modern-day Artic ration. The contents of a modern sledging box containing twenty man-days of food: twenty days of food for one man or ten days of food for two men.
Courtesy of Paul Ward.

on foot. After the pole, the team had a fight on how far to go each day, with Messner trying to cover more distance and Fuchs not wanting to walk as long, sometimes walking for twelve hours a day and hungry. The food rationed was very little; they lost a lot of weight and eventually suffered from muscular atrophy. They arrived at the coast on February 13, 1990. Afterwards, Messner would call Everest "a child's play compared to the Antractic."

In polar expeditions when the body needs heat to warm itself to keep vital organs functional, the need for energy increases dramatically. On top of that when a person is hauling a sledge, the need for energy increases even more and becomes about 6,500 calories a day, three times more than regular daily dietary need. This is provided with the food that is carried which must be light, well-packed, and concentrated with calories.

Today, food taken on Antarctic journeys is much more sophisticated. There are light and compact freeze-dried foods containing high calories, and they are easy and quick to prepare which saves fuel as well as time. Freeze-drying means that the weight is much less, and modern packaging is significantly lighter than the tins that used to be taken along. Dehydrated food is also more varied in recipes than in the past. Despite attempts to introduce variety, much sledging food tastes quite similar today. It is also costly, more than twice that of feeding someone at the main base, due to expensive dehydrated food.

And what happened to the pemmican? Why did it not remain as an Antarctic "favorite"? In light of all other canned, dried, freeze-dried, or concentrated modern food of today, maybe the words of the late Bishop of Saskatchewan from 1902 explains why pemmican did not retain its popularity even in Canada, considered the home of pemmican. He is said to have stated before a distinguished audience in London the following discouraging words: "Eating pemmican was like chewing a candle."[35]

CHAPTER 4

Mountain Expeditions

Rising from the ground toward the sky, mountains are close to heaven and gods. They have been sacred for many cultures. For some, they are intimidating; for others, they are inviting. Early mountain expeditions were extensions of mountain walks with their yet-to-be-improved gear and often lavish meals carried with a caravan of porters. Although some of the Alps peaks were climbed in the late eighteenth century, travel was slow and mostly on foot; no trains or cable cars took travelers to the foot of the mountains. Professional guides were few and not always consulted as advisers, but often taken as porters or servants.

Mountaineering did not emerge as a sport until the nineteenth century. Climbing of mountains with the objective to ascend the summit was recognized as a sport after 1854 when Sir Alfred Wills climbed Wetterhorn. Three years later, the Alpine Club was founded and the period known as the golden age of alpinism started. In the early years of the golden age, climbs were scientific as well as sportive. It was not uncommon for mountaineers to carry instruments up the mountain and make scientific observations. Mountaineering slowly became an exertion with symbolic results. Triumph rather than observation became a pursuit on its own and was measured in firsts, fastests, and mosts.

A Letter from Mont Blanc

The *dame* of the Alps, Mont Blanc, the highest mountain in Europe, with its white dome arching over the border of Italy and France, was totally unknown up until the middle of the eighteenth century. The Swiss named the dangerous mountains in the Chamonix valley "the cursed mountains." Swiss engineer and cartographer Pierre Martel mentioned and measured the height of Mount Blanc in 1745. In 1760, Horace Bénédict de Saussure, who was an aristocrat from Geneva, offered a financial reward to anyone who could complete the first ascent of Mont Blanc. After some trials and attempts, it was Michel Gabriel Paccard, a doctor from Chamonix, who accomplished the first climb to the summit with his guide Jacques Balmat, on August 8, 1786.

We have to remember that at that time men had no rope, no crampons, and no ice axes like today. They only had a long and heavy alpenstock. Moreover, they were carrying Paccard's scientific equipment, particularly his heavy mercury barometer in a long wooden case.

Neither of the two left a published record of their ascent. Others wrote their story and gave the credit mainly to Balmat, downplaying Paccard's role. When British climber Ernest Hamilton Stevens published Paccard's lost narrative of the first ascent of Mont Blanc in the *Alpine Club Journal*, he showed how both had been to the top by sharing the summit notes of Paccard, and this put an end to the Paccard-Balmat controversy.[1] According to these notes on the second day of their two-day climb, the men left their bivouac in Montagne de la Côte and walked for 14.5 long hours, a feat of courage and endurance, before they reached the top. They reached the summit after hours of constant climbing, over some very steep slopes and crevasses. If they had to stay in the mountain for one more night, they would freeze to death. Paccard later wrote: "At the top, when we wanted to write and eat, we found the ink in my pocket ink-bottle to be frozen, and so was some meat that Balmat had in his bag."

With this first ascent, Balmat and Paccard inspired generations of mountaineers including Eric Shipton, who became an important figure in Himalayan mountaineering, nearly being the first person to climb Mount Everest. Shipton would later write, "Theirs was an astounding achievement of courage and determination, one of the greatest in the annals of mountaineering. It was accomplished by men who were not only on unexplored ground but on a route that all the guides believed to be impossible."[2]

Not the first or the second but the nineteenth climb to Mont Blanc raised tremendous interest after it was published in a book.[3] In 1827, John Auldjo, a Scottish Canadian geologist, arrived at the summit with six guides and a bottle of wine. From the summit, he wrote an affectionate letter to his sister Annie. This was the first ever letter written from a summit. It is still preserved and kept at the Alpine Club in the United Kingdom. In this letter, the odd spelling and Auldjo's shaky handwriting and confusion over the date (he signed it 1825) signals the effect of altitude.

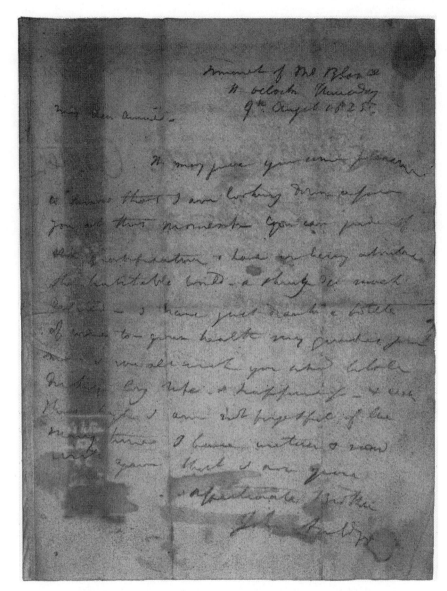

The first summit letter, by John Auldjo to his sister from summit of Mont Blanc, 1827.
Alpine Club Photo Library, London.

My dear Annie,

It may give you some pleasure to know that I am looking down upon you at this moment. You can judge of the gratification I have in being above the habitable world—a thing I have much desired. I have just drunk a bottle of wine to your health. My guides join me & we all wish you well while drinking—long life and happiness—& even this high I am not forgetful of the many times I have written & now write again that I am your

Affectionate brother

John Auldjo

At the time, taking wine to Mont Blanc was not a strange affair. The food list of later expeditions resembled not the provision for a mountain ascent but the shopping list for a Victorian feast. Supplies for a climb to Mont Blanc on August 12, 1851, with five climbers and four guides were dominated by liquor, in amount and in cost.[4]

60 bottles of vin ordinaire
6 bottles Bordeaux
15 bottles St. Jean
8 bottles Cognac
1 bottle syrup of raspberries
6 bottles of lemonade
2 bottles champagne
20 loaves
10 small cheeses
6 packets of chocolate
6 packets of sugar
4 packets of prunes
4 packets of raisins
2 packets of salt
4 wax candles
6 lemons
4 legs of mutton
4 shoulders of mutton
6 pieces of veal
1 piece of beef
11 large fowls
85 small fowls

What was still seen as strange, however, was women climbing mountains.

Walking the Mountains in a Skirt
and on a Champagne Diet

When women started entering mountain summits in the late nineteenth century, it was definitely threatening for men who attached great importance to climbing as a means to prove their manliness. In this period, women were not as submissive and tamed as commonly thought. They engaged in many activities in literature, philosophy, and natural history; however, competitive sports and extreme exercise were inaccessible to them. This was largely due to the advice that the doctors were giving against strenuous exercise, based on the perception that women need to protect their reproductive system and their roles as mothers and wives. Medical journals even published articles on dangers of menstruation and how to manage it. There was an agreement among doctors that women must rest during this period. This did not mean, however, that women were compliant. Upper middle class women in the towns and cities of England were inquisitive, educated, and sometimes spoke foreign languages. This inevitably led to some of them being critical about medical advice and challenging to prove it wrong. It helped that around that time medical professionals also received a lot of criticism. At a time when epidemics, early death, and disabilities were common struggles, doctors were not always respected. Some women and their families ignored medical advice and started cycling and exercise. In this context, women were quick to follow men in the golden age of mountaineering. By the mid-1870s most alpine summits were climbed by women, and mostly in style.

In 1830, when Mademoiselle Henriette d'Angeville was attempting an ascent of Mont Blanc, in her luggage were a feather boa, a black velvet mask, and a pigeon in a cage. Next to her warm clothes and walking stick, she also carried what she called "for the convenience of the journey" a straw basket with small inside pockets, a phial of vinegar salts, a phial of eau-de-Cologne, a folding pocketknife, a small and a big fan, a friction brush, in case of numbness, a shoehorn "for changing my boots," a rubber pillow, the indispensible notebook, with half a dozen sharp pencils, a small looking glass, a first-class telescope, a thermometer, a box containing cucumber pomade, two flasks, with their own beakers, one containing almond milk and the other lemonade, a small spirit kettle "to make tea in five minutes or to heat soup" and a box containing tea.[5]

Before setting off to climb Mont Blanc with six Chamonix guides and six porters, Henriette d'Angeville consulted her doctor, prepared her will, and then she made an inventory for the trip. She ordered "enough food for the men to be in good health and not suffer from lack of nourishment: 2 legs of mutton, 2 ox tongues, 24 fowls, 6 large loaves, 18 bottles of St Jean, 1 bottle of brandy, 1 bottle of *syrop*, 1 cask of *vin ordinaire*, 12 lemons, 3 pounds of sugar, 3 pounds of chocolate, 3 pounds of French plums." It seems that she needed six porters to carry all this food, and she needed all this food to sustain the men. For herself she took only a few things with her: some lemonade, a pot of chicken broth, a private *blancmange* in a flask, and a few prunes. How she carried a *blancmange* in a flask remains a mystery, as this is a white pudding made of sugar, milk, or cream thickened with starch and gelatin.[6]

Such was the bountiful account of first female climb of the highest mountain in Europe. The first only if we do not count another woman, who was literally dragged by the guides to the top, for very different motives. Maria Paradis, a peasant born in Chamonix valley, was taken to the mountain by Jacques Balmat, twenty-two years before d'Angeville in 1808. "The guides told me you are a pretty girl and you need to earn money. Travellers will ask to see you and they will tip you well."[7] The eighteen-year-old Paradis set off with Balmat and two guides. By the end of the next day, she was begging Balmat: "Throw me in a crevasse and go where you want." Instead, the guides pulled her to the top by her arms. After this frightful climb, she became one of Chamonix's most famous residents, adopted the name "*Maria de Mont-Blanc*" and opened a well-visited tearoom at her home in Les Pèlerins.

So when twenty-two years later D'Angeville was on the summit of Mont Blanc, something surprising happened that would make her be remembered as the highest person *ever* on Mont Blanc. Her guide Couttet said, "You must go higher than Mt. Blanc." He and another guide, Desplan, interlocked their hands to form a seat, on which they made her sit and lifted her from the snow as high as they could, thus in fact elevating her to a greater height that had never been attained by any other man or woman before her. On the summit, she wrote a few notes in her little book as well as some letters to her friends. Her thoughts were selfless and mostly reflected her astonishment with nature. When her eyes met the border of her country with Italy, she became patriotic: "My soul framed an ardent invocation for the glory and good fortune of France." This was the right moment to release the pigeon, which was carrying a note attached to its foot to announce the good news to the count of Paris. The pigeon project, however, was not as successful as planned. The note never arrived in Chamonix and the pigeon never returned to the dovecote. It was most likely shot down while flying over Les Contamines.

After an hour on the summit, D'Angeville and her party started their journey back. The fact that she was in better condition than the men was no surprise to her, considering her will and motivation which they lacked, "Those who, unlike me, had not come for pleasure, found that time dragged and their sufferings were hard to bear. I made my way back to them, and as soon as I saw the condition of my poor fellow-climbers, I hesitated no longer." She inscribed her favorite proverb on the snow before departure: "*vouloir c'est pouvoir* (to want is to be able to)."[8] The next day at tree level they found men waiting with a mule to carry d'Angeville. She was, however, in very good shape and insisted on entering Chamonix on foot.

In the second half of the nineteenth century, more and more women joined mountaineering history. At the same time, more women continued to be guided to the wonders of a mountain with no ambitions to climb it. In 1854, a husband and wife team made a joint expedition that would certainly not be as spectacular as climbing Mont Blanc but had its own special reward.

Sir Alfred Wills, who was a pioneering mountaineer in the Alps, had just gotten married and desired to introduce his new wife to the high Alps. He decided to spend the night at Mer de Glace in a bivouac with a secret arrangement by no other than Jaques Balmat as their guide. Balmat employed an old man and a *bon garçon* (good boy) as porters. They set out on August 28, taking a considerable amount of equipment, a mattress, blankets, sheets, a coffeepot and a supply of glasses, with knives, forks, and spoons. The old man carried all these while the *bon garçon* carried the vast amount of provisions to celebrate the occasion. They walked all day up to the glacier, lunched near Trélaporte, and continued up to the Mer de Glace. On this delightful afternoon, when they reached their bivouac spot, the lady sat down and started sketching while the porters started preparing the banquet. At seven in the evening, on a large flat rock, Balmat took out a tablecloth and spread delicacies on it: chicken, mutton, bread, butter, cheese, biscuits, raisins, salt, sugar, cream. Potatoes were roasting, and coffee was boiling. Glühwine accompanied the feast. "A more delightful evening was never passed," wrote Sir Alfred Wills. After all, Balmat was known to do things nicely. And despite the cold night and below-freezing temperatures that followed, this was a high-class honeymoon for a young bride of Victorian drawing rooms.[9]

In the early 1860s, all of the summits of the great peaks were reached one by one. Finally Matterhorn, a pyramid mountain with four challenging faces, also known as mountain of mountains, became the subject of an international competition. In 1865, Edward Whymper and his party finally summited Matterhorn, but on the way back a disaster occurred. A slip, a broken rope, and four deaths later, mountaineering became almost a dirty word in Europe. Two years after the tragedy, a group of Italians tried to climb Matterhorn from the Italian side with Whymper's rival J. M. Carrel and his party, including his own daughter Félicité. She nearly became the first woman to climb Matterhorn. Nearly, because only 300 feet below the summit, a terrible storm caught them and turned her dress over her head. She was wearing a *crinoline*, a structured petticoat, a stiff fabric under her dress. Her father and the rest of the party struggled but achieved to disentangle her and yet they had to abandon the climb. The spot of the incident was marked as Col Félicité and this is how the young woman left her fame in the mountain.[10]

Four years later in 1871, Henriette d'Angeville would die at the age of seventy-seven, before she could know that later that year Matterhorn was to be climbed for the first time by a woman. This woman was Lucy Walker, another female mountaineer who was very well prepared for this challenge. With this, the golden age of mountaineering for women began.

Lucy Walker was a British woman mountaineer who started climbing at the age of twenty-two when her doctor recommended it as a cure for her rheumatism. This was still the second half of the nineteenth century, and not many women were climbing mountain summits, let alone climbing above the snowline. Although Lucy was not the first woman to climb in the Alps, she was the first who climbed so many. By the time she died at the age of eighty-one, she had completed ninety-eight expeditions. Lucy Walker had achieved some first ascents: the Lyskamm (1868), the Matterhorn (1871), and the Weisshorn (1873). Sadly, she did not move her pen as much as her feet, and she did not leave any written personal record of any of these achievements.[11]

Walker was the first woman on many peaks. She turned into a famous climber when she became the first woman to climb Mount Matterhorn, at a time when women were still thought to be better off walking in the safety of valleys instead of mountaintops, where "even" men had died. She was a large young woman with pace, endurance, and determination no less than that of any man. Next to this, she also was a lady who spoke many languages, was an expert in needlework, and entertained people as a charming hostess at her home in Liverpool. What was remarkable was how her Victorian lifestyle had penetrated her climbing style. She would climb mountains in her white print dress. Her diet in the mountains was sponge cake and champagne.[12] This made her fans and foes cheer for her with great enthusiasm, as we see from the lines printed in British weekly humor and satire magazine *Punch*, shortly after her climb to Matterhorn.

A lady had comb to the Matterhorn's summit,
Which almost like a monument points to the sky;
Steep not very much less than the string of a plummet
Suspended, which nothing can scale but a fly.

This lady has likewise ascended Weisshorn,
And, what's a great deal more, descended it too,
Feet foremost; which, seeing it might be named Icehorn,
So slippery 'tis, no small thing is to do.
No glacier can baffle, no precipice balk her,
No peak rise above her, however sublime,
Give three times three cheers for intrepid Miss Walker,
I say, my boys, doesn't she know how to climb![13]

Lucy Walker is considered one of the pioneers of women climbers. Clearly climbing the mountains in dresses was not practical. The proper dress for climbing had been an issue that some innovative ladies got around by sewing loops in the hems of their skirts or attaching strings with which they raised or lowered their hems when they were on the walk. In contrast to Walker, who always wore dresses, Marguerite "Meta" Brevoort, who followed in the footsteps of Walker in the Alps season after season, was the pioneer for wearing trousers.

As an American living in England, Brevoort made a number of important ascents in the Alps. She had had the ambition to be the first woman to climb the Matterhorn until her role model Walker made it to the summit a few days before Brevoort arrived.[14] Her experiments with clothing started when she devised a scheme with a cord run through a series of rings around the bottom of the skirt by which the skirt was lifted up. These experiments proved to be useless after which she gave up trying and reverted to the absolute taboo: trousers. She was said to sing the *Marseillaise* on the summit of Mont Blanc after drinking champagne.

Brevoort mostly climbed with her nephew Coolidge but another unusual lady accompanied them. This lady was a beagle called Tschingel, because she made a successful crossing of Tschingel Pass. She was not an aristocrat, but a dog with a simple lineage. Tschingel was first believed to be a male until she started giving birth to puppies.[15] In her eleven years, she climbed thirty peaks and crossed thirty-six passes, perhaps thanks to her diet of red wine and warm weak tea.[16]

Historians mostly overlooked women climbers because they either did not write about their experiences or wrote more about the environment and the nature, describing their external observations. When we look at the fame of women climbers, we come across their eccentric champagne and cake habit. However, at the time men also traveled with luxurious foods and liquor to the mountains. Historian Clare Roche claimed that the "New Women" were already climbing and walking in the mountains before they became a phenomenon, as evidenced by the records of clients in the guide journals archived in the Alpine Club library. This "new woman" was presented as an educated, unmarried, and independent woman who refused motherhood. However, women mountaineers were a mixed group. Some climbed with husbands, some with fathers, brothers, or friends. Not all women wanted to climb summits either. Some enjoyed walking, drawing, and writing. For women in general, it was a mixed motivation to be in the mountains. For some, it was a physical endeavor and for others, a personal journey. Their motivation was also reflected, not so surprisingly, in the eating habits of these women. Some were very competitive and could even do without eating. Katherine Richardson, for example, raced to the Dauphiné region of the Alps in 1888 because she heard that a woman was planning an attempt to the last unclimbed Alpine peak, the Meije. She arrived there only to find that the lady they were talking about was none other than she herself. One guide commented: "she does not sleep, she doesn't eat and she walks like the devil." On an ascent, she was said to stop for forty-five minutes to wait for her guide to recover.[17] When she did eat, her modest diet consisted of bread and butter, with honey or jam, and tea.[18]

There were many other women with impressive lists of achievements in the mountains: the Pigeon sisters, Mrs. Mummery, and Mary Paillon to name a few. There were also other Victorian women travelers as globetrotters and voyagers. These women were active at the end of the nineteenth century and beginning of the twentieth century when women's emancipation was gathering momentum among middle-class educated women. It was the Victorian passion to improve oneself, which found an outlet in world travels. What was common to all of them was the growing desire for independence. Their motivation for travel might have been writing, painting, photographing, or missionary. To avoid accusations of self-promotion, which was against social norms, women kept private journals, penned letters, and wrote anonymous publications instead.[19] This might very well be the reason they wrote about food too.

One of the globetrotters of that time was Isabella Bird, a woman from a middle-class background, set free from her world when the doctors recommended she spend time outdoors. Her travels started with Australia; she went around the world even more after her husband passed away. She was known to have a cast-iron digestion for food and for facts and sights, covering thousands of miles on horseback over high mountains and distant rivers, on a handful of rice and raisins. Her trips were missionary pursuits which she funded herself and did not have a budget to allow luxuries. As trips extended to different geographies and geographical nature, carrying tons of food supplies from England was out of the question. She had to make do with local food. In *Journeys in Persia*, she wrote of having enjoyed "the food of roast mutton, rice, chapatti, tea and milk, without luxuries or variety." Another globetrotter, Marianne North, roamed Europe with her father and when he died, she went on long journeys to Jamaica and Brazil. She had long had the dream of going to tropical countries to paint their peculiar vegetation. Her staple diet in her travels was bread and butter, displaying the diversity of the eating habits of lady travelers.[20]

Some women did not compromise style for achievements. American-born May French Sheldon was from a wealthy family. In her travels, such as her Kilimanjaro safaris, she had with her a caravan carrying her dainty cloth to spread, napkins and enameled dishes, and an array of cutlery for each course where she would sit at a dinner on a trail in her silk dress.[21]

Also Aubrey le Bond, the first president of the Ladies Alpine Club, was known to eat well. For the *Alpine Journal*, the magazine of the Alpine Club, she reviewed her food experiences over the years. Her favorite foods were jams and *pâté-de-fois-gras*. She found that huts were few and did not provide any food. However, after half a century of climbing she was impressed with the variety of preserved foods available in the 1930s. When thermos bottles were finally available, she declared them a boon for modern climbing. The best food experience she had while in the mountains was in the Arctic Norway. "The provisions we took on our expeditions were the most delicious any climber could wish for. Slabs of salmon-trout just caught, good bread from Tromsö, excellent butter and jam; while for drink, tea freshly made whenever wanted with thick cream from a tiny farm close to our camp, was a diet voted perfection for the mountaineer."[22]

Around the same time far away in Australia, Freda du Faur, wearing a skirt below the knee over knickerbockers and long puttees, expressed her fulfillment in the mountains, and the attitude some women had toward the basic needs such as food: "all the primitive emotions are ours—hunger, thirst, heat and cold, triumph and fear—as yard by yard we win our way to stand as conquerors and survey our realm."[23]

Everest and Thin Air

After the Alps, the world turned to the Himalayas. In the beginning of the nineteenth century, the British had already started the Great Trigonometric Survey of India to determine the location and names of the world's highest mountains. In 1856, they established the highest of them all, measured at 8,840 meters, and the Royal Geographical Society gave it its English name after Sir George Everest, the geographer and former surveyor general of India. In searching for the food history of mountaineering, looking at the history of Everest gives us a lot of clues about eating on foot at the edge of human capabilities.

The British always viewed Everest as their own mountain. This is because they were controlling the border with India and no other country had access to it. The British mountaineers wrote much of Himalayan mountaineering history. The first recorded efforts to climb it started in 1921 with the British reconnaissance expedition. In 1922, a group of British mountaineers made the first climb to Mount Everest with the intention to summit the mountain. The group included George Mallory, who would later also join an expedition with Andrew Irvine; the men disappeared, and Mallory's body was found seventy-five years later, below the summit. The 1922 expedition was the first where oxygen bottles were used. The Tibetan and Nepalese porters nicknamed these oxygen bottles as "English air."

Early expeditions were seen as if they were military operations. This was partly due to the national funding and symbolism of the attempts and partially due to the army background of mountaineers. Even the words used in expeditions reflected that. In many records of climbs of the early 1900s, summit attempts were called "assaults." The approach to food was also militaristic. Food for the mountains was the food of the soldier, not because it suited the mountain but because it suited the planning. It represented what was needed: control over nutrition, weight, and eventually performance. In the trip reports published the year after, General Bruce reported how food was seen in high camp, "Practically speaking, we hardly considered by which name our meal should be called, but only what would seem nice to eat or convenient to produce, when we next wanted food or drink. Among the supplies I classify some as 'standard pattern'—such things as we know were always to be had in abundance, the *pièce* as it were, of our whole *ménage*— three solid foods, two liquid food and one stimulant (meaning tea)." The three of standard pattern were ration biscuits, ham, and cheese. The two liquid foods were pea soup and cocoa. Ham and cheese were very popular.[24]

In the 1920s at the time of the first climb to Everest, the leading climbing manual *Mountain Craft* by the British climber Geoffrey Winthrop Young emphasized the importance of food in the mountains and the link between food and foot. "Mountaineers are sound men, and have usually only two weak points, the feet and the stomach. New boots or overwork attack the first, unaccustomed food, changing atmospheric pressures, and revolutionary hours of sleep, food and exercise upset the second."[25] Young advised that as food that is not palatable or eaten with pleasure is of little benefit and that high altitude suppresses appetite, climbers should be provided with "pleasant luxuries that go down easily." Accordingly, early mountain expeditions took

British Everest expedition breakfast at camp during approach, March 1922.
Alpine Club Photo Library, London.

large quantities of food, which included delicacies such as *fois gras* and truffled quails, as well as wine, champagne, and whiskey. The 1922 expedition included sausages, sardines, herrings, sliced bacon, soups, ox tongues, green vegetables, peas, and beans. As for luxuries, they had quails in truffles, some sweets such as crystallized ginger, figs, and prunes, and Heinz spaghetti.[26]

Although the 1922 attempt did not prove to be successful, Mallory did not give up and tried to raise more money to go to Everest again. When people asked why he wanted to climb the mountain, he famously said: "Because it is there."[27] However light this statement seems, climbing Everest had become a national pride, especially when climbers of other countries also wanted to start attempting it, only hindered by the private access of the British.

In 1924, in the footsteps of George Mallory, another British mountaineer named Edward Norton attempted Everest. He brought tins and bags of food to Camp V, a stick of pemmican, some tea, sugar, and condensed milk, a tin of sardines or bully beef, and a box of biscuits: the familiar food of arctic expeditions. Norton explained the difference in eating in high climbing: "Herein lies one of the difficulties of high climbing. One eats from a sense of duty, and it is impossible to force oneself to take enough food even to begin to make good the day's wastage of tissue."[28]

The new light way style of expedition came after the 1930s, which included eating local food at lower altitudes but still taking supplies for the high altitudes when energy and morale was needed the most. However, Raymond Greene, who was the expedition doctor of the British team in Everest in 1933, complained that the secretary in London took no notice of the wishes of the expedition members about what they wanted to eat.[29] Still, the 1933 party had special high-altitude rations consisting of toffee, Kendal mint, maple sugar, tinned and preserved fruits, jams, tinned coffee au lait, Ovaltine, cocoa, Bournvita (a chocolate malt drink mix), biscuits, and Brands Essence (chicken extract).

Above 18,000 feet, the diet of a mountaineer was monotonous and unpalatable. Eric Shipton on the 1935 Everest expedition noted that the caloric intake was reduced to 1,500 to 2,000 calories between 18,000 feet and 21,200 feet. At this altitude, mountaineers desired a lot of sugar, up to 14 ounces a day. They consumed this mainly in beverages, without any adverse taste effects, because beverages taste less sweet at higher altitude. Despite the lack of appetite, climbers often enjoyed cooked food, and some of them craved special foods such as salmon, sardines, and tinned fruit. The effect of sugar in relieving fatigue and the increased appetite for sugar at high altitude was interesting considering the experiments done on animals that showed that mild hypoglycemia sensitized the cerebral cortex to the adverse effects of lack of oxygen. This meant that desiring more sugar was a way for the body to deal with the lack of oxygen.[30]

Frederick Marshman Bailey was a British intelligence officer who spent a lot of time in the high Tibetan region and in unknown parts of China. He had relied on tinned products and local supplies until he got married and his wife considered tins "inefficient housekeeping." In Tibet, he could always find a sheep, yak's milk, butter, and cream, and he could bake bread each day with flour he carried on the trip, and biscuits he found useful to overcome the altitude sickness. In an article published in Geographical Journal in 1948, he advised large teams going to Everest region to supply their fresh vegetables in a very unique way. "On our annual trip from Sikkim to Gyantse we had vegetables specially grown for us. I suggest that for an Everest expedition, vegetables should be grown in the Arun or some other adjacent valley and a load of these carried up to the base camp every few days." Furthermore, he had recommended that a first-class chef at base camp, preferably a European or a really good Indian hillman, could prepare a first-class meal. This prospect would give the climbers coming off the mountain a great moral advantage. However, at that time teams on Everest were much more technically oriented in their meal planning.

The 1938 expedition took the diet to an extreme. Tilman took the weight of food to an absolute minimum, causing his team to complain of hunger and blaming the lack of food for their lack of success. Tilman thought simple foods were better than processed foods and eliminated jam, reduced the amount of rations, and depended largely on monotonous local foods.[31]

In 1952, British physiologist Griffith Pugh collected data at 25,000 feet at Cho Oyu. He predicted that on the summit of Everest people would be at the edge of their limit and staying alive would be difficult. He also was the first to understand that hydration was crucial to avoid the thickening of the blood, which prevented efficient transportation of oxygen in the body. He urged the climbers to drink 3 to 4 liters a day. He also understood that adding sugar to water would ensure ingestion of enough calories and would be easier than chewing solid foods at high altitude. Another important discovery of this expedition was pressure cookers. As the party became convinced of the value of a pressure cooker, it was decided to take it along in 1953. In many ways, 1952 expedition paved the foundation for a scientifically solid 1953 climb.

During the 1953 Everest climb, besides measuring the effect of oxygen support and physical performance, Dr. Pugh was also in charge of the expedition food. He was in a team with George Band, the youngest of the expedition. While Pugh reviewed the scientific evidence from dietary research he did on Cho Oyu the year before, Band had sent out a questionnaire to ask the climbers what they preferred to eat. Some climbers were very specific about what they liked and didn't, whereas others seemed fully uninterested. Ed Hillary and George Lowe gave a long list of their wishes including tinned fruit, salmon, dehydrated soup, dried fruit, chocolate, pressure cookers, fresh stew, and honey. They also explicitly mentioned what they did not like. In this black list we see the all-time least favorites: pemmican, grape-nuts, service biscuits.[32]

Himalayan expeditions of the past were a mixture of local foods with bulk foods from England. Below 10,000 feet, they would use rice, *dhal* (lentils), and *atta* (stone-ground wheat flour); above 10,000 feet, potatoes and *tsampa* (roasted barley flour mixed with yak butter and tea). Eggs and chicken were available up until 13,000 feet; yak and sheep could be purchased between 12,000 and 14,000 feet and sent up to 18,000 feet. Most of the meals in a Himalayan expedition were consumed at two meals, breakfast and supper, and these had to be very large meals to provide the daily caloric requirements (4,000 to 4,500 calories). Still sometimes mountaineers experienced problems in consuming the calories planned. In his expedition report, Noyce recounted difficulties they had with some of the food: "Breakfast 7.15. A large plate of porridge to which I add Grapenuts. Neither Gregory nor I feel like bacon. I don't think this is the height's fault, but the bacon's. In other ways we are eating well; only the yak stew last night defeated us."[33]

Cooking was done over wood fires up to 18,000 feet. Above that, cooking and getting enough liquids was difficult. Paraffin stoves were used. Snow was melted to make water for tea. This took a long time and used a lot of fuel. The difficulty of making water and the reduced sensation of thirst made it difficult to hydrate. Because at higher altitude water boils at a lower temperature (80 degrees Celsius or 176 degrees Fahrenheit at 20,000 feet), it does not get hot enough to cook food efficiently and costs a lot of fuel. Until 1951, pressure cookers donated by manufacturers were rejected by mountaineers. However, in the Everest trip of 1953 they used pressure cookers for meat and potatoes. The Sherpa cooks even improvised pressure cookers of their own "consisting of a biscuit tin with the lid forced on, and a small hole stoppered with a stick acting as a safety valve."[34] By 1954, pressure cookers would become acceptable by mountaineers.

Pugh saw that he had to make some adjustments to the diet of the mountaineers for the 1953 expedition to be successful. He had seen the importance of food and the well-being it provided at high altitudes. He wanted to develop rations that were lighter, sweeter, and also catered to the liking of mountaineers. He broke tradition and used composite rations from small-unit army troops. He took two types of rations: one type was the general purpose ration of tinned foods for fourteen and twenty-eight days combined in a different menu each day. Their weight was of no importance, and they would be supplemented by rice and potatoes. The second was an assault ration for use above 20,000 feet, where weight was economized and no tins were used. He also asked each climber before the expedition what they would like to be able to eat at high camps. These were packed in bulk and were called "luxury boxes." This way they could substitute what they didn't like from the assault ration with something they liked from the luxury box. At base camp, Pugh discarded the most unpopular items such as pemmican and the army biscuits. To the pleasure of everyone, he modified the assault ration to include rolled oats, milk powder, sugar, jam, sweet biscuits, cheese, *Kendall* mint bar or banana bar, boiled sweets, salt, cocoa, tea, soup, and lemonade powder. Yak meat, mutton, rice, and potatoes supplemented the general-purpose composite rations. During the assault, climbers ate most of the sugar and milk in their rations; they otherwise subsisted on items such as sardines, salmon, cheese, tinned fruit, and French *saucissons* from the luxury boxes, and Vita-Wheat, *Knäckebrot*, and honey salvaged from the Swiss expedition of the previous year. The diet of the porters was instead a simple *tsampa* and *atta*, which they consume in the form of a paste or dough taken at three meals in the day. Eight pounds of *tsampa* was the standard ration for a man for the 3.5-day journey, which was equivalent to 35,000 calories per day. They also had a large supply of sugar and plenty of tea. With these adjustments, the fitness of the climbers was much better than the year before. This could be measured as the body weight loss of the men. While in 1953 the average weight loss after the first month, or 13,000 feet, was 2 pounds, the year before it was 11 pounds. In 1953, even after the second month, the weight loss was merely 4 pounds.[35]

After the 1953 expedition, Pugh and Ward wrote that eating more sugar was offering relief at higher altitudes. "In the Western Cwm (20,500–22,000 feet) on Mount Everest, individual differences in tolerance to altitude began to be obvious. Going for too long without food caused unusual fatigue more than at lower altitude, which could be relieved by taking sugar."[36] There was also salvation coming from salvaged supplies. One of the youngest members of the 1953 expedition, Wilfried Noyce, recounted the joy of finding the Swiss boxes from the expedition of the previous year when they arrived at Camp IV. "At last. A glance to the left and there are the boxes. Two hundred slow yards, and we have arrived . . . Ovosport, Nescafe, cheese, orange juice—these luxuries have been refrigerated for us through the winter. Now they can be used to give variety to our diet."[37]

Finally on May 29, 1953, Edmund Hillary and Sherpa Tenzing Norgay, supported by of a team of 362 porters, 20 Sherpa guides, and 10,000 pounds of baggage, stood on top of the world.[38] When the summit was finally "conquered," a radio message announced it from Namche Bazar to the British Embassy in Kathmandu. A few days before, the *New York Times* had called Mt. Everest "earth's third pole."[39] When the expedition was finally successful, in big part thanks to his new oxygen sets and new approach to diet and hydration, Pugh wrote in his diary: "The ascent of Everest is another milestone in the progress of man's conquest of his environment."[40]

Pugh's contribution to high-altitude mountaineering was tremendous. His science, combined with the leadership of John Hunt and the total teamwork, demonstrated what was possible in the Himalayas. In just three years after the first climb of Everest, all the world's highest mountains would be climbed. This was the beginning of the golden age of Himalayan mountaineering and women were quick to follow.

It was not long before the first women planned an expedition to the Himalayas. When Elizabeth Stark organized the food for the first female expedition to the Himalayas for her and two of her friends, Monica Jackson

Tenzing Norgay and Edmund Hillary drink a celebratory cup of tea at Camp IV in the Western Cwm after their successful ascent of Mount Everest. Image by George Band, May 30, 1953. © Royal Geographical Society (with IBG).

and Evelyn Camrass, in 1955, she asked advice of men experienced in Everest, Kanchenjunga, and Antarctica. She drew up a packing plan of dividing food per week. For the weeks in high altitude, she prepared different boxes containing more high-altitude rations. She found this task rather difficult just as early explorers in the Arctic found out: some foods came in bigger boxes and she had to split them into proper quantities. Her climb mates challenged her to take more of their favorites, treats for Evelyn for when they felt low and more sardines because Monica liked them. Luckily, many companies supplied them with food for free or on special terms. Some companies even commented that she did not ask for enough food. They also gave Mingma (their expedition Sherpa) money to buy food and tea for the Sherpas at or below the base camp. Sherpas preferred their own food, rice, *dhal*, and *atta*. However, during their trip they would sometimes discover that Sherpas did not mind some of the western foods, like the jam that disappeared from their supplies. After a confrontation, the ladies received eggs and potatoes in exchange for the missing jam.[41] It turned out that Sherpas were mixing the jam with snow to make a dessert.[42] The jam and snow dessert was also mentioned in the 1953 Everest expedition reports of Wilfried Noyce as one of the few foods they had appetite for when they arrived at Camp IV:

"Some 'raspberry jam snow' and some chocolate. We don't feel like eating much."[43]

As expected, the women ate a lot more at the base camp than anywhere else. Mainly because their cook had much more time to prepare meals. They would eat soup and hot potatoes, and drink orange juice and lemon fizz. They would have tea and more potatoes, biscuits and jams and sardines, only as an aperitif before supper. Higher up, however, they were not hungry and during their walks they could only manage to eat chocolate, mint cake, dried fruit, or boiled sweets. In the evening, their appetite improved, and they had rice with *masala* (curry spices), *dhal*, and vegetables.[44]

This expedition paved the way for more women to head to the Himalayas, and those were not only mountaineers. In 1958, three women, practically homemakers, set off on an adventure. They drove through ten countries to India in six weeks and crossed 300 miles on foot into Zanskar in twenty-one days. Zanskar was then part of Tibet and forbidden to foreigners. They were the first Europeans to cross this land, and they even climbed a virgin peak and named it *Biri Giri* (Wives' Peak). One of them, Eve Sims, had the task of organizing food for the trip, although she was a self-described "recent wed with no experience in cooking." She asked the Ministry of Agriculture, Fisheries and Food for dehydrated food, read expedition books, and wrote down the names of the companies that supplied their food. She made a ration list and sent this to the other team members, Anne Davies and Antonia Deacock, for approval. They accepted everything as is, and only changed one thing: the brand of coffee. Sims then received all supplies as donations or at a reduced price: dehydrated meats, vegetables, fruits and fish, powdered milk, condensed milk (which they mixed with snow to make caramel *glacé*), sugar, biscuits, jams and marmalades, sweets and chocolates, lemonade powder, mustard, bedtime drinks, potato powder, instant coffee, and tea. She ordered so much tea that this became a topic everyone talked about. She sorted, packed, and listed all items and divided them for the outward journey, for the mountain trek, and for the journey back. The last two were sent to Bombay by sea.[45] After five months, they returned to England and never climbed again. Eve Sims's words prove that her motivation to explore the mountains was no less noble than another, "I'd been my father's daughter, my husband's wife, but this time I was somebody on my own."

By the 1970s, seeing women in the European mountains was commonplace. Yet in Japan, husband and family still came first for women, when Junko Miyazaki was planning the first female expedition to Everest. She first became pregnant, to meet her duties, and then started planning the trip. Her climbing permit was granted when she was four months pregnant, and when she finally attempted Everest in 1975 her daughter was 2.5 years old. Despite enormous difficulties both culturally and financially, Junko organized this trip for ten women. It would take her three years. Their food menu was economic, consisting of basic non-luxury dishes, but still it had 190 different kinds of food. It reflected the Japanese food culture and was a testimony to how food on trails represented food at home. For the base camp, they took *gyozas*, egg soup, *gomaku/zushi* (a rice dish), bamboo shoots and potato, *kanappe* (stiffed bread), *tshumami* (roasted potatoes), fruit jelly, and *sake*. For breakfast, they would eat boiled rice, *miso* (bean paste) soup, *mezashi* (fish), fried egg, and dried and braised seaweed. For the evening meal, boiled rice, omelette, *miso* soup, sausage, and stir-fried vegetables were planned. On Camp II, they would eat bread freshly made at base camp with butter and jam, tinned ham, cheese, and tea, which remarkably resembles European assault food (except for the fresh bread), merely from the necessity to carry lighter food on higher camps. On Camp II mornings, they would also eat *zoni* (thick soup and rice cake), pickled vegetables, and green tea, and in the evenings *takikomi yohan* (rice pilaf cooked with chicken and vegetables), *miso* soup and seaweed, salad, dried instant mashed potatoes, pickled vegetables, and tea. Unfortunately, they had not reported their food on further camps. What was recorded, however, was that on their final climbing day after three cups of coffee, Junko ascended the final stage of the mountain with Sherpa Ang Tschering alone as resources did not allow more people to go with her. On May 16, 1975, Miyazaki became the first female climber who set her feet on top of the world.[46]

Nutrition of the High Mountains

Surviving and performing at a high altitude has always been a great challenge for mountaineers. Thin high mountain air has less oxygen. Although the body can adapt to carry oxygen more efficiently by increasing its hemoglobin, red blood cells, the body never fully adapts. Hence, no native civilization lives above 5,100 meters.

When mountaineers who live in lower altitudes ascend to areas of high altitude, their body suffers from exponentially reduced oxygen, as they climb up. They suffer from headache, nausea, dizziness, trouble sleeping, fatigue, rapid pulse, and swelling of hand, feet, and face. These are symptoms of acute mountain sickness, which by itself is not very hazardous but if it is ignored and remains untreated can lead to more serious life-threatening high-altitude cerebral edema and high-altitude pulmonary edema. Also neuropsychological disturbances were frequently reported. In the early expeditions to

Everest, bizarre changes in perception and mood were reported. During the 1933 expedition, mountaineer Frank Smythe gave a dramatic description of a hallucination. He saw pulsating cloud-like objects in the sky. He reported a strong feeling that he was accompanied by a second person. He even divided his food to share with this imaginary companion. In the same expedition, Eric Shipton had aphasia at 7,000 meters. "If I wished to say give me a cup of tea, I would say something extremely different, maybe tram-car-cat-put," he recalls. "I was perfectly clear headed but my tongue refused to perform the required movements."[47]

Researchers have tested oxygen tubes in various forms and oxygen-increased respirators, which concentrate the density of oxygen in the air breathed through a mask by increasing total atmospheric pressure in the mask. There have been benefits demonstrated at altitudes up to 5,300 meters with such a mask.[48] Still to this day, there is no quick and easy solution to the thin air above 5,000 meters.

In 1960, Edmund Hillary and Griffith Pugh set up a project called The Himalayan Scientific and Mountaineering Expedition, also called The

Evans and Bourdillon resting at Swiss Camp V while breathing oxygen from their closed-circuit sets. Hunt's oxygen set in the foreground, May 2, 1953. Image by John Hunt.
© Royal Geographical Society (with IBG).

Silver Hut, which established an insulated hut at 5,800 meters (19,000 feet). Hillary and Pugh knew each other from previous trips to Cho Oyu in 1952 and to Everest in 1953. In this laboratory, which was set up 16 kilometers south of Everest, high-altitude physiologist Pugh carried out extensive studies on high-altitude acclimatization. The hut was occupied by people for up to nine weeks. There was weight loss in all expedition members ranging from 0.5 kilogram to 1.5 kilogram per week. This was the case despite the availability of sufficient freeze-dried and canned food, as well as fresh meat, potatoes, and eggs. Pugh concluded that this altitude was too high for permanent living mainly because the lung and the heart functioned at two-thirds capacity versus at sea level and fatigue limited physical work.[49]

After the first climb on Everest, it would take mountaineers twenty-five years to prove that standing on top of the world without oxygen support was possible. In 1978, Reinhold Messner and Peter Habler successfully ascended the mountain without the use of supplementary oxygen. This achievement provided the definitive answer to the question as to the ability of humans to survive in this environment.

The Silver Hut expedition also inspired the 1981 American Medical Research Expedition to Everest (AMREE), the first of its kind dedicated to studying human physiology at extreme altitudes. A prefabricated laboratory was set up at Everest base camp at 5,400 meters and other labs at 6,300 meters and 8,050 meters. One of the objectives of the expedition was to study nutrition and weight loss at high altitudes. This study found similar results to the Silver Hut study that despite the availability of high-caloric, tasty foods, people at high altitude lost appetite and weight even more than expected based on calorie intake and energy expenditure calculations. They have concluded that the fuel one uses, and therefore the food one eats, is not much of a limiting factor in performance, even at extremely high altitudes, and that what matters more is the appetite. They found that fatty foods were distasteful and western food tasted insipid. As the sense of taste is dulled at high altitude, stronger flavors such as curries and herbs were needed to whet the appetite. Moreover, expedition members desired what was not available. Therefore, at recreational altitudes (8,000 to 12,000 feet), they recommended eating what you feel like eating.[50]

Since then, many men and women have climbed Everest without supplemental oxygen. Still to this day, every year thousands of people attempt the summit and only about 15 percent achieve the summit and come back successfully. Success depends on many factors, including sufficient food and hydration. In 2008, a group of scientists, including among others an anesthetist, a statistician, a vascular surgeon, and a computer analyst, studied the causes of death on Mount Everest over eighty-five years from 1921 until 2006. They examined the circumstances of death from sources such as direct reports and interviews, and based on indirect sources such as journals, books, and the Himalayan database. They looked at a database of more than 14,138 climbers, 8,030 of which were mountaineers and the rest Sherpas. In total, only 3,058 people achieved the summit ascent. The mortality rate was 1.3 percent and climbers typically died during descent from the summit. They confirmed that the death rate on Mount Everest is greater than that of lower mountains attempted by similar populations of climbers. They also found that most climbers on Mount Everest die above 8,000 meters, what is known as the death zone, usually during descent from the summit. They often developed cognitive impairment and ataxia, symptoms of high-altitude cerebral edema. Interestingly, common symptoms of altitude sickness at 2,500 to 5,000 meters (respiratory issues, nausea, vomiting, and headaches) were rarely noted. Their conclusion identified water as one of the determining factors by writing that "above 8,000 meters a common problem is a decrease in intravascular volume as a response to high altitude and dehydration due to the difficulties of melting sufficient snow to make water."[51] It is recommended to drink more water at altitude to overcome the drier air, the higher respiration rate, and natural diuresis (urinating more). In reality, one only needs an additional liter to a liter and a half of water at altitude, because too much water is harmful and can dilute the sodium levels of the body (which is called hyponatremia) causing weakness, confusion, seizures, and coma. As a rule of thumb, mountaineers check their urine color to see if they are properly hydrated: clear urine indicates adequate hydration, whereas dark urine suggests dehydration and the need to drink more water.

Water is definitely one of the problems and remedies of altitude. Another one is carbohydrates. When exertion is combined with not eating enough, it drains carbohydrate reserves. Signs of low blood sugar resemble hypoxia and hypothermia, confusion, dizziness, even hallucinations, especially in diabetics. A carbohydrate-based diet is recommended at altitude also because it requires less oxygen to burn. Climbers prefer a high-carbohydrate and low-fat diet, and find fatty foods distasteful. This is very different than the preferences of polar travelers, who indulged in seal meat and blubber. This can be due to the possible effects of fat malabsorption at high altitude. Absorption and healthy bowels are a rarity at high altitude. Even though this is not proven by research to this date, it is believable that the gut bacteria, much like humans, would act differently at high altitude and produce different amounts of gas under such conditions. Bill Tilman, who is an iconic expedition mountaineer, said that the mountaineer's worst problems were hemorrhoids and bedsores.[52]

With all these problems of breathing, eating, and digestion adding up, weight loss during high-altitude expeditions is a fact. Expedition food is not always appetizing, and climbers with reduced appetite don't eat enough food to compensate for the caloric intake they need to keep the energy balance of their body. After weeks of such a diet, vitamin deficiencies can also occur. This can be a very good reason for taking vitamin supplements during mountaineering expeditions. Although not recommended as a weight loss program, today it is generally accepted that a mountaineer who goes to climb Everest and takes six to eight weeks to acclimatize and wait for the right weather to attempt the summit would be a few kilos lighter when he comes back home.

When asked what he likes to eat on a mountaineering expedition, Dr. Schoene, MD, who was a member of the AMREE expedition, called for any diet that encourages eating, not excluding luxury items such as caviar. When he planned the meals for the 1981 AMREE trip, he went to a grocery store and wrote down the names and addresses from labels of foods that he thought he would want, and wrote letters to those companies asking if they would donate to the expedition. "Almost as a joke, I wrote a letter to the owner of Romanoff Caviar. Surprisingly, he wrote back: 'You can have all the caviar you want!'"[53]

Luxury and camp food might sound like an oxymoron, and caviar to travel 8 kilometers up from the sea might seem an oddity. However, this was not so for Russian mountaineers. Reinhold Messner recounted that when it came to food in the mountains, the Eastern Bloc countries had the best of the best. "We had plenty of food but the Russians for example, they took caviar with them on the eight-thousanders." Did he think it made a good mountain food? "For sure. You don't want to eat boring, tasteless food up there. That's no good at all. It has to taste good or it just gets left."[54]

Was caviar even good to eat? Persians used caviar as an ancient medicine and a provider of energy, like Italians in the middle ages. The Persian name *chav-jar* means cake of power, cake referring to the way it was pressed into a round shape. Once Persia became Muslim, sturgeon fish was considered to be unclean and caviar never had the place in Iranian life as in Russia. It was still used by a minority as a seaside snack and eaten in the mountains with bread and milk. In Iran, the sturgeon and its roe was considered *haram* (forbidden), as only fish with scales could be eaten according to Islamic law. Russians benefited from the fisheries in the Caspian Sea in the middle of the nineteenth century with concessions from the Iranian government. When the

1927 agreement expired, the government did not renew it and nationalized Iranian fisheries in the Caspian Sea. Caviar production and export became a state monopoly, and caviar export brought the Iranian treasury millions of dollars in revenue. After the revolution of 1979, the Islamic state remained between two evils, losing the sales of caviar or allowing a *haram* food to be sold. After careful consideration of clerics and fisheries experts, the traditional ruling was reversed, and caviar was declared *halal* (permitted).[55]

Caviar on Everest was not a luxury reserved to Russian mountaineers. In 2009, the founder of the United Kingdom's biggest importer of caviar, known as the Caviar Queen, Laura King took nine friends to Everest's base camp and held the highest breakfast in the world. In this trip, she raised 68,000 British pounds for the charity St. Davids Care, catering for young adults with moderate to severe learning disabilities. What she served was of another altitude: chocolate, sliced smoked salmon, champagne, and caviar. Caviar is extremely perishable. However, it can last for four to six weeks when kept unopened and refrigerated. After opening, it will last for only three to four days.[56] At the Everest base camp, it is possible to indulge in luxuries, whereas during the summit push the food looks much more Spartan.

In his 1924 Everest attempt, Edward Norton recounted another foreign food story. On their way to camp V, they discovered the remains of a Korean camp. With AngPhu Sherpa, they moved into the tent and found some food that had been left behind. Among this food was some seaweed. "I was very skeptical about this at first, because in fact it just looked like a sheet of black paper." Nonetheless, Norton thought he ought to try it just once. "So I did and in fact the leaves tasted quite excellent, of course they weren't very filling."[57]

Norton's anecdote is interesting because it emphasizes the western view on which food was normal and which was strange. Here we see various food cultures intersecting: those of the western world, those of the eastern world, and those of the expedition world. Mountaineers bring with them their national culture as well as what they think belongs to the culture of the mountains or challenges of the expeditions. Little information is available in English from historical Asian climbs in the Himalayas. However, when we look at the food taken to the mountains today by Korean, Japanese, and eastern European teams, we can see the diversity of the foods that comfort and support climbers of other cultures.

Kenneth Koh, an Everest climber and a self-described adventure nomad, recounts: "Some of the stuff that works well for me are the local *ikan bilis* (sun dried anchovies and fried peanuts with a sugar and chili)—sweet, salty and spicy! Nutritionally, that provides me with a seafood based, whole food source of minerals and iodine, which can be lacking in the mountains. You

Chilis above 8,300 meters, 2011.
Courtesy of Jamling Bhote/Kenneth Koh.

can eat it as is, like a snack, or added to a rice or noodle dish. I also carry some barbequed pork. It's our form of jerky. They sell it vacuum packed for travel. Once it's open, it will last about a week. Sometimes, I'll take two packs, and open them various times during the trip. Sometimes on trips, there isn't enough protein, both these fill the gaps. And a lesson from Everest: some hot sauce or powdered chili or chili flakes. Nothing like a little spice to help something unpalatable go down."[58]

Today, there are some natural remedies recommended for high-altitude illness, although with some doubt from the scientific medical world, such as coca leaves, ginkgo biloba, and garlic. There are also other alternative ayurvedic solutions to high-altitude illnesses highly researched in alternative medical circles, such as *Shilajit*, which is a herbal drug composed of a gummy exudate that oozes from the rocks of the Himalayas in the summer months; however, these are frowned upon by the medical field.

Despite its widespread use for prophylaxis in South America, there is no evidence that coca in the form of chewed coca leaves or coca tea is effective at preventing acute mountain sickness. As for ginkgo biloba, there are mixed results. It was shown to prevent or to reduce symptoms of acute mountain sickness in some controlled trials. However, there are also multiple studies showing the opposite results. The discrepancy is likely a result of differences in the source and composition of gingko products used in these studies.[59]

Sherpa guides in Nepal have been recommending their guests to have garlic soup as a remedy for altitude illness for years. Garlic is said to thin the blood and help ease blood circulation and might help high-altitude symptoms. Modern-day alpinist and co-author of *Extreme Alpinism*, Mark Twight proposed garlic as an essential cold-weather supplement. "It's a better anti-clotting agent than aspirin and reduces the stickiness of platelets, which improves overall blood circulation." He also noted that mountaineers including Reinhold Messner used garlic supplements for high-altitude climbing because physiologists claimed they improved vascular elasticity.[60] Garlic is also used for the treatment of fatigue, although the mechanisms involved remain unclear. In animal studies, garlic has been shown to promote exercise endurance. Differences in the methods of processing garlic result in differences in the intensity of its anti-fatigue effect, and the most favorable form of processing has been shown to be extraction of raw garlic followed by its natural aging for a long period in a water-ethanol mixture. In human studies, it has been confirmed that garlic produces symptomatic improvement in persons with physical fatigue, systemic fatigue due to cold, or lassitude of indefinite cause, suggesting that garlic can resolve fatigue through a variety of actions. Currently available data strongly suggest that garlic may be a promising anti-fatigue agent, and further studies are needed to have conclusive advice on its use in high altitudes and in general.[61] In another study, garlic was tested against high-altitude pulmonary edema in rats. The study demonstrated that after a high dose of garlic over five days, hypoxic pulmonary hypertension was blocked.[62] Although the medical evidence on garlic may not be conclusive, it sure adds a lot of flavor to foods in the mountains.

So, just in case it works, here is a garlic soup recipe from Gelbu Pemba Sherpa Chawa, in his own words: "Well about garlic soup, you have to prepare one soup bowl of hot water, one spoon of corn flour, you have to mix it first and you can put some green onion and 5/6 pieces of garlic you have to cut or grind. And salt and pepper that's all, but you can use garlic in any kind of soup."[63]

Messner's Load

During the 1970s and 1980s, the technical standards and scale of lightweight Himalayan climbing gathered huge momentum. This was the true golden age of mountaineering with light equipment, clothing, and food. Alpine-style climbing with no oxygen support and relying on less equipment became a philosophical idea. Climbers were walking light and fast, which made them exposed to danger for a shorter time but once there was trouble with weather or with navigation, the teams would be in bigger trouble.

In June 1970, Reinhold Messner and his brother Günther joined a team of mountaineers to be the first to climb the summit of Nanga Parbat, an eight-thousander in Pakistan and one of the toughest mountains of the Himalayas. The night before the summit day, the Messner brothers agreed that Reinhold would try to summit alone as bad weather was closing in. Yet, after Reinhold set off in the early hours of the morning, Günther caught up and unexpectedly joined him on the way to the summit plateau. The brothers climbed the summit right before sunset and stayed near the summit overnight in an emergency bivouac. They started the descent following a different route than planned and they got stuck in a difficult part of the mountain face. A couple of nights passed and help did not arrive. Despite the thin air, they could understand the options: to stay and die or to move and potentially live. The brothers descended traversing the mountain despite the dangers of an avalanche. After four days of no food and water, hallucinations started: they kept hearing running water as if there was a spring nearby. Günther had altitude sickness and felt very ill. Reinhold felt stronger and went ahead as the route finder. After a while when he realized that his brother was not following and returned to look for him, it was already too late. Günther was nowhere to be found. He was most likely killed by an avalanche. Facing the loss of his brother, exhaustion, and severe frostbite, which would cost him seven toes, Reinhold continued down to the Diamir valley until he met some local shepherds that helped him survive. Besides the devastation of having lost his brother, Messner experienced a lot of criticism upon return, blaming him for his brother's death.

This tragedy showed how little margin of error there is in alpinism. Messner brought with him no gear and only a little food, a handful of emergency nuts and raisins and effervescent vitamin tablets. At that altitude, every gram of extra weight counted. However, the nuts were too little to sustain. After 1.5 days of not eating and drinking, they tried the vitamin tablets, but there was no water to dissolve them. They tried to dissolve the tablets in the tube with snow. "It was too cold, you couldn't melt it in the tube in your hands. The foam was undrinkable, just a thick broth," Messner recounted in his memoir. "If only we had been able to get a mouthful of soup down us."[64]

It was eight years after this tragic experience, in 1978, when Messner set off to climb Mount Everest with Austrian mountaineer Peter Habeler.

Everything was calculated to be efficient yet sufficient. "I generally count on about half a kilo of gas and about 600 to 800 grams of food per day for two people—packet soups, bacon or salami, but not too much fat. It's harder to digest food at high altitudes. The stomach doesn't get enough oxygen either."[65] In this trip to Everest with careful planning and despite the opposition of scientists and doctors, Messner proved to the world that it was possible to climb Everest without oxygen support.

The mountain adventures of Messner continued until he became the first man to solo-climb Mount Everest and to climb all fourteen eight-thousanders of the world. He is considered the world's greatest mountaineer that has ever lived. He climbed with mountaineers from all over the world. After his mountaineering career, Messner set out to be the first man to cross Antarctica, Greenland, and the Gobi desert on foot. He was often guided by indigenous people: Eskimos in Greenland, Tibetans in Chang Tang plateau, and the Uighur at the edge of the Takla Makan Desert. He considered them his mentors and the guardians of our planet. Messner experienced the difference between an adventurer and a local firsthand. "Adventure as an end in itself is a crazy notion for many people out there. The Tibetan nomads just try to survive out there with their yaks their whole lives long."[66] Messner was saved on many occasions by the wisdom of the locals, who are familiar with the environment and have adapted to the challenges of living there. On the months-long eastern Tibet trip when he was back tracing the ancient migration trail of the Sherpas from Nepal to Tibet, he had met a yak caravan and stayed with them for a few days. Locals gave him *tsampa* and *sha kampo*, dried meat. Messner never pretended to belong to the wilderness. "Wilderness, rock and desert are transitory places, they can never be our home," he said, "By going to places where I don't belong I experience the art of living."[67]

In August 2005, remains of a climber were found on the Diamir face. Reinhold Messner recognized the shoes of his brother, which were made especially for the trip, just like his. DNA tests confirmed that it was Günther. After many search expeditions to search for this brother and despite continued criticism from the climbing world, this discovery allowed Messner to consider himself relieved from accusations that he left his brother in the mountain. What exactly happened in the mountain rests in the private memories of Messner. A month later, the remains of Günther were burned at the foot of Nanga Parbat in Tibetan tradition. The participants sang, "*yelo Lak*, the gods were merciful," and threw rice into the air.

CHAPTER 5

Desert Travel

For some explorers, crossing the arid land of deserts was the calling. Their intentions were mostly scientific and sometimes geographical, such as examining the potential petrol reserves under the sand bed. Desert exploration offered solitude and required persistence. Desert travel was not about conquering the environment but rather about enduring it. It also called for the help of locals like no other geography.

Besides the coldest desert of Antarctica, the Arabian Desert and the Sahara attracted the most European attention and the toughest footsteps. But before Europeans set foot on deserts for exploration, Marco Polo crossed the Taklamakan and the Gobi Deserts in Asia in his epic journey that lasted twenty-four years.

Marco Polo and the Gobi Desert

Venetian merchant traveler Marco Polo was not the first European to reach China but he was the first to leave a detailed chronicle of his experience, which inspired Christopher Columbus and many other travelers (*The Travels of Marco Polo*, c. 1300). His father and uncle had met Kublai Khan, the emperor of Mongolia, in present-day Beijing. Kublai Khan asked them to give a letter to the Pope, requesting one hundred Christians acquainted with the seven arts (grammar, rhetoric, logic, geometry, arithmetic, music, and astronomy) and oil of the lamp in Jerusalem. When they came to Venice for this task, they met Marco for the very first time and took him along in their journey in 1271. This is how their travel of almost 15,000 miles (24,000 kilometers) began.

They sailed to Acre and then rode on camels to the Persian port of Hormuz. As their ships were not strong enough to sail straight to China, they continued overland through the Silk Road. They crossed the salt desert of Kerman and the Pamir Mountains, called the *Roof of the World* by local people. The mountains were so high and the air so thin that he noted "fire gave less heat and the food did not cook well." They walked at the edge of the Taklamakan Desert but crossed the Gobi Desert before entering China. Polo was impressed by the vastness of Gobi. "The stock of provisions should be laid in for a month, that time being required for crossing the desert in the narrowest part. To travel it in the direction of its length would prove a vain attempt, as little less than a year must be consumed, and to convey stores for such a period would be found impracticable."[1]

Marco Polo described nomad Mongol tribes and how they relied mainly on meat and milk. Some had large flocks of goats, oxen, and sheep, and they ate whatever they could catch, including dogs and rats. In their saddlebags they carried strips of dried horsemeat and cakes of dried milk. They drank *kumis*, fermented mare's milk that was according to him slowly intoxicating.[2] In Marco Polo's writing, we also find the explorer's surprise at the diet of the locals, which contrasted very much the diet of Europe at the time. About the Mohammedans of Hormuz, he wrote[3]:

> They sow their wheat, rice, and other grain in the month of November, and reap their harvest in March. The fruits also they gather in that month, with the exception of the dates, which are collected in May. Of these, with other ingredients, they make a good kind of wine. When it is drunk, however, by persons not accustomed to the beverage, it occasions an immediate flux; but upon their recovering from its first effects, it proves beneficial to them, and contributes to render them fat. The food of the natives is different from ours; for were they to eat wheaten bread and flesh meat their health would be injured. They live chiefly upon dates and salted fish, such as the *thunnus*, *cepole*, and others which from experience they know to be wholesome.

Three and a half years later, the Polos reached Kublai's summer palace in Shangdu, near present-day Zhangjiakou. Marco was about twenty-one years old. Here he has said to have worked for Kublai. Eventually via Persia and the Black Sea he returned home to a Venice at war, where he would be imprisoned. It was in prison that he dictated his story to his cellmate Rustichello da Pisa, who wrote the famous book, with so much exaggeration that some historians questioned its veracity, and even whether Marco Polo

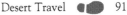

had ever been to China. Nonetheless, he left the first record of European exploration into Asia, "creating the Asia for the European mind."[4]

Perhaps it is not surprising that the first European explorer who explored Arabia on foot and with camels, for the sake of exploring it, was a Victorian eccentric. Geologist and linguist Charles Montagu Doughty had been planning his journey for eight months when he managed to organize a secret place in a pilgrim caravan of six thousand men and twice as many camels traveling to Mecca. Although he was not very successful in his disguise, he safely made it to Hejaz, where he left the caravan and joined another one, which carried butter to Mecca. He completed his trip with commercially unsuccessful books written in archaic English, which no one would read, but inspired and informed many explorers to follow in his footsteps. One of them was Thomas Edward Lawrence, also known as "Lawrence of Arabia."[5] Having survived water shortages and lasting on little or no water for one or two days at a time, he managed to arrive at the north edge of the desert after a year and saw the Persian Gulf. "I saw before me the sea . . . with the promise, after desert diet, of incomparable Arabian hospitality."[6]

Two other men left their mark on Arabian desert travel, although neither of them were the first in crossing it: Philby and Thesiger.

Philby's Copper Coffeepot

Harry Saint John Bridger Philby was the first European to cross Arabia from east to west on foot in 1917 when he was working in British intelligence in World War I. In 1925, he settled in Jeddah and set up a trading company. In 1928, he started making plans to cross the Empty Quarter. However, he could not become the first man who crossed the Empty Quarter because Bertram Thomas crossed it from south to north only a few months before Philby departed in 1931. Bertram Thomas was a financial adviser to the sultan of Muscat and was planning this trip secretly. Learning this, Philby was devastated but he planned a trip from north to south instead, with men, camels, and supplies for three months. He explored the area more intensively than Thomas. His trip was completed in 2.5 months and almost all food was consumed. Once back, he published his trip with great details on what they ate in the desert. He was surprised that food was "Among the Badawin the commonest theme of conversation."[7]

Dates and rice were the main staples, whereas coffee, tea, sugar, and butter with condiments such as cardamom, cinnamon, onion, salt, and pepper were not forgotten. However, they forgot to take flour, so they could not bake bread the whole trip. The longing for bread was heartfelt in Philby's notes: "There is nothing more satisfying than a lump of coarse bread cooked in the ashes and kneaded with dates or sugar and butter to make the mess they call *Hunaini*." He had a dozen tins of biscuits, which he carried mainly for their boxes; once they were empty, he would store insects in them. But the biscuits were sweetened and he couldn't use them up quickly enough to empty their boxes.[8]

When food was scarce, they reverted to other solutions such as making a substitute tea of cardamom and sugar. Philby was happier when they had plenty of food to eat. "Salih set apart at a second fire and cooked us a modest breakfast of rice liberally buttered from the leather jug he carried at his saddle-bow. That certainly filled me with cheerful strength."[9] Philby carried two tins of fruits with him from Mecca to Hufuf and from Hufuf to Empty Quarter, saving them for a crisis. And when he decided that it was the right moment to eat one, he realized that he was with ten other people. Not wanting to share them at all, he finally resolved to share it only with Sa'dan (his personal attendant) and flattered his conscience. "The fruit and juice were lukewarm with the day's heating but delicious; and I lay down to sleep as I had never slept before, while the clouds gathered about us with the music of distant thunder."[10] There are other instances where he mentions a private stash. "I had, it's true, a private supply of tea for emergencies, but this I was saving for the hoped-for final attempt on the waterless desert. So for the next few days I was without the comfort of tea."[11] He suspected that the others also had secret stocks.[12]

Philby had converted to Islam before this trip. He spent Ramadan in the desert and joined the fasting of the Bedu. This meant that he had not eaten or drank water all day for fifty-five days, only tea and freshly drawn camel's milk, once at dawn with a bowl of rice and again at dusk. Arriving at Shanna, he wrote: "A good meal of rice and and butter and dates after sunset made everyone happy and cheerful."[13] His companions sang a desert song when they arrived in Shanna with lots of specimens and no food to eat except for onions[14]:

We came to Shanna and saw foemen three;
We fled away for fear of treachery,
Seeking the Wadi where good onions be!

From time to time in the extremity of his hunger, Philby browsed on the raw flowers as they marched along. The Manasir made rice mixed with the flowers of *abal* (a plant with white edible flowers). They made a dish of *Makika*, which they recommended not to eat with meat as it is known to harden leather, though it seemed to have other hardening effects even with no meat. Philby discovered that the dry twigs of *abal* slightly crushed in a mortar and mixed with hot water made a fairly satisfactory substitute for tea. "Its colour was all that could be desired but the liquid was somewhat bitter to the taste and constipating in its effect—an antidote, as I was to learn, to the powerful salts of the Naifa water."[15]

In his memoir, there are dozens of times he mentions enjoying coffee and dates. He mentions being accustomed to eating dates dipped in butter or milk, a habit deep-seated in the Arabian character. They celebrated the end of the journey with coffee and tea.[16] "We have good things in plenty, and coffee."[17] And coffee emerges as an item that gives joy: "the coffee and dates had put fresh life into the men, who chatted and sang despite the risk of singing in the dark which might attract an oryx."[18] "Tales of hospitality in desert booths of great shaikhs with the coffee and the meat that make glad

Curved-beak Arab coffeepot (*dhille*) given to Harry Philby (1885–1960) while he crossed the Rub 'Al Khali (The Empty Quarter), January 1, 1932.
© Royal Geographical Society (with IBG).

the heart of man."[19] When the coffeepot appeared, it signaled time to rest. Philby wrote: "the time draws high for a short halt, with coffee to cheer the heart of man." Philby's copper coffeepot is now among the artifacts of the Royal Geographical Society, marking the significance.

In the harsh desert environment, it seems that the explorers made a big effort to be like their guides, or perhaps this was the main reason why they were attracted to the desert. Also Bertram Thomas believed that he should sacrifice his comforts and get along with Bedu: "I eschewed tobacco and alcohol to win a reputation for orthodoxy that would ultimately help me in the crossing of the Great Desert."[20]

But no one has adopted the Bedu lifestyle like Wilfred Thesiger did. He was the most affectionate witness of Arabian hospitality.

Thesiger and the Bedu Way

While the world was struggling with war, genocide, and colonialism, Thesiger was crossing the Empty Quarter, the largest sand desert in the world, in the area of today's Yemen, Saudi Arabia, United Arab Emirates, and Oman. He was sent there by the Food and Agriculture Organization in Rome to collect information on locust movements. The Empty Quarter was one of the last pieces of land uncovered on foot. With its towering sand dunes and extreme climate with daytime temperatures reaching 50 degrees Celsius and nighttime plummeting to freezing, it was a harsh environment. Thesiger had no house, no car, and no family, and regarded these as the reasons for his freedom to explore the world.

He recounted his travels in the Empty Quarter of Arabia between 1945 and 1950, where he claimed to have spent the best five years of his life. "One learnt to appreciate a drink of clean water, the luxury of eating meat. And then the ability, after you'd marched about 14 or 15 hours to surrender to sleep. These are the things."[21]

Thesiger traveled 2,000 miles over seven months with the company of some tribes of the Bedu on this journey, as in all his journeys. He was rationing himself and his party to 2 pints of water a day and 8 pounds of flour a month. As a consequence, they were always thirsty and hungry, besides being pursued by raiding parties. Although others traveled across Arabia before him, he opened new routes and described the vanishing way of life of the Bedu. If Lawrence was of Arabia, Thesiger was of Bedus.

Thesiger hoped to be part of the environment and accepted by tribal people: by the Beduin and by the Marsh people. He didn't go out and look at places; he went instead to stay there a bit. In each of these environments,

Thesiger adopted the customs, cultures, and attitudes of the inhabitants, including their food. He dressed like the Bedu, he wore no shoes like they did, and he ate what they ate. He learned to travel light and to eat local food rather than relying on tinned foods. In fact, the only time he ate tinned food was in Abu Dhabi, when he was hosted by the governor of Taif, the king's grandson, at a new hotel with rooms decorated in Victorian furniture. Otherwise, he ate with his group, simple meals of porridge from a common dish. When he was passing by villages, the villagers fed him. For his journeys, he bought rice, flour, dates, sugar, tea, coffee, and liquid butter. As rice took too much water to cook, flour was often the biggest staple, used in making a simple, unleavened bread. He traveled for travel's sake for almost forty years. He was the last Victorian traveler. When, in one of his earlier trips, a servant brought him a bowl of camel's milk from a nomad encampment nearby, he was so content that he declared then and there that the desert "claimed him."

As the conditions of travel on foot were so unique and the trespassing required such a complete adaptation, Thesiger's narrative of the food became the story of the Bedu ways. For breakfast, they baked bread if not in a hurry. Otherwise they ate leftovers from the meal the night before, sometimes with sweet and black tea and often with bitter black coffee. After breakfast, they set off on foot and walked for the first two or three hours until they started riding the camels. On long days, they would march for ten hours or until grazing was found for the camels. When the camels were loaded and without water, they walked rather than ride them. If they stopped in the middle of the day, they would unload the camels, let them graze, and cook bread or porridge or most often just eat dates. They always drank coffee. Coffee and dates were staples of the desert. The ringing of the brass coffee mortar invited everyone to the ritual. The server would pour a few drops in a small cup, standing, and hand it to each one in turn, bowing as he did. Each person was served again, but no more than three times, until the one drinking shook the cup signaling that he had enough. Thesiger was as much part of this ritual as everyone. Only after shaving his beard and going back into his European clothes after the journey, was he no longer one of them. He was once more different, a stranger, a Christian. As they brought him coffee, someone asked, "Do the Christians drink coffee?"

They carried supplies and water in goatskin bags. Four or five people would form a group and carry their combined food. One person would be assigned to do the cooking when there was enough water. Dinner would be rice, but generally bread, due to lack of water. The cook would dampen the flour, add a little salt, and mix it into a thick paste; then the cook would divide the dough in equal parts and pat them between his hands into half-inch discs,

Muhammad bin Al Jabari (on the right), one of Wilfred Thesiger's Bedouin guides, at a campfire in Ramlat ar Rabbad sands.

while someone would start the fire with flint from the desert and steel of the blade of a dagger, using a small piece of their clothes for tinder. Discs of bread would be put on glowing fire, turned over immediately, and buried under hot sand and embers. They would sit in a circle and dip pieces of this bread, which tasted like sawdust, into a small bowl of melted butter or soup.

The water in the desert was brackish. The first time he tasted it, Thesiger thought it tasted like Epsom and spat it out. Often the Bedu added a few drops of milk to make it taste better, but camel's milk also tasted slightly salty. Sometimes, Thesiger took his water without milk but mixed it with crushed cinnamon, cardamom, ginger, and cloves to make it into a tea. He was often hungry, but thirst troubled him the most: "I was always conscious of it. Even when I was asleep I dreamt of racing streams of ice-cold water, but it was difficult to get to sleep." When he was thirsty, swallowing bread was difficult, making him even hungrier. When it rained, the water did not relieve them but made them drenched, cold, and still thirsty. And no wood was dry enough to light a fire. And when they did find water, they carried a limited amount of it so as to not put too much weight on the camels.

Goatskins in which the Arabs carried their water were a piece of gear that stood the test of time. These goat bags were light, and when empty they could be rolled up and stowed away. They would be rubbed with butter from the inside to completely seal them. If they leaked, holes were plugged with splinters of wood. The bad news was that this also meant that the already foul-tasting water also tasted of goat. Flour, rice, and dates were packed in other goatskins and slung along the saddle to balance the weight of water on the other side. Butter instead was carried in lizard skins about 18 inches long.

The Bedu had no desire for variety of food. They would eat happily the same food twice a day for months, caring about quantity over quality. When they were hungry for weeks, they were talking about food, the food they have eaten, and the food they planned to eat. They often went hungry and thirsty because either the wells they found were dry or because they had to share their food with travelers who came their way. Thesiger described at length the feeling of hunger. After weeks of hunger, he tried to persuade himself that he was not hungry and that he was used to or indifferent to it. For the first day, his hunger was a feeling of emptiness. He could overcome it like a toothache. By lying on his stomach or pressing it down, he tried silencing the cries of his hunger. In the evening, he dozed and dreamt of food. At night, he woke up and thought of food. He could not concentrate on anything: as he tried to read he would slack and find himself thinking once more about food. He started looking at camels and thinking of them as food. In these difficult moments, he consoled himself thinking that he would rather be here in the desert than in London, sitting in an office, but with food.

If any animals were shot, that would be a feast. "They craved hungrily for meat, for our unvarying diet was of unleavened bread, baked in the ashes of the fire, or of porridge if the water sufficed."[22] Sometimes they could buy a goat. However this didn't mean that they could always enjoy it themselves. In the desert, one could never turn a guest away. And when there was meat for themselves, its division was always tricky. The Bedus never wanted to appear greedy. When there was occasionally meat to share, no one wanted the bigger piece. They had to pull sticks to determine who would get each piece. Otherwise, everyone insisted that they received a bigger piece and wanted to change it. Judgment of others was the tribal law and the basis for cultural codes, also relating to food. Another code was about the use of hands. When there was rice with gravy, for example, the right hand was dipped into rice. The right hand molded the rice until it became a ball and then put neatly into the mouth. Eating was always done with the right hand, as the left one was reserved for washing after relief.

Thesiger was a hunter. After his trip in Arabia, he brought back ibex skin and horns, gazelle skin and horns, oryx skin and horns, gerbil, leopard skin, and jas, jird, and jerboa. Once they shot a gazelle and placed half of it in the bush for the day after. When they woke, it was gone, taken away by a fox. They tracked it down, found the meat buried under another bush by the fox. They brushed off the sand and took it back to eat.[23]

They fed once a day at sunset and sometimes had a few dates at midday, which was a luxury. Although camels gave some milk, it was very little due to lack of grazing and long marching hours. Thesiger's biggest trouble was with water. He found it unpalatable as is and drank it only in black coffee or tea flavored with ginger. So for two months, he drank no water but he records being fine without water, as the weather in his trip was more forgiving, with cooler temperatures even during the day.[24]

The Bedu called Thesiger "Umbarak," the blessed one. He referred to the Bedu as "My Arabs." He understood and respected the fact that the Bedu were the desert, and to get along with the desert he had to get along with the Bedu, on their terms. He thought it was better to live among them as one of them, helping in the everyday tasks and sharing in common the food and water, rather than apart in a tent or tended by a servant. He understood that to the Bedu it would be unthinkable that a man should travel with them and yet refuse to share his food among them, for they would share theirs, however short, with all comers. He looked for a sense of acceptance and equality among them. He loved them for their freedom, courage, and generosity.

As much as he admired the Bedus for their total loyalty and nobleness, there were also moments when Thesiger was quite frustrated with the situation. In one such event, when they had not had any meat for days, they caught a hare in the morning and talked about how to cook it all day. When they arrived at their campsite, the decision was to make a soup of it. As the hare was cooking, the cook looked up and saw three Arabs coming over to them across the dunes. Seeing the guests, Thesiger's group stood up, made them welcome, and gave their food to them, saying god has brought them and that they were a thousand times welcome. They also made some coffee and served dates to the guests. To Thesiger's amazement, when the guests offered the hosts to join them, the others said, "No, no, you are our guests and you are welcome. Eat." Thesiger had no other option than to watch them eat the hare, which they had been talking about all day. He felt murderous but could not say a thing other than joining the others to assure them that god had brought them on this occasion.

On another occasion, they saw some tents but did not want to stop because Thesiger wanted to avoid Saudi patrols in the area. A man came out of one of these tents running to them and shouting, "Why are you avoiding my tents? Come and I will give you meat and fat (which means he would kill something for them)." When Thesiger's party said that they wanted to continue walking, the man insisted, "You either come into my tent or I'm going to divorce my wife." So they accepted to go over and watch him kill one of his camels, and they ate for three days. This was a typical and awe-inspiring example of Arab hospitality, which Thesiger could not fully comprehend but fully respected.[25]

With three companions, short of both food and water, when they traveled across the sands of Uruq al Shaiba to the well at Khaba, near Liwa Oasis, they did not drink until sunset. Only then each person received a ration of 1 pint of water mixed with camel's milk. On arrival, after having crossed the Empty Quarter, Thesiger reflected that the journey was not important, however excited he had been at the chance to do it. "It was a personal experience," he wrote, "and the reward had been a drink of clean water, nearly tasteless water. I was content with that."[26]

The second time Thesiger crossed the Empty Quarter, he had to be saved from the angry king as he went there as a foreigner with no permission and was caught. His savior was none other than Philby, who had crossed the Empty Quarter before Thesiger under the auspices of Abdul Aziz Ibn Saud, the first king of the modern state of Saudi Arabia. Philby sent a letter to the king to save his British friend and luckily it was accepted. One can always ask what the point is in enduring all of these hardships. In fact, for Thesiger, exploration was a personal venture. He went there to find peace in the hardship of the desert travel and the company of the desert peoples. The goal of the journey was rather unimportant but the achievement required great effort and sacrifice, which made the journey worthwhile. Thesiger thought that some experiences did not have to bring material achievements because he believed that the way to get there is what matters. He found that the harder the journey, the bigger the reward.

Twenty-seven years after his last trip, in 1977, Thesiger returned and saw everything in Arabia had changed; he found that he was the only one not adjusted to the new Arabian world.

Crossing the Sahara on Foot

The writings of Philby but especially of Thesiger inspired many men for centuries, yet until the end of the twentieth century no one had yet crossed the biggest desert on foot, the Saharan desert.

Fourteenth-century-traveler Ibni Battuta had crossed the Sahara from south to north with a caravan of camels in 1352. He traveled luxuriously, with donations from Muslim rulers. In his travels, he was interested in food. His memoirs are found doubtful in his exaggeration as well as accuracy of information. He described dates and locusts as the desert food available in the area and referred to milk and mangoes. Milk is believed to be coconut milk and mangoes must be another fruit similar in name.[27] Moreover, some of his descriptions of Tuwat (current-day south Algeria) being a saline swamp with no cultivation were in discrepancy with the notes of Muslim historian Ibn Khaldun, who said that the area was full of palm trees and streams.[28]

Geoffrey Moorhouse, a British journalist and another admirer of Thesiger, had tried to cross the Saharan desert in 1972. "It was because I was afraid that I had decided to attempt a crossing of the great Sahara desert, from west to east, by myself and by camel."[29] He went on foot with two camels and one guide, but failed. He was too lonely and afraid in the desert and was having many nightmares, including those where his food and water were stolen.

In the 1980s, the Saharan desert was still not crossed from west to east on foot. Another British man, an author and historian who wrote a biography on Thesiger, was to admire and even idealize the nomads. Michael Asher, just like Thesiger, claimed that while living with the nomads he wanted simply to become one of them, but realized that this was ultimately impossible, as their world too was on the brink of change. Unlike Thesiger, Asher did not claim that the nomads were better off staying the way they were. He instead accepted that the nomads themselves had to decide their own future. Nonetheless, he became a member of the deep ecology movement against industrial civilization and decided to cross the Saharan desert from the Atlantic in Mauritania to the Nile Valley in Egypt. He set off in August of 1986 with his wife Mariantonietta Peru and three camels, and arrived in the Nile Valley 271 days and 4,500 miles later, marking the first recorded crossing of the Saharan desert on foot.

When Michael Asher lived with the Kababish nomads in Sudan for three years, he learned to eat as they did. He recounted to me how he was eating together from a single dish with his right hand. "This is a far more efficient system than we have, because it means that you don't get bogged down with cutlery or crockery—there is only one vessel to be cleaned (usually with sand, not water)."[30] They ate no vegetables or fruit except onions, when available. Yet he was impressed that in the three years he lived with them he never got sick. Their diet was basically a polenta made of *asida* (sorghum-flour) served with camel's milk or with *mlah* (a kind of gravy) made of dried tomato powder and other spices. They got asida, tea, and sugar from farmers by trading their animals. They also ate dates (the hard type rather than the sticky type). Camel's milk (fresh or soured) was their sacred staple with customs and rituals attached to drinking it. The Beja nomads of eastern Sudan prefer coffee like those in Arabia. The nomads he lived with only drank tea with masses of sugar—if no sugar was available, they drank it with dates.

When possible, they would slaughter a goat, sheep, or (only for special occasions) a camel. They also hunted, mainly dorcas gazelles, but would eat hares, some birds such as pigeons, and other animals such as monitor lizards (including their eggs), fennec foxes, and kangaroo rats, which they roast on the fire in the skin. Meat was often sun-dried (known as *tishtar* in the western Sahara and *sharmoot* in the eastern Sahara) until it became so hard that it could be smashed into powder with a stone, later to be sprinkled on the polenta. The head of the animal was considered the best part, and everything was eaten, including the tongue, nasal membranes, eyes, and brains—the head was usually cooked in the sand under the embers of the fire. "If a camel was slaughtered, the liver and hump (a gelatinous substance) were eaten raw—juice from the camel's gall-bladder is squeezed over it: they refer to camel gall-bladder as the 'desert lime' because it has a lemony taste."[31]

In the western Sahara, the staple of nomads is couscous rather than sorghum flour. It's a very efficient food for the desert as all the water is absorbed, none wasted, and the water does not have to be boiled, so less fuel is required. (Nomads cook exclusively with firewood, not charcoal.) They drink *zrig*, which is a mixture of milk, water, and sugar.

Traveling alone or with his wife, Asher usually ate as the nomads do, carrying sorghum flour, etc. He made his own *sharmoot* usually by drying the meat of a slaughtered goat on bushes in the sun. He also carried tins of sardines as a supplement. "I cook on the same kind of fireplace [made of three stones] and eat with my hand."[32] On trek with clients, he ate differently, with individual plates, knives, and forks. They ate mainly tinned food including tinned fish and meat, but quite frequently they bought a goat on the way and slaughtered it for fresh meat. They carried onions and fresh vegetables, such as tomatoes and aubergines, which they sometimes replenished on the journey. For breakfast, they had cereal, eggs, bread, both commercial and desert-baked, coffee, tea, and dried fruits. They carried some fresh fruit, at least for the first few days, and a variety of imported food such as cheese, couscous, rice, and pasta. They had tea, coffee, and a range of sauces and condiments. Meals were cooked on charcoal, which was carried, as the heat was far easier to regulate than that of firewood when cooking for large numbers. They had several camels for carrying provisions. Water was taken from wells and pools but treated with iodine, which is not something he does when traveling alone.

Is the life of the nomads still as it was when he lived with them? "No—I last visited the Kababish two years ago and found that though life is superficially similar—people still ride camels and live in tents, etc.—the feeling of being in "a different world" has gone. The women now wear full garments with the *hejab*, men wear imported cotton shirts. Many nomads now have mobile phones, and there are many more motor vehicles. The tents I saw were mostly repaired with old sacks, which suggests that the women no longer practice the art of weaving. The old clan-migrations that I witnessed no longer continue. Many settlements now have schools, although most seemed to be unused. In camel-handling many more synthetic materials are used."[33]

In Chad, however, the nomads seem more traditional, still making their own waterskins, camel-gear, etc. They don't have mobile phones or many motor vehicles around, perhaps making it the last desert to explore like the traditional nomads of once upon a time.

Western Sahara and the Want of Salt

As much as the Sahara was a source of salt with giant slabs in the desert, West Africa had a big need for it. In pre-colonial West Africa, salt was the most important mineral, next to iron and gold. In the tenth century in Gao, the capital of Songhai, salt was so rare that it was kept in the store of the royal treasury. This is not surprising, because salt was sometimes exchanged for gold on a weight-for-weight basis. At the coast, salt was obtained by boiling seawater. Inland, however, it was harder to come by. Major deposits were in the Sahara. Slaves dug out salt, and camels transported it. Salt was exchanged for grains like millet, rice, and corn.[34]

When the Scottish explorer Mungo Park explored West Africa in 1795, he was the first westerner known to have traveled to the central portion of the Niger River. With two guides, he started for the unknown interior. He crossed the upper Senegal basin and traveled through the semi-desert region of Kaarta. The journey was full of difficulties. In Ludamar, he was even imprisoned by a Moorish chief for four months. On July 1, 1796, he escaped, alone and with nothing but his horse and a pocket compass, and on July 21 reached the long-sought Niger River at Ségou, being the first European to do so. He followed the river downstream 80 miles (130 kilometers) to Silla, where he was obliged to turn back, lacking the resources to go farther.

On his return journey, on July 29, he took a route more to the south than that originally followed, keeping close to the Niger River as far as Bamako, thus tracing its course for some 300 miles (500 kilometers). At Kamalia, he fell ill and stayed in the house of a man for seven months. Eventually, he reached Pisania again on June 10, 1797, returning to Scotland by way of Antigua on December 22. He wrote his account of the journey in a book, which gave Europeans a glimpse of what Africa was really like. His book described how locals in The Gambia ate corn, made couscous, used *shea* butter, and hunted horses for food. In the interior country, the greatest of luxuries was salt. Historically, farmers got salt from the blood, milk, or meat of animals when they traded with herdsmen. He saw children suck a piece of rock salt as if it were sugar, from the need of salt. He too suffered from the want of salt: "I have myself suffered great inconvenience from the scarcity of this article. The long use of vegetable food creates so painful a longing for salt that no words can sufficiently describe it."[35]

Mungo Park was not as lucky in his second journey to Niger in 1803. He never came back. He drowned in a river while escaping hostile locals. His journal was never recovered.

Patagonia and the Want of Meat

Another big desert to be explored was Patagonia. Often early pioneers to South America did not walk much on land but sailed the coasts. Spanish conquerors anchored and came ashore mainly to take possession of the land with a ceremony before looking for information and riches while living off their ships. When they did step off their ships, their description of abundance in food was heightened, next to their often meager and rotten rations on board. Food such as fresh fish, butter, rice and other grains, tropical fruit, and local wine offered by locals to the travelers fit the image of a fertile land to inhabit. Sooner or later, explorers had to go deeper inland on foot to seek treasures, native people, and food. Not all of the ventures ended with success, and lack of food was often the reason.

When America was discovered, Spain sent many pioneers to colonize the new domain. As such, Patagonia was given to Simon de Alcazaba to conquer and to populate. He prepared a crew of 250 men and set off with two ships. Soon they were challenged with leaking ships and rotting fish and meat. They found the solution in switching to a hardtack ration. When water started becoming a problem, they resorted to drinking wine. Despite having lost contact, the two ships entered the Strait together. The men built a settlement of mud huts, each man took a generous 20 pounds of hardtack as his food ration, and they started their march northwest into the Patagonian plains. After only 44 miles (70 kilometers), Alcazaba (who was older than the crew and worn down from the trip) gave up and returned. The rest continued walking on arid landscape of immense plains studded with basalt. They followed a river and came across an Indian settlement where they learned how to recognize the edible roots and vegetables. An old woman became their guide and told them where they could find gold. By then, the precious hardtack was finished and they were living off the land. When ten more days of walking had not delivered any gold, they resigned and started walking back. A rebellion in the group and a shameful discovery of hidden sugar, bread, and raisins in a tent split the group. While some men walked back to the river to inform Alcazaba, the others went toward the coast with hunger and desire for revenge. When the second group arrived first at the ship and killed Alcazaba, others who arrived later were left at the port to eat roots and whatever they could find. Soon a new rebellion in the ship reduced the number of men even more: some were beheaded, others were thrown into the sea with weights around their necks, some others were hanged, and some more escaped. The remaining men took the ships and left, eventually transferring to one of the ships when the other wrecked. After all this misfortune, they had to sail to the nearest port as the scarcity of their food made it impossible to go back to Spain. This is how of the 250 men who left Spain, only 75 arrived in Santo Domingo in September 1535.[36]

Three centuries later, when Charles Darwin explored Patagonia, he fell in love with the land. Darwin surveyed Patagonia and Tierra del Fuego in 1831 and 1832. He wrote in his diary that after seeing parts of the Chilean coast, Lima, Galapagos Island, and the Blue Mountains in Australia, he was

most impressed by the plains of Patagonia, without habitation, water, trees, mountains, and only some dwarf plants. "The plains of Patagonia are bound-less, for they are scarcely passable, and hence unknown, they bear the stamp of having lasted, as they are now, for ages, and there appears no limit to their duration through future time."[37]

Darwin also observed difficulties of cooking at altitude in his survey of Patagonia, when he camped with his party in Mendoza[38]:

> At the place where we slept water necessarily boiled, from the diminished pressure of the atmosphere, at a lower temperature than it does in a less lofty country; the case being the converse of that of a Papin's digester. Hence the po-tatoes, after remaining for some hours in the boiling water, were nearly as hard as ever. The pot was left on the fire all night, and next morning it was boiled again, but yet the potatoes were not cooked. I found out this by overhearing my two companions discussing the cause, they had come to the simple conclusion "that the cursed pot (which was a new one) did not choose to boil potatoes."

In Tierra del Fuego, Darwin found a mushroom that grew on trees which was eaten by the natives. With the exception of a few berries, this was the only plant food the natives ate; he wrote that this was the only country where a cryptogamic plant was a staple food. The climate and vegetation did not afford any other way. "The Fuegian savage, the miserable lord of this miserable land."[39] The Fuegians impressed the captain of Darwin's ship *Beagle* Robert FitzRoy when he received the testimony of three Fuegians. They would eat humans, after a hostile encounter and when pressed by hunger. "Those who are vanquished and taken, if not already dead, are killed and eaten by the conquer-ors. The arms and breast are eaten by the women; the men eat the legs; and the trunk is thrown into the sea. During a severe winter, when hard frost and deep snow prevent their obtaining food as usual, and famine is staring them in the face, extreme hunger impels them to lay violent hands on the oldest woman of their party, hold her head over a thick smoke, made by burning green wood, and pinching her throat, choke her. They then devour every particle of the flesh, not excepting the trunk, as in the former case. Dogs however were not eaten, like older women, because 'dog catch *iappo* (otter).'"[40]

When Darwin was in southern Argentina in his exploration in 1833, he met Bernantio's friendly tribe, going to a *salina* for salt and noted, "The Indians eat much salt, their children sucking it like sugar. This habit is very different from that of the Spanish Gauchos, who, leading the same kind of life, eat scarcely any."[41] Gauchos mainly ate meat and did not need salt. Dar-win also observed that Gauchos ate a lot of fat, which helped them digest meat in large amounts and not get hungry when they did not eat for a while.

"We were here able to buy some biscuit. I had now been several days without tasting anything besides meat: I did not at all dislike this new regimen; but I felt as if it would only have agreed with me with hard exercise. I have heard that patients in England, when desired to confine themselves exclusively to an animal diet, even with the hope of life before their eyes, have hardly been able to endure it. Yet the Gaucho in the Pampas, for months together, touches nothing but beef. But they eat, I observe, a very large proportion of fat, which is of a less animalised nature; and they particularly dislike dry meat, such as that of the Agouti (a type of rodent)." He quotes the doctor on John Franklin's overland expedition to the Polar Sea, having observed in 1829 that "when people have fed for a long time solely upon lean animal food, the desire for fat becomes so insatiable, that they can consume a large quantity of unmixed and even oily fat without nausea."[42]

Desert Ultramarathons—When Walking Is Not Fast Enough

Negotiating mountains to climb them, cross them, or to circle around them is not new, neither is seeing runners suck on small water bottles, gels, and energy drinks during marathons that run through cities. What is relatively new and increasingly growing in popularity is another way of pushing personal limits on foot. A trail running community who run (when they can, and walks when they have to) long distances and on difficult trails. These are often ultramarathons, footraces that cover a distance longer than a marathon (42.195 kilometers). In trail runs where distances are much longer and terrain, climate, and altitude much more challenging, the preparation of food focuses on survival. Runners not only try to finish these races but to finish them without losing a lot of weight, which can be dangerous and cause runners to quit the race with serious health problems. Some of the famous races are Tor des Géants in Italy (330 kilometers), Badwater Ultramarathon in the United States (217 kilometers), Ultratrail du Mont Blanc (166 kilometers), and Ultra Trail Mount Fuji (161 kilometers). Another foot challenge is called skywalking, which is not only running a long distance but also running it on elevations higher than 2,000 meters. These runs started in the Alps on Mont Blanc and Monta Rosa in the early 1990s and spread to the Himalayas, Mount Kenya, and Mexican volcanoes. However, there is no limit to geography: runs are on mountains, on desert, and on ice. On desert, the famous race takes place on the Saharan desert.

When the twenty-eight-year-old Frenchman Patrick Bauer decided to traverse the Sahara desert on foot, alone, completely self-sufficient, carrying a

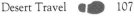

rucksack weighing 35 kilograms with water and food, it was the starting point of what was to become the *Marathon des Sables*. It took him twelve days to cover 350 kilometers where he wouldn't come across a single village, oasis, or watering place. The first running event was in 1986; twenty-three pioneers took part in the first edition of this legendary multi-day running event in the Moroccan Sahara covering a distance of 250 kilometers on foot. The Marathon des Sables is now the mother of all ultra-trails on extreme conditions. It is a six-day, 251-kilometer (156-mile) ultramarathon, equivalent to six regular marathons. This multi-day race is held every year in southern Morocco. Participants must carry his/her own backpack containing food, sleeping gear, and other material. Temperatures can exceed 40 degrees Celsius in the sun, putting the body under strain and making it difficult to eat enough calories to sustain it. It is considered the toughest footrace on earth.

Two brother runners, Lahcen and Mohamad Ahansal, born to a nomadic family near Zagora in the Sahara desert in Morocco, have dominated the *Marathon des Sables* ultramarathon for two decades. Lahcen won it ten times and his younger brother Mohamad five. In an interview, the Ahansal brothers explained what they eat during a run. Lahcen eats pasta, couscous, and dried fruit, whereas Mohammed takes cans of dates or *khobz chahma* (a Berber stuffed bread). "On the MdS [Marathon des Sables] I eat dates, dried fruit, pasta, rice, *sellou* (a dessert of nuts and spices ground to a fine powder) and dried meat."[43]

Raffaele Brattoli is an Italian ultramarathon runner who has completed twenty desert runs so far, including the grand slam of four deserts: Gobi, Atacama, Sahara, and Antarctica. This all together means 1,000 kilometers on foot under some of the most difficult conditions on Earth. He runs races on desert with auto sufficiency, which means taking care of his equipment and food for himself in a small backpack with no support or resupply. In the beginning, Brattoli was buying precooked dehydrated foods like many others, until he started making his own dehydrated meals and packing them under vacuum, ready to prepare quickly by adding water. He makes a mix that can be added to different kinds of bases to make three different types of dishes. His recipes are reflecting his northern Italian food culture.

Brattoli mixes 30 grams of cooked dehydrated polenta with 30 grams of dehydrated *bresaola* (an Italian dried salted beef) in very small pieces, which he dehydrates himself. To this he then adds 30 grams of grated *grana padana* cheese and 20 grams of oil, one spoon of vegetable or beef broth, and a bit of pepper. He alternates this meal with a potato purée powder or a risotto base of boiled and dehydrated rice, and dehydrated vegetables like zucchini, potatoes, carrots, onions, and any seasonal vegetables, all cut into small pieces and also dehydrated.[44]

For during the race, he likes to nibble on his own sweet and savory energy bar from dried fruits, nuts mixed with candied fruits and honey, cheese, and *bresaola*. Sometimes, he takes marzipan paste or ready snacks like biscuits or chips. Rules dictate that racers must take in 2,000 calories per day minimum, but usually they need to exceed this and reach 5,000 calories while running 50-kilometer days. Calorie-dense foods like this help keep the weight on. How about the appetite?

"Appetite is difficult to get while running in the desert. Concentrated and dehydrated tomato paste helps me for appetite and gives me enough salt to retain moisture."[45] Brattoli has done stranger things, such as putting Nutella chocolate paste in empty toothpaste tubes to take it along as a dessert, especially for in the evenings when he wanted something sweet.

As he runs toward the desert sun, he sees shapes forming in front of his eyes, men, animals, the devil, linked to his stress and fears. Does he dream of foods while running? "Yes, a lot." He dreams of an ice-cold beer, ice cream, sparkling water, Coca Cola, and watermelon. "All the things one dreams of on a hot day in the beach."[46]

Other runners sometimes share food mostly to try out of curiosity. He tried, for example, a dehydrated cola drink from Japan. He didn't think it tasted the same as the real thing. A trick he learned from an Australian runner that helps him is to put a small rock under the tongue when the mouth is very dry. This, he says, is a trick from the Aboriginals to keep salivating. Australia was also the origin of the strangest food he ate while running: dried snake, shark meat, and dried alligator.

In races Brattoli carries a small plastic plate but the way he prepares the meals is to cut a plastic bottle in the middle and prepare the dehydrated meal inside it to then eat the meal out of this plastic bowl. Some people take plastic ice cream containers. It is an effort to reduce weight to carry.

The longest desert run Brattoli did without stopping was three nights and two days in Oman. When he was running the Oman race, a group of Bedouins in an old pick-up truck stopped him in the desert and took away his food. He still had water, but he could not survive without food for very long. He started seeing black and sent a GPS emergency signal right before he passed out. When he opened his eyes an hour later, he was at a checkpoint. After recovery for over five hours, he was allowed to continue running and finish the race. He still doesn't know which misery led them to behave like this.

Another ultramarathon or trail is the Iranian Silk Road. The race is scheduled in two formats: 250 kilometers and 150 kilometers. The soil is various with sand dunes, marshes, and rocky stretches. Doctors and nurses support checkpoints. Runners carry their backpack of about 10 kilograms with clothes, food, and mandatory safety equipment. Athletes depart from the tented camp in the morning. Camps are dismantled from the staff on-site and reassembled at the end of the stage after the athletes have started the daily stage. Each camp includes sleeping tents, supplies of hot and cold water, and a medical tent (doctors, nurses, and medical equipment). At the end of each stage, the athletes arrive at a tented camp for the night. The organization supplies about 10 liters of drinking water per day per person at checkpoints and at camps. Alberto Tagliabue is a racer who was just back from this race when I talked to him.

Tagliabue is another talented Italian runner who left the asphalt for the love of trails. He recounted a similar story to Brattoli: taking polenta, *parmigiano* cheese, *mocetta* (another type of dried meat from Northern Italy). He proudly adds: "Other people take dehydrated pasta meals. When we are eating our meal they are all looking at it." To have a sense of bread, he takes *taralli*, small pretzel-type crackers from Puglia in the south of Italy. He learned to eat constantly every hour a gel or something else. Otherwise he says, "My legs get tired." Granted, during races he also dreams of food, of a cold Coca-Cola, pasta, and pizza. Tagliabue summarizes very well in the end what it is all about: "Food is very important. When you are away from home for one week, you look for comfort and something that you like."[47]

CHAPTER 6

Pilgrimage

In the history of walking, some people walked with different motivations than discovering the limits of the outside world. Pilgrims walked to a geographical destination to arrive in a place within themselves. Pilgrimage was a spiritualized walk. The spiritual and the material, thinking and doing were connected through the act of walking. To arrive was to earn it. The harder the journey, the bigger the rewards. And the journey on foot was always harder.

Many religions still have strong tradition of pilgrimages to locations that are important in the history of that religion as a path to retreat, enlightenment, and spiritual growth. The pilgrim often goes on foot, sometimes to holy cities, temples, or tombs, sometimes to holy mountains, caves, or rivers. Putting aside political pilgrimages such as the Salt March of Gandhi in 1930 (which was done as a walk to produce salt from seawater to protest the taxation on salt production set by the British government), traditionally pilgrimage is done for healing for one's self or a loved one. There are a few walking trails that stand out in their historical importance and the number of visitors. Camino de Santiago is such a trail.

Pilgrims Fare on a Scallop Shell

Legend holds that the remains of St. James were carried by boat from Jerusalem to northwestern Spain, where he was buried on what is now the Cathedral of Santiago de Compostela in Galicia. The Catholic pilgrimage route to the shrine of the apostle St. James, also called St. James Way, originated in the ninth century. In fact, the trail follows an earlier Roman trade route.

According to a medieval legend, Compostela is derived from the Latin *Campus Stellae* (i.e., "field of the star"). In 813, the light of a bright star guided a shepherd at night to the burial site in Santiago de Compostela. The shepherd reported his discovery to Bishop Teodomiro of Iria. Bishop Teodomiro declared that the remains belonged to Apostle James and notified King Alfonso II in Oviedo. On the spot where the remains of St. James were said to have been found, a cathedral was built.

Concerning this, French alchemist Fulcanelli offers another explanation. In French, Compostela is called *Voie lactée*, the Milky Way. Greek gods followed this route to go to the palace of Zeus, and the heroes followed it to enter Olympus. The popular Spanish name for the astronomical Milky Way is *El Camino de Santiago*. According to a common medieval legend, the dust raised by traveling pilgrims formed the Milky Way.

In the Middle Ages, diverse walkers occupied the trails: lords traveling with their escorts, ordinary people in neighborhood groups or with people they met along the way, pilgrims in chains ordered by the civil court for humiliation, and people who walked on behalf of the rich.

Once a pilgrim was initiated, he wore a uniform to show his commitment to his new life. In 1406, an English pilgrim, Richard Alkerton, wrote, "the pilgrim shall have a staff, a sclavein, and a scrip." The sclavein was a long tunic. The scrip was a pouch in which he kept his food, mess-cans, and money. This was their attire at the end of the eleventh century. The origin of the pouch is not clear, but it was also used by migrant monks of Egypt in the fourth century. Although it can be said that a pouch is essential to any traveler on foot, the pilgrim's pouch became a symbol of almsgiving because it was too small to hold much money, indicating that he needed charity for his livelihood.[1]

Pilgrimage depended on the compassion of others, along the way and in monasteries. The Benedictine rule required that monasteries offer food and shelter to pilgrims. This introduced serious financial problems to some of the abbeys. Especially in places such as Montserrat in Catalonia, carting the food up the steep mountain tracks to the church was difficult. For this reason, in the fourteenth century, preachers started asking pilgrims to bring their own food unless they were poor or disabled.[2]

Today, there are many ways to walk the trail, and the most famous one is the *Camino Francés* or the French route, a trail since the Middle Ages (and the first European cultural trail). This trail crosses from France over the Pyrenees into Spain and continues along the north of the Iberian Peninsula to Santiago de Compostela, which marks the end of the trail. This route is done on foot and can start anywhere. In the Middle Ages, pilgrims started from their house, wherever that might have been. A typical walk on the Camino Francés took at least four weeks, allowing for one or two rest days on the way.

The scallop shell is the symbol of the Camino. It acts as a metaphor, the grooves representing the various routes pilgrims travel to arrive at a single destination. It also had a practical purpose: the pilgrims could use it for gathering water to drink or for eating out of as a makeshift bowl. Another emblem of the pilgrimage is the gourd, which the early pilgrims used as a water bottle. At one time possessing a scallop was sufficient proof that one had completed the pilgrimage. The French word for a scallop is *coquille St. Jacques* (shell of St. Jacques). The English name James is derived from Jacob in Latin. In French, Jacob is translated "Jacques."

The scallop shell is also the symbol of baptism, and it is found frequently on baptismal fonts. The dish used by priests to pour water over the heads of a catechumen (a person under instruction in the rudiments of Christianity, as in the early church) in baptism is often scallop-shaped. Scallop shells

Pilgrim's scallop shell and gourd on Camino de Compostela.

symbolize birth, and for many people the Camino is connected with rebirth or the beginning of a new life.

British poet and explorer Sir Walter Raleigh likened the pilgrimage to the point of death in his poem "The Passionate Man's Pilgrimage,"[3] which he wrote after his condemnation, on the day before his death (although some academics believe that this is claimed only for dramatic effect):

> Give me my scallop shell of quiet,
> My staff of faith to walk upon,
> My scrip of joy, immortal diet,
> My bottle of salvation,
> My gown of glory, hope's true gage,
> And thus I'll take my pilgrimage.
> . . .
> Blood must be my body's balmer,
> No other balm will there be given,
> Whilst my soul, like a white palmer,
> Travels to the land of heaven;
> Over the silver mountains,
> Where spring the nectar fountains;
> And there I'll kiss
> The bowl of bliss,
> And drink my eternal fill
> On every milken hill.
> My soul will be a-dry before,
> But after it will ne'er thirst more;
> And by the happy blissful way
> More peaceful pilgrims I shall see,
> That have shook off their gowns of clay,
> And go appareled fresh like me.
> I'll bring them first
> To slake their thirst,
> And then to taste those nectar suckets,
> At the clear wells
> Where sweetness dwells,
> Drawn up by saints in crystal buckets.

Most pilgrims carry a document, called the *credencial*, which gives access to inexpensive, sometimes free, overnight accommodation in *refugios* along the trail. This "pilgrim's passport" is stamped in each town in a cathedral or church or in a *refugio* at which the pilgrim has stayed. It provides pilgrims with a record of where they ate or slept, and serves as proof to the Pilgrim's Office in Santiago that the journey was accomplished according to an official route. This way, the pilgrim qualifies to receive a *compostela* (certificate of completion of the pilgrimage). Many of the small restaurants and cafes along the Camino also provide stamps. The stamp can be associated with something of a ceremony, where the stamper and the pilgrim can share information. As the pilgrimage approaches Santiago, many of the stamps in small towns are self-service due to the greater number of pilgrims.

The *compostela* is a certificate of accomplishment that no other walker receives; it is for pilgrims arriving in Santiago de Compostela who have walked at least the last 100 kilometers with a religious motivation. At the Pilgrim's Office, the *credencial* is examined for stamps and dates, and the pilgrim is asked to state whether the motivation in traveling the Camino was "religious," "religious and other," or "other." In the case of "religious" or "religious and other," a *compostela* is available; in the case of "other," there is a simpler certificate in Spanish.

Talking about "other" motivation, this trail today offers a culinary pilgrimage as well as a spiritual one. On each stop, one can stay at a bed-and-breakfast usually offering the bounties of the land one crosses all daylong walking. The soul searching under the endless sky leaves itself to the search of local delicacies and wines in the evening. The trail passes culinary stops of Navarra, Rioja, Castilla y León, and Galicia. When viewed from a food culture, the trail reads like a menu.

Navarra's favorite is a trout, stuffed with slices of *jamon Serrano* before put on the grill to cook, and crispy *menestre de verduras*, a great mix of vegetables sautéed together in oil and garlic. Navarra is also known for its wines. Then comes Rioja, with its majestic wines and stuffed red bell peppers. Game meat and wild mushrooms can be seen on the menu in hunting season. Castilla y León, on the other hand, is the land of wheat fields, roasts, and stews paired with robust red wines. Galicia offers green hills and mountains as well as the green soup called *Caldo Gallego*, Galician stew. It is filled with leafy collard-like greens, white beans, potatoes, pork and sausages, onions, and garlic. Another Galician specialty comes from the area around Padrón, the town where legend says St. James's martyred body arrived. Padrón is known for Padron peppers, *pimientos de Padron*, brought here by a monk returning from the new world. These are green finger-sized peppers that are thrown whole in a pan with olive oil. They are served on a plate crispy and with a splash of sea salt. Galicia is also home of fresh, succulent shellfish and fish, and this is often handled simply, with a quick grilling or steaming, a bit of olive oil, and sea salt. Inland, the forests give chestnuts to make chestnut soup. Another specialty is *empanada gallega*, Galician savory pie filled with pork, onions, and red bell pepper.

Most people, however, stay at pilgrim accommodations and have a pilgrim's menu, which is a simpler fare than the local specialties and wine. There is also the possibility to cook in some of these places and share meals with other travelers.

A Nourishing Pilgrimage through Italy

Another world-famous pilgrimage trail is Via Francigena. The walk of Sigeric, the Archbishop of Canterbury, to Rome to visit Pope John the XVth marks the beginning of this trail. The full route covers 1,700 kilometers, starting in Canterbury in England and passing through France and Switzerland to arrive in Rome. In medieval times, the records of these spiritual journeys were full of food impressions. Especially in the thirteenth century, economic exchanges and food were described even more, even though the trail was no less religious. Pilgrims were often hungry or sick because of food adulterated or served old at the inns.[4]

Pilgrims in the old days would receive a pilgrim passport from their bishop or church, which was called *credenziale* in Italian, and this would be stamped along the way and presented to get food and accommodation. Pilgrims would carry a scrip (a small knapsack), carrying very little food and water. Sigeric gave a long list of locations for pilgrims for services, accommodation, and food in the notes of his journey in the tenth century. Interestingly, he invited the pilgrims to proceed more slowly, to increase the frequency of stops to let them enjoy the good things that these areas offered. In Valdelsa, for example, there were eight stopping points in an area which was not so difficult to walk to justify the higher frequency of stops. It was instead presented as a kind of "promised land," for the fertility of its soil, the richness and variety of its agriculture, and the many small towns and even more numerous villages. His notes were written by his secretary on the way back from Rome and constituted the first "guidebook" for pilgrims to follow. There were pilgrims who completed this trail on horseback or even on camels, but the majority went on foot because of the bigger merit they would attain.[5]

Until a few decades ago, interest in the Via Francigena was limited to scholars. This began to change when many, after traveling the Camino de Santiago in Spain, wanted to make the pilgrimage to Rome on foot as well. This brought popularity to Via Francigena, and the trail and paths began to be marked for religious tourism. The religious and local government agencies tried to recover the original route. Where possible, today's route follows the ancient one but sometimes it deviates from the historical path in favor of paths and roads with low traffic. Once the potential for the tourist trade in Italy was recognized, some people have worked hard to divert the path so that it passes around their bar or restaurant.

What remained from the Middle Ages are a few famous ingredients along the trail like the onion of Certaldo, saffron of San Gimignano, and some more substantial dishes, which developed after sugar and other ingredients became widely available. Visitors of the trail benefit from the many medieval recipes, which continue to be made for tourism and help keep local traditions alive.

Along the Tuscan route, some dishes can still be found, such as vegetable soups made using day-old bread, *acquacotta* (broth-based soup, literally meaning cooked water), onions, chickpeas, or lentils. Another example is *Testaroli* in the Lunigiana area, which is a type of fresh pasta made from flour dough that is squished between *testi* (special cast-iron baking dishes) and then briefly cooked in boiling water. Or *Torta d'erbi* from the Lunigiana, which is a stuffed pie made with flour, water, vegetables, and herbs. A nourishing cake to give to the walking pilgrims was a sweet cake called *Spongata*, made from two layers of dough and stuffed with honey, bread, dried fruit, herbs, and spices. In the Garfagnana mountains, the specialty was *Biroldo*, a loaf-shaped sausage with a dark red color, soft texture, and a strong aroma of spices mixed with pig's blood.

Some recipes have changed over time due to availability of ingredients since the Middle Ages. For example, in Siena a medieval cake called *Panpepato* was made with abundant pepper and other spices in its dough. Today, the white version, called *Panforte Margherita*, is made softer, sweeter, and with candied fruit, almonds, and spices. In addition, Crusaders carried panforte with them on their quests, and some believe that panforte was first prepared for this purpose.

Nowadays, it is possible to coincide the walk with some of the most interesting food festivals organized along the trail, such as the champagne festival in Reims, Beaujolais Festival in Beaujeu, food truck festival in Lousanne, Valtidone wine festival in Piacenza, truffle fair in San Miniato, or pecorino cheese festival in Tuscany. In fact, with so much food to eat today, the path is a joy for religious and non-religious food pilgrims. The slower the journey, the bigger the rewards.

Mount Kailash—A Walk of Respect

Mountains are symbolic for arrival. Climbing to the summit can be associated with virtue and closeness to the creator. However, there is one mountain that preserved its holiness by people not climbing its summit. Mount Kailash is a sacred mountain in western Tibet that sits at an altitude of 6,718 meters. It is unclimbed, not because Kailash is a particularly hard or risky climb, but out of respect for its status as home to the Hindu god Shiva. It is considered a sin to set foot on its slopes, as it is a sacred place in four religions: Bon, Buddhism, Hinduism, and Jainism. In 1926, British mountaineers Hugh Ruttledge and Colonel R. C. Wilson found it feasible to climb the mountain but ran out of time.[6] In the mid-1980s, Italian climber Reinhold Messner declined a Chinese offer to ascend Mount Kailash out of respect to Tibetan beliefs. Although in 2001 the Chinese gave permission for a Spanish team to climb the peak, in the face of international disapproval it was stopped. All attempts to climb the mountain are now forbidden.

Instead, the mountain is walked around in a clockwise direction. The path is 52 kilometers (32 miles) and usually takes three days to complete. Some pilgrims believe that the entire walk around Kailash should be made in a single day, which is not considered an easy task for an average walker who faces uneven terrain, altitude sickness, and cold. It is the arduous mode of walking chosen by some of the pilgrims that makes Kailash one of the most difficult pilgrimage routes. These pilgrims measure the path by the body length. Captain John Noel, who was a mountaineer in Tibet and the Himalayas, observed this walk in 1931 with awe: "They prostrate themselves on their faces, marking the soil with their fingers a little beyond their heads, arise and bring their toes to the mark they have made and fall again, stretched full length on the ground, their arms extended, muttering an already million-times-repeated prayer."[7] In this way of walking, the pilgrimage takes three weeks.

While some of the pilgrims can stay in guesthouses on the path, most stay in their own tents. And the only food they can find is dried noodles and yak butter tea, sold at teashops along the trail. American-Norwegian photographer Mikkel Aaland described his own pilgrimage to Mount Kailash in 2013. His dinner consisted of freeze-dried chicken with noodles while his guide ate tsampa, roasted barley mixed with yak butter, tea, and sugar. For breakfast, Aaland took along *gjetost*, a brown goat cheese from Norway, and ate it with a whole wheat bread from a shop in Kathmandu.[8]

This majestic mountain with its conical shape continues to be respected for its unattainable and snow-covered dome.

Shikoku—The Pilgrimage of Offerings

Shikoku is the smallest and the least populated island in Japan. It is also known for its eighty-eight-temple pilgrimage associated with the ninth-century priest *Kūkai*, who propagated Buddhism in Japan. The walk does not focus on the temples but the way between the temples. Its aim is to allow the walker to look inwards and come out as a better person after the walk. This was a trail for monks, until a monk wrote a guidebook in 1687 and others started walking it.

The standard walking course is approximately 1,200 kilometers (750 miles) long and can take anywhere from thirty to sixty days to walk. The old-fashioned method is to complete it by foot, and some earlier pilgrims walked barefoot. After the Second World War, bus tours started an eleven-day journey on the road. The health consciousness of the 1990s woke up the interest in walking on foot again.

The pilgrims wore white jackets emblazoned with the characters reading *dōgyō ninin*, meaning "two traveling together," the traveler and *Kūkai*. Pilgrims carry a notebook and collect red stamps at each temple, walking 30 kilometers or more each day. In the past, women were forbidden to enter mountain huts. Today, only the peak of Mt. Omine is forbidden to women. For the rest, the Shikoku pilgrimage is popular among women and for some it has become a family field trip.

There is a custom of offering gifts to the walking pilgrims, which is called *settai*. It includes food, drinks, accommodation, and even towels. It is an offer to help the pilgrimage, to participate in the journey of the other. *Settai* was seen as early as 1690 where, in the book of Shikoku Henro Kudokuki, Shinnen admonishes the people to give lodging and food to the poor and the pilgrims. One type of food villagers gave to pilgrims was *mugikogashi* (ground barley). During the Bunka period (1804–1818) in the summer, it was mixed with cold water to make a drink, or sugar was added to make porridge. The traveler Jippensha Ikku, who traveled around Shikoku in 1821, offered an explicit account of the kinds of food given as *settai*. He received such foods as *chameshi* (tea rice), *mugikogashi/hattaiko* (ground barley), *kowameshi* (boiled pounded rice with red beans), *mochikome* (pounded rice), *miso*, *umeboshi* (pickled plum), tofu soup, red bean rice, seaweed, and fried vegetables with meat. Charity extended from food to a haircut or a free place to stay. Sometimes, inn owners offered some of the meals on the menu for free as well. In another book from 1825, a traveler recounted that along the pilgrimage path throughout Shikoku *waraji* (straw sandals) and *dango* (sweet, round dumplings made from rice flour) were hung on pine trees. If you took a *dango*, you were to put two *mon* of money in the container. There were also other gifts from the devoted villagers: rice, chestnuts, *hie* (barnyard millet), *nanba* (mountain Japanese apricot and *kibi* (millet), *soba* (buckwheat noodles), *sōmen* (noodles), *irimame* (parched beans), *hattaiko* (parched flour), *satsumaimo* (sweet potato), and *gomasu* (sesame vinegar). When pilgrims had extra *sekihan* (red rice) and *mochi* (pounded rice) after they finished eating, they would give the rest to the son of the inn at which they stayed the night after, for waking them up.[9]

Offering tea to travelers has been another deep-rooted custom in Japan. Toward the second half of the sixteenth century, pilgrims were given tea. As time passed, increasingly more *chayas* (tea buildings) were observed around temples or shrines, and the drinking of tea became popular also in Shikoku. By the late seventeenth century, tea was served in all inns, taverns, and roadside food stalls, and in many huts set up in the fields and mountains.

This tradition of giving food and shelter was also explained by the wish of the island people to prevent any problems that were present in the past when pilgrims came to the island with diseases and needs, and collapsed on the way from hunger and sleep. As well as healing and spirituality, poverty was one of the motivations for pilgrims. In 1833 to 1839 because of the period of famine, people who were starving and had no money or jobs came here, as they could get food donated along the way. Pilgrim numbers grew. Sometimes they kept walking even after finishing the round of the island. Japanese folklorist Katsurai stated that in lands far from villages a great number of pilgrims died on the way because poor village families killed them for their money. In these stories usually a family welcomes a pilgrim to their house and when they discover that he has a lot of money they kill him and steal his money. First the family becomes rich but after a while all sorts of misfortunes follow: illness, quarrels, the birth of mentally ill children, and premature death. Such families would be stigmatized and cursed for generations; villagers would avoid marriage with them and believed that many misfortunes would come to these families for generations.

This mysterious side of strangers made pilgrims both welcomed and feared. In general, villagers were kind to pilgrims. But their extreme kindness did not help the pilgrims either. As a rule, a pilgrim had to beg for his food at least twenty-one times during one period of pilgrimage and this was very difficult when village people donated food or inns provided food for free. Until the early twentieth century, there were organized associations in Japan that were set up to help pilgrims by bringing them food and supplies: rice, red beans, pickles, pickled *ume* (plums), tofu, soy sauce, dried persimmons, *miso*, firewood, some money, and sandals. Also until recently on Shodo Island, individual families would give pilgrims rice, *mikan* (mandarin oranges), cakes, and money. Another way pilgrims were supported was the community groups collecting rice, red beans, and rice cakes, and cooking for pilgrims in the Fuji temple in Tokushima.[10]

Pilgrims today usually carry their lunch and rely on inns and guesthouses for breakfast and dinner. They can also stay in some free lodges along the route. Japanese *minshuku* and *ryokan* inns provide room, dinner, and breakfast. Lunch

Local people giving rice to pilgrims along the Shikoku pilgrimage route by Jippensha Ikku in 1821.
Courtesy of David Moreton.

can be eaten as a set price menu in restaurants or made with ingredients bought at food stores along the way. These stores also sell *bento* (boxed lunch).

Each region in Shikoku has a local specialty. Tokushima has ramen noodles, *wakame* seaweed, or lotus root. Kagawa has *udon* noodles. Many of the inns are close to the ocean so they serve freshly caught seafood. A rather simple traditional food worth mentioning is *katapan*, hard and crunchy sweet crackers. It was in fact conceived as a food for military personnel in 1896 and at first called *Heitai pan* (soldier bread). It is made with wheat flour and sugar, which are kneaded together and stretched out, then cut, baked, and dried. Since 1913 after visiting the seventh-fifth temple of the Shikoku Pilgrimage, Zentsu-ji Temple, pilgrims often buy *katapan* from the Kumaoka Kashiten (Kumaoka Sweet Shop). Another *settai* tradition that seems to stay unchanged is the villagers offering citrus fruit, which is plentiful in the area.

On the Shikoku trail, there are some Shugendō sites. The religion of Shugendō, a Buddhist sect, did not have temples and shrines but believed in the power of mountains. Shugendō pilgrims were called yamabushi, "those who lie down in the mountain." They wore, like all Japanese pilgrims, white robes, the color of the dead, and they viewed themselves as having crossed

Pilgrims (David Moreton and David Turkington) receiving Japanese citrus fruit "natsu mikan"
settai, 2006.
Courtesy of Tom Ward.

into the realms of the dead when entering the mountains. While traveling
up the mountain, they gained spiritual strength; on returning to the foot-
hills, they were reborn in this world.

Fuji has always been an image of an ideal mountain, religiously and
aesthetically, albeit from a distance. However, the ascent of Fuji became
an objective only after the introduction of Chinese culture and Buddhism
and Shugendō. During the Meiji Period in 1872, Shugendō was considered
superstitious and was banned. Mount Fuji was closed and practices were carried out in secret, until it reopened in 1945 with the Japanese Culture Act.
Practices in Fuji and other mountains always included fasting and abstinence
from water. Shugendō was a blend of pre-Buddhist folk religion, tantric Buddhism, and Taoistic magic. Buddhist ethics, particularly the six virtues, are
also incorporated into Shugendō doctrine and adapted to mountain ascetic
practice. These were charity, observance of precepts, patience, devotion,
meditation, and wisdom, which dictated sharing food with another who is
hungry or sharing water with who is thirsty, carrying another's luggage when
he is tired, abstinence from improper food and drink, and not complaining
when hot, cold, hungry, or thirsty.[11]

Another group of pilgrims, Tendai Buddhist monks, have been walking on trails at a fast pace, earning the name "marathon monks." It is important to note that sport is a way of self-fulfillment in Japan. Names of sport end with –do, such as judo and kedo, do meaning "the path" or "the way." The practice of searching for self-fulfillment *is* the path. Marathon monks walk a route on Mount Hiei and other nearby mountains in the northeast of Kyoto. They walk long distances, up to 80 kilometers a day, for more than a hundred days in a year. Enlightenment is achieved after one thousand days over seven years. They wear a hat made from woven *hinoki* wood, with both sides rolled up. Their robes are white, which is associated with death in Japanese culture. Their footwear, *waraji*, represents lotus petals and this is changed to *tabi* after the first three hundred days have been completed. It is said that the pilgrims carry a dagger and hemp rope with which to kill themselves if they are unable to finish their practice. Once he completes the one thousand-day walk, a monk practices a Shugendō asceticism of seven days with no food, no water, no sleep, and no lying down. The idea is to bring his body as close as possible to death.

In modern Japan, asceticism might have died out, although in 1967, there was a Shugendō pilgrimage group that climbed Fuji. They were being held by their legs and dangled over a cliff; when they arrived at the ascetic hut, they had a thin rice gruel of thirty-six grains of rice in a tea bowl. Once on the summit, they circled the crater, confined themselves in a hut for ten days, and at the end they cooked the celebratory red rice and descended the mountain on the eastern slope. Back in the villages, they performed fire rituals and recited prayers, receiving food in return.[12]

At the foot of Mt. Haguro in Yamagata, an old tradition is still preserved that is more than just travel on foot and further removed from eating. Every year on August 24, pilgrims arrive at the Shozennin temple. The pilgrims are not monks; they have normal jobs and they come here for various reasons. At the start, they are treated to a small feast. They then start their journey by participating in a funeral ritual, after which they are considered dead. They do not eat for three days, after which they are allowed to eat a small meal of soft rice and vegetables. During the day, they traverse the mountain for long distances and at night they return to the hut. Days 5 and 6 are spent with chanting and praying and at the end they drink rice wine together. On the seventh day, August 30, they travel to places where their ancestors' spirits live. On August 31, they travel back down the mountain. On the ninth day, September 1, they feast to their hunger, they put bandages on all their scars, and they say goodbyes to depart. After ceremonies of chanting and exorcism rites such as throwing spices onto hot coals to expel bad spirits, four days of the pilgrimage are completed. Before they depart, a fire is lit and they jump over the fire, celebrating their rebirth.[13]

From Inca Pilgrims to *Feliz Viaje*

The great Inca trail was a network of roads in South America. In the Inca Empire, these roads were leading to each of the four corners of the empire, which came to be shaped like the Milky Way. This road system (*qhapaq ñan*) covered 30,000 kilometers from north to south with side roads going west to east, connecting today's Colombia, Ecuador, Peru, Bolivia, Chile, and Argentina. Roads were reserved for the empire but the nobles, the army, and the pilgrims could use them too. Permission was required before others could walk on the roads, and tolls were charged at some bridges. These Inca roads served pedestrians as well as caravans of packed llamas. They were built in such a way that about every 20 kilometers, one day's journey, the state-built *tambos* (hospices) would serve travelers a place to sleep and get a meal, water, and even weapons.[14] Staple foods in the Inca Empire were corn, potatoes, quinoa, and beans. *Aji* (chili peppers) were a common condiment, and coca was used for rituals and medicinal purposes.[15]

Not far away, in Bolivia near the Peru-Bolivia border, at the Copacabana pilgrimage site, which is sacred to the pre-Columbian sun god, there is the Titicaca Island and the ruins of the Inca Temple of the Sun. The Incas saw the island as the cradle of creation, and in the fifteenth century the island temple became one of the principal pilgrimage sites of the empire. Across the Copacabana peninsula, the Incas built a wall and inspected the pilgrims before they walked on farther. From that moment on, they had to refrain from eating meat, salt, or chili peppers. If they were poor, they could take some other foodstuff from the state storehouses. Pilgrims would walk three hours from there to then take a boat to the island where they would visit a number of sites and give their offerings. As for offerings, archeologists have found llamas, alpacas, and children buried at this site, as well as clothes and remnants of foodstuff. After the island of the sun, pilgrims would visit the island of the moon. Generally, pilgrims would take corn that grows on this island, which they believed would ensure fertility of their home fields. Nowadays, Christian pilgrims visit the shrine of Copacabana on February 2 and August 5, approximately when the sun reaches its highest and lowest position in the sky at Lake Titicaca. And instead of taking corn back with them, the pilgrims now take ceramic or metal models of the houses and trucks they pray the Virgin of Copacabana will grant them.[16]

Inca pilgrims sometimes went on the road to reach mountain peaks and to make sacrifices. *Qhapaq hucha* was the Inca practice of human sacrifice. Children were mainly sacrificed because they were pure. They were selected to be physically perfect and healthy, and they were fed and fattened before the sacrifice in order to offer the most precious of all gifts to the gods. The children would eat their last meals while the Incan high priests took them to high mountaintops. In a long and arduous journey, they fed the children coca leaves to aid them in their breathing. It also made them less conscious of the trip. Upon reaching the burial site, the children were given an intoxicating *chicha* drink made from corn to minimize pain, fear, and resistance. The Inca believed intoxication opened channels to the spiritual realm, and *chicha* was an important element of social and ceremonial gatherings, where ritual drunkenness was often obligatory. They were then killed either by strangulation, a blow to the head, or by leaving them to lose consciousness in the extreme cold and die of exposure.

When archaeologists begun to find these victims on Andean mountaintops, their bodies were mummified and preserved due to the freezing temperatures and dry, windy mountain air. Their stomachs still contained coca leaves. In 1995, the body of an almost entirely frozen young Inca girl, later named Mummy Juanita, was discovered on Mount Ampato. Two more ice-preserved mummies, one girl and one boy, were discovered nearby a short while later. All showed signs of death by a blow to the head.

In 1999, near Llullaillaco's 6,739-meter summit, an Argentine-Peruvian expedition found perfectly preserved bodies of three Inca children, sacrificed approximately five hundred years earlier, including a fifteen-year-old girl, nicknamed *La doncella* (the maiden), a seven-year-old boy (the llullaillaco boy), and a six-year-old girl, nicknamed *La niña del rayo* (the lightning girl). The latter's nickname reflects the fact that (sometime in the five-hundred-year period the mummy spent on the summit) it was struck by lightning, partially burning the preserved body and some of the ceremonial artifacts left with the mummies. Today the three mummies are exhibited at the Museum of High Altitude Archaeology in Salta, Argentina. Researchers analyzed their scalp hair and found traces of coca and alcohol, suggesting ingestion in the lead-up to death. At the site, some artifacts were found: wooden drinking vessels (*keros*), ceramics (e.g., *aribalos* for liquids), and richly decorated textile bags (e.g., *chuspas* for coca) that retained their more ephemeral foodstuff contents—offerings including corn, peanuts, and coca leaves—with dried camelid meat also found within the burials. The findings also revealed what The Maiden was chewing in her last moments. A coca quid was found still clenched between her teeth, and there were remnants of chewed leaves around her mouth.[17]

On the famous Inca trail today, the only sacrifice one makes is to share it with many other tourists. Coca leaves are still chewed today by Peruvian porters and guides, and the leaves are given to tourists made into a bitter tea but mostly to fight *soroche*, altitude sickness.

The Inca trail is one of the two main ways to approach Machu Picchu coming from the Inca heartland. The spectacular Inca trail, a very uneasy route, rises as much as 4,200 meters to cross the "Dead Woman Pass." The travel from Cusco to Machu Picchu following this route took at least four full days for the Inca on foot. It has been also proposed by some scholars that Machu Picchu was a sacred center, a pilgrimage site. At an altitude of 2,400 meters, the site was built as a condor's nest between two peaks, Huayna Picchu (the young peak) and Machu Picchu (the old peak). When Hiram Bingham, a Yale lecturer with a passion for exploration, found Machu Picchu in 1911, he thought it was the lost capital of the last Inca reign, Vilcabamba. Today, although still not known why and when Incas built the town, it is believed to be the royal estates of the Inca Pachacuti.

It appears that the classical Inca trail was conceived mainly as a ceremonial route, not as a functional one, at least in the dry season. Its very existence contributes to serious doubts on the royal estate theory: indeed the ruler traveling to Machu Picchu to spend the winter (dry) season there did not need such a long, uneasy way to arrive to his estate. Because for the dry season (May to September, which is also the season during which Machu Picchu is supposed to have been visited by the Inca), there is another, much easier and natural way from Cusco to Machu Picchu, following the Urubamba valley up to the Machu Picchu ridge and then ascending up to Winay-wayna and the town. This path could become dangerous or even impassable in case of heavy rains, but in the dry season it allowed a three-day-long, quiet travel. One more Inca path ascending directly from the river to the town was found in the deep forest on the east flank of the Machu Picchu ridge in 2004. All of the other trails support the ceremonial role of the classical Inca trail.[18]

The Inca trail is a popular trekking site today. On the Inca trail nowadays, porters outnumber the clients to provide a comfortable experience. The four-day trip takes travelers into the forest, experiencing altitude gain and Peruvian dishes cooked by the expedition cooks. Peruvian staples are prepared on campgrounds: *quionoa*, in soup or as rice, potatoes, chicken, beef, and corn. To make the experience even more memorable, cooks have started

Feliz viaje (happy journey) cake on the Inca trail, 2015. From left, Modesto Franco and Toribio Condory, cooks of the Inca trail.
Courtesy of Hyun-Jung Kim.

making cakes to celebrate the special dates of their clients, such as wedding anniversaries and birthdays. The cake is called *feliz viaje* (happy journey) cake and is baked without an oven. Cooks bake the cake inside a pot on a stove over low heat for forty-five minutes to an hour. They then decorate it with whipped cream. "The porters are in charge to carry all the ingredients for cooking, including the eggs. They must be very careful to carry them in order not to break them."[19]

Food in the the Holy Land

The Holy Land is the area where modern-day Israel, Palestine, Lebanon, western Jordan, and southwestern Syria reside. Jerusalem has been the holiest city in Judaism since the tenth century BCE. During classical antiquity, it was considered the center of the world, where God lived. The Western Wall or "Wailing" Wall of the First Temple, at the site of Temple Mount today, remains in the Old City of Jerusalem and is the most sacred and visited site for Jews. Jerusalem is also a holy city in a number of religious traditions, including Judaism, Christianity, and Islam.

The concept and experience of pilgrimage was so strong in medieval Europe that it fired the imagination of the age and set the tone for travel of all kinds. In literature, the concept of the sacred journey structures Dante's *Divine Comedy*, which recounts the author's own transformation through hell and heaven. The earliest Christian pilgrims wished to see the places where Jesus and the apostles had lived on earth. This meant journeying to the Holy Land. This was a relatively easy feat in the fourth century, when the Roman Empire still unified the Mediterranean world. However, the Crusades to win control of the Holy Land were a particular kind of pilgrimage.

Jerusalem pilgrims traveled on land at the end of the tenth century. The route was less popular in the twelfth century, and after the end of the thirteenth century most pilgrims traveled by sea. Journey on land was difficult and meant 30 to 40 kilometers a day on foot, at least for those who could not afford a horse. A traveler had to cross high mountains and face illness, bad weather, being robbed, and even being murdered during travel. Travel over the sea was hardly any safer. Pilgrims complained about noise, rats, seasickness, hunger, thirst, and food that was infected with maggots. Quite a few pilgrims died of food poisoning, and there could be piracy. After arrival, some pilgrims complained that they were rushed through the holy sites in ten days, a very short time considering the long and painful ship journey to get there.[20]

In Jerusalem, pilgrims relied on services on the street, as not all households had an oven. In the twelfth century, ready-to-eat cooked meals and bread were sold to the pilgrims in the central market of the city on a street, which was called *Rue Malquisinat* (Vicus Coquinatus), meaning street of bad cooking in French. On *Rue des Herbes* (the Street of Herbs), herbs, fruit, and spices were sold. Just outside the southern wall to the west of Temple Mount, there was a cattle market and a pig market. The existence of the pig market indicates French residents and pilgrims, as many inhabitants of the city, including Christians of Palestine, whether Melkite, Syrian Orthodox, or Armenian, did not eat pork as a result of the centuries-long influence of Islam.[21]

One of the Italian Jewish travelers to the Holy Land, Meshullam ben Menahem, got very ill in his stomach and recorded in his travel memoir his surprise that not all pilgrims die on this journey. He was in Jerusalem for a month, mostly ill, and he visited the sites in two days. He fondly reported that "the land flows with milk and honey" and fondly mentions *karob* honey, date honey, as well as wheat, barley, pomegranate, and all kinds of fruits.

Nonetheless, in his account what is striking is the difference between the habits of the Jews in the Middle East and those in Italy. He was particularly surprised that Jews were eating by hand and not using napkins, calling them "pigs at their eating." His conclusion displays the awe of the traveler once more: "I could not eat and enjoy their dishes, for they are different to our people's and strange to a healthy man, much more so to a sick man like me." He recovered after the care of Ashkenazi Jews from Italy prepared for him a diet of familiar food.[22] The account of Obadiah from Bertinoro, a fifteenth-century Italian rabbi, shows that the experience of pilgrimage was a matter of mind-set as well. He was amazed by the markets that sold cooked meals. Middle Eastern Jewish food was considered a sophisticated cuisine. A saying advised "to sleep in a Christian bed and to enjoy Jewish food."[23]

Both Christian and Jewish pilgrims to Jerusalem took a boat from Venice to Jaffa. For the ship journey they typically packed a bed, a rope to hang the bed up during the day, and a keg for drinking water. They would also buy a barrel of red wine at Padua along with ham, salted beef tongues, hard cheese, figs, a hard biscuit, dates, sugar, almonds, syrup, and medicines against the heat. They would buy a food chest to carry these for the ship's journey. In 1533, French crusader Greffin Affagart wrote: "Whoever undertakes this expedition must have a good intention, a good heart, a strong stomach and a good purse."[24]

During the Middle Ages when Christians could not visit the Holy Land, other sites closer to home became favored places of pilgrimage: St. Peter's in Rome and Santiago de Compostela in Spain. In England, the most favored pilgrimage destination was Canterbury Cathedral and its shrine of Archbishop Thomas Becket, martyred in 1170 on the orders of King Henry II. Century after century, pilgrims journeyed to Becket's shrine. Their trek was immortalized by Chaucer's *Canterbury Tales* (1385–1400), a collection of stories of twenty-nine pilgrims seeking healing and transformation as they travel as pilgrims to Canterbury. The tales reveal their motives for pilgrimage. The pilgrims are made memorable by their relationship to food and drink. Chaucer's tales are a game of food, and his awareness of food and analysis on food distribution are based on his own experience, not as a pilgrim but as the controller of customs in the port of London where he oversaw the import and export of foodstuffs for twelve years.[25] Food in these stories represents the characters of the people and helps Chaucer create a parody of their indulgences and weaknesses. In part of a verse from Franklin's portrait, we can sense the satire[26]:

His bread and ale were always fresh and fine,
And no one had a better stock of wine.
Baked meat was always in his house, the best
Of fish and flesh, so much that to each guest
It almost seemed to snow with meat and drink
And all the dainties of which one could think.

Clearly, Franklin is a rich man of power, as food represents the material status of people who can afford opulent feasts. And the reference to bread and wine recalls the sacred bread and wine of Christian mass, communion, where bread and wine are changed into the body and blood of Jesus Christ. Strikingly, in the tales, the Cook prepares quite luxurious meals that the faithful were to eat. The menu includes chickens boiled with marrow bones, *mortreux*, which is a mixture of chicken, pork, liver, sugar, yolks, and spices; pies; and *galingale*, which is a kind of marmalade made of honey, wine, ginger, cinnamon, and *galangal* (a kind of herb similar to ginger).

The profile of the cook reveals the state of cooking and trading of food in late medieval England[27]:

They had a cook with them for the occasion,
To boil the chickens with the marrowbones
And sharp spice powder and galingale.
He could easily recognize a draft of London ale.
He could roast and boil and fry,
Make "Mortreux" and bake a pie well.
But it was a shame, it seemed to me,
That he had an ulcer on his shin.
He was among the best at making "Blankmanger."

Contrasting the Cook's talent in his trade is how often he gets drunk and how he lacks personal hygiene.

Chaucer's work represents the strife for heaven, despite the weaknesses of the pilgrims coming from all layers of society: the commoners, the nobility, and the clergy.

Hajj to Mecca

And announce the pilgrimage to humanity. They will come to you on foot, and on every transport. They will come from every distant point.

—Quran 22:27[28]

The Hajj is the annual Islamic pilgrimage to Mecca, Saudi Arabia. Every year, more than two million Muslims perform hajj during a five-day period from the ninth through the thirteenth of *Dhu Al-Hijjah*, the twelfth month of the Muslim lunar calendar. The hajj pilgrimage is one of the five pillars of Islam and, according to Islamic teachings, has to be undertaken by Muslims who can afford it at least once in their lifetime.

In pre-Islamic Arabia, Kaaba was still the center for worship. Pagan Arabs were worshipping idols and images and maintaining silence or performing their pilgrimage in a naked state. After Mecca was conquered by Muslims in 630 CE, Mohammed declared new hajj rules and in 632 CE, shortly before his death, he performed his only and last pilgrimage with a large number of followers on foot, teaching them the rites of hajj and the manners of performing them. When the pilgrim is about 6 miles (10 kilometers) from Mecca, he enters the state of holiness and purity known as *ihram*. A pilgrim wears seamless white garments, consisting of two sheets wrapped around the body. Hajj has an ascetic quality in that the pilgrim must abstain from sex and cannot cut either his hair or his nails until the pilgrimage rite is over. He must not kill any animals for food, which was considered a pagan ritual and abolished.

During medieval times, tens of thousands of pilgrims would go to Mecca in caravans from Syria, Egypt, and Iraq. There were three pilgrimage routes: the Kufa route from central Asia, Iran, and Iraq; the Damascus route from Anatolia and Syria; and the Cairo route from Africa, al-Andalus, Maghrib, and Egypt.[29] Numerous pilgrims walked next to caravans. Caravans included tens of thousands of camels carrying people, merchandise, food, and water. Rulers appointed official guards of pilgrims called Amir al-Hajj. A hajj pilgrimage meant risking one's life. The journey took more than three months. Although Bedouins along the route would sell water, food, and camels to the caravans, they also sometimes raided the Hajj caravans. The Ottoman army ensured the security of caravans and negotiated the cost of a safe passage with the Bedouins, which was still not guaranteed. For example, the raid of 1757 entered history as the most famous Bedouin raid against the hajj caravan where an estimated twenty thousand pilgrims were either killed or died of hunger or thirst; senior officials were executed for their negligence or involvement. Depending on their contract with the caravan leader, pilgrims would either carry their own food or receive it from the caravan leader. Also in Mecca and Medina, in order to prevent food shortages, Ottoman rulers sent grains from Egypt to make bread and *desise* (a porridge of crushed wheat and fat).[30]

Due to lack of settlements en route, food shortage was a serious problem. The lack of water was even a bigger problem when temperatures could rise to 50 to 60 degrees Celsius and all wells dried up. Moreover, the available water was not clean and would lead to typhus and cholera outbreaks among the pilgrims. All these reasons led to the construction of the Hejaz Railway from Damascus to Medina in 1908, making the journey safer. Although the Bedouin resisted the building of the railway at first, some tribes slowly started selling goods like meat, cheese, and milk to the pilgrims.[31] The railway closed in 1920 after the fall of the Ottoman Empire and never reopened.

In the early days, hajj was done entirely on foot or on camels. Nowadays, most pilgrims fly into Jeddah and take a bus to Mecca. By foot or by bus, the pilgrim then travels 8 kilometers to the massive tent city of Mina, where most pilgrims are housed in air-conditioned tents.

Rarely, pilgrims who cannot raise the funds walk across borders, which are often in conflict. As such, in 2011, Banovici, a pilgrim from northeastern Bosnia, walked the 3,540 miles across Bosnia, Serbia, Bulgaria, Turkey, Syria, Jordan, and Saudi Arabia to finally reach Mecca. He left his home with just a 20-kilogram backpack, containing only basic equipment and two hundred euros, and slept mostly in mosques, parks, and occasionally in the streets. In an interview, he particularly praised the Syrian people who showed him the safest routes and gave him "oranges and apples" in the streets.[32]

At dawn on the ninth day of *Dhu al-Hijja*, pilgrims begin a 14.4-kilometer walk to the plain of Arafat, where the Prophet Muhammad delivered his final sermon, passing Muzdalifah along the way. The route has cool mist sprinklers. Hajj ambulances and medical stations are set up along the route. Pilgrims spend the day in supplication, praying and reading the Quran; it is the pinnacle of most pilgrims' spiritual lives. After sunset, pilgrims begin the 9-kilometer walk back to Muzdalifah, where they sleep in the open air. At sunrise on the tenth day of *Dhu al-Hijja*, pilgrims collect small pebbles at Muzdalifah and carry them to Mina for the Stoning of the Devil at the Jamaraat ritual. During this ritual, pilgrims throw seven tiny pebbles (no larger than a chickpea) at each of three white pillars. Traditionally, after Jamaraat, pilgrims sacrifice an animal to symbolize the ram that Abraham sacrificed instead of his son. More recently, pilgrims purchase a "sacrifice voucher" in Mecca and have this sacrifice performed for them. After returning to Mecca, pilgrims go immediately to the Grand Mosque, which contains the Ka'aba, the most sacred site in Islam, and perform a *tawaf*, circling the Ka'aba seven times counterclockwise, which can take hours. In addition to *tawaf*, pilgrims may perform *sa'i*, walking or running seven times between the hills of Safa and Marwah and then drinking *zamzam*, holy water, from the Well of Zamzam. According to Islamic belief, zamzam is a miraculously generated source of water pre-Islam, when Abraham's infant son Ishmael was thirsty and kept crying for water and the well was revealed to Hagar, the second wife of Abraham and mother of Ishmael. This route, which used to be open air, is now enclosed by the Grand Mosque and can be crossed via air-conditioned tunnels, with separate sections for walkers, runners, and disabled pilgrims. After a final *tawaf*, the pilgrims leave Mecca. Many pilgrims extend their trip to Medina to visit the Mosque of the Prophet, which contains the tomb of Mohammed and is the second holiest site in Islam.[33]

Drinking zemzem water cleans the pilgrim from greed and unjust gains. Islam sees the stomach as the source of all lust, which is why taming the stomach through fasting is an important religious practice.[34]

Eating less is a virtue in the context of body and soul dichotomy as a metaphor for moral struggle, which is shared by most other religions.

CHAPTER 7

Army Rations

Military food dates back to ancient times. Spartan soldiers subsisted on black broth, a mixture of boiled pigs' legs, blood, and vinegar, so disturbing in taste that it was interpreted as another sign for the soldiers' fearlessness.[1] The Roman legions instead ate considerably well, at least when stationed. They kept a herd of cattle and grew corn, other crops, and vegetables. Food was plentiful with wine and beer accompanying it. The Vindolanda tablets listed the food items of Roman Britain: cereal, venison, beans, wheat, barley, apples, fish sauce, oil, spices, pork fat, olives, oysters, eggs, ham, pepper, chicken, salt, wine, sour wine, and beer.[2] Also many Roman soldiers depended on care packages sent from home.

When in campaign and on marches, however, the story was a little different. The soldiers were back to basics. They carried sickles to forage food and a ration for three days. The ration included 1.4 kilograms of bread, 1 liter of sour wine *posca*, and 50 milliliters of oil per person per day. Each soldier carried a bread ration. They also made their own bread. As the grain of wheat conserved much better than flour, each group of soldiers living in the same tent carried a wheat ration and a small portable hard stone hand mill to grind the grain. This flour was either baked into a flat bread; made into pancakes with flour, wine, and oil; made into a simple porridge with flour, water, and salt; or made into whatever else he had in his disposal, perhaps garlic and onions. They baked bread under a *clibanus*, a clay pot with a lid in the shape of a bell or an inverted bowl. Meat was often carried "on the hoof" as herds of animals and often they chewed on *lucana*, a dry sausage. When possible, soldiers would supplement their food with purchases from merchants as well as whatever they could catch, kill, collect, or steal.[3,4]

Napoleon famously said that an army travels on its stomach. Though army food existed much before Napoleon was an army general, it was around his years that it started to become modernized and structured. Since then, cooks but mostly scientists have worked for years to produce high-caloric food that lasts for months in sealed pouches and tins. However, it was also important that they were safe to eat and did not cause any food poisoning. After all, an undercooked egg could be just as dangerous to an army as the enemy. Army food was not only about sustenance, it served also as morale booster, a reminder of home in a hostile, alien place. In this regard, it had to also be tasty and this was probably the biggest challenge of all.

In early wars, troops lived off the land; on occasion, even animals were taken along with the troops. Such supplies were difficult to sustain, and rations had to be developed to support the needs of military troops on trails and sometimes under extreme climates and conditions. Advances in food processing and nutrition have paved the way for effective army rations. Throughout history, important developments in food preservation came from trying to meet the needs of military operations. At each war, the rations evolved with new packaging or processing techniques. What helped the planning and development of food tremendously in the First World War was the invention of the conservation process by the French confectioner Nicholas Appert in the 1790s. Appert developed a method of conserving all kinds of food substances in glass jars, practically inventing canning. He received 12,000 francs from the Ministry of the Interior's Bureau of Arts and Manufacturers on the condition that he published details of this process. But glass was not as practical to use in the field. Englishman Peter Durand patented the idea of using tin cans. Tin plates were already used to keep food but with less success. Sometime around the middle of the eighteenth century, the Dutch Navy began to supply foods such as roast beef and salmon preserved by packing them in fat in tinned iron canisters. However, the commercial packaging of foods in metal containers began only in the early nineteenth century. By the 1820s, canned foods were a commercial article in Britain and France.[5]

One of Nicolas Appert's canning experiments was on canned soups. However, a much older product, pocket soup (also called portable soup or veal glue), was already mentioned in cookbooks for the first time in 1681. In 1679, Papin invented the steam digester or bone digester for extracting fats from bones in a high-pressure steam environment, which also rendered them brittle enough to be easily ground into bone meal. The bone digester was the forerunner of the pressure cooker, just as portable soup was the precursor of the bouillon cube. Basically, a soup was prepared with, for example, "three legs of veal and one of beef, with ten pounds of lean ham, all cut very small, a quarter of a pound of butter, four ounces of anchovies, two ounces of mace, a bunch of celery, six carrots washed well, a large bunch of sweet herbs, a spoonful of whole pepper, and a hard crust of a penny loaf."[6] The soup was cooked; its fat was skimmed, reduced until it was a glue-like jelly, and dehydrated into powder and stored in tins. Portable soup was similar to today's bouillon cube: lightweight, portable, nutritious, filling, and easily reconstituted; one just needed to add water. By the mid-nineteenth century, scientific advances permitted the mass production of several foods based on pocket soup, including meat extracts and stock cubes, which became iconic travel foods for soldiers, explorers, and travelers.

Another turning point for army rations was when American Gail Borden created the process of evaporation and canning of milk in Texas in 1853. Interestingly enough, Borden started out with manufacturing a version of pemmican, which he called "meat biscuit." He was selling these to gold seekers in California. He also sold some to the Arctic explorer Dr. Elisha Kent Kane, a medical officer who was a member of two of the unsuccessful Arctic expeditions to rescue the polar explorer Sir John Franklin. Borden won a golden medal for his meat biscuit at the 1851 International Exhibition in London. After this, he tried to persuade the US Army and Navy to buy his biscuits. Failing to do so, he finally turned to the condensed milk business. When the Civil War broke out in 1861, a large demand for condensed milk came in from the Union Army. This eventually made him a fortune and condensed milk a familiar product in the army.[7]

Freeze-drying was another technique developed during World War II. It involved freezing the food, removing almost all the moisture under vacuum, and sealing it in an airtight container. First, it was a useful invention for preserving blood plasma that had to be transferred under no refrigeration. Later, freeze-dried food made its way into army rations in cans. Instant coffee led the way. After the war, freeze-drying was used for preserving other types of foods. Although it was (and still is) a more costly method of conservation, freeze-drying allowed more lightweight foods to be taken along on foot. Not only fruits, vegetables, and meat, but entire meals could be preserved.

The invention of portable stoves in the nineteenth century was another big milestone for army food. In 1855, one of the first French celebrity chefs, Alexis Soyer, went out to Crimea in charge of the catering for the British Army at a time when the soldiers were depleted by disease and poor diet. He designed innovative kitchens, catering equipment, and foods. One famous invention he made was a stove. The soldiers in Crimea were cooking meals on open fires, and the army was running short of fuel. Soyer designed a stove that consisted of a drum with an enclosed furnace below. It cooked for more people and used much less wood. It also worked on coal, gas, and peat. His stove remained used in the British Army for more than a decade. Soyer also designed a Scutari teapot, which had a filter to hold the tea, and provided the troops with better tea. "War," Soyer said, "is the evil genius of a time; but good food for all is a daily and a paramount necessity."[8]

Developments in army food also influenced explorers who relied on rations in their expeditions. Most provisions were originally designed for the army and later used in mountain and polar expeditions. Bovril was one of them.

Bovril—The Fuel of Armies and Explorers

In the second half of the nineteenth century, when concentrated long-life foods had become an acceptable idea, a product was developed by a Scotsman for Napoleon that would later become an icon of British culture. In 1874, during the Franco Prussian War, Napoleon ordered one million cans of beef to feed his troops. As Britain did not have enough beef to supply the French demand, the French Army gave the contract to Scotsman John Lawson Johnston, who had emigrated to Canada and set up his business just a few years prior. Johnston gained his butcher skills (and his namesake) from his uncle John. Eventually, Johnston took over his uncle's butcher shop in Edinburgh. He used beef trimmings to make his own *glace de viande* (meat glaze, made from beef stock by heating it until it became concentrated, viscous, and took a dark brown color), which sold so well that he opened a second shop and a factory. While there, he developed Johnston's Fluid Beef, later called Bovril. His meat glaze was different from conventional meat glaze. Gelatin was present in all meat glazes and made them solid at room temperature. In his glaze, instead gelatin was hydrolyzed with alkali to make the mixture semi-liquid. This made his product easier to package, measure, and drink. Moreover, Bovril had a very strong name, *bov* came from the Latin word *bovem* meaning ox and *vril* from a popular novel at the time in which *vril* was an electromagnetic substance that gave strength to the people of a superior race. In this, Bovril meant strength from ox.[9]

Bovril also made its way to Everest expeditions. It was the fuel behind England's beloved and successful mountaineer Chris Bonington, who had first ascents in the Himalayas and climbed Everest four times. He was featured in a commercial in 1979 on top of a snowy mountain looking enthusiastic about a big mug of beefy Bovril, saying, "We boil up snow and ice to make hot strong Bovril to thaw ourselves out and how that beefy taste cheered us."[10]

Bovril also made its way to the ice-covered mountainous island off the coast of Antarctica in the Southern Ocean. Bovril was part of the ration that would barely last the men before they could be rescued after 4.5 months of being stranded on Elephant Island. Bovril later used quotes from Shackleton in their advertisements such as: "The question of the concentrated beef supply is most important—it must be Bovril." Bovril Company also produced a supplement called Virol. It was dark and thick liquid like molasses sold in a stoneware pot. Virol Bone Marrow contained bone marrow from ox rib and calf bones, whole eggs with the shells, malt extract, and lemon syrup.

The history of Bovril nicely ties with the history of food on foot across different times and geographies. But Bovril was first a "war food" in World War I. Afterwards, Bovril was a popular food in England thanks to heavy advertisement of its nutritional strength in the twentieth century, even depicting it as one of the two infallible powers: the Pope and Bovril.

Army Rations—Eating the Alphabet

For rational reasons, army rations have simple names. This makes them classified based on their objectives and codes their purpose rather than the content. Military rations are named like vitamins (A, B, C) and sometimes like secret service agencies (LRP, MCI, or MRTE). Many of the world's rations are based on the rations of the American army. It is therefore very interesting to understand its historical evolution, which parallels the developments in nutrition, product development, and logistics, as much as the well-being of the soldiers, although their wishes for taste *might* have been compromised.

In the eighteenth and nineteenth centuries, from the Revolutionary War to the Spanish-American War, the available ration was called "garrison ration." It consisted of meat, salted fish, hardtack, and vegetables. This simple food was given to troops based at a station. During the Civil War, the difficulties in food logistics led to the development of army rations. By World War I, garrison rations had improved based on advances in nutrition, but they were lacking in vitamins due to the lack of availability of fresh foods. During World War I, American forces used the reserve ration, the trench ration, and the emergency iron ration. The iron ration was the first attempt to make an individual ration. It was created in 1907 and consisted of cakes made of beef bouillon powder and parched, and cooked wheat, chocolate, salt, and pepper packed in tin. This later became the reserve ration and consisted of fresh bacon, canned meat, hardtack, coffee, sugar, and salt. There was also tobacco and cigarette rolling papers. This evolved further, and, in 1938, it became what is now known as the C-ration.

This letter-naming convention was based on preparation needs. A-rations were fresh rations and served in dining halls with kitchen and refrigeration facilities. B-rations were prepared with canned or preserved ingredients but still in field kitchens. There were also five-in-one and ten-in-ten rations intended for a group of people and much like the B-rations they needed a kitchen to prepare. C-rations, on the other hand, were individual rations completely pre-cooked and ready to eat. A D-ration was an emergency ration containing high calories from chocolate mixed with other ingredients. A J-ration was developed for troops in tropical regions. The K-ration was designed for assault forces. The M-ration was the mountain ration developed for use by US troops operating in European mountains during World War II.

At the outset of World War II, nutritional value was the primary requirement for special ration items. After the war, a subsistence research laboratory was established where its personnel tried to develop food components with the greatest nutrition in the smallest volume and weight. Acceptance and palatability were secondary. Actual experience showed that troops would not eat what they did not like, no matter how great they were nutritionally. As the war progressed, acceptability became more and more important, admittedly rather an issue. The developments in the C-rations in the later years had to take this into account.[11]

The K-ration was introduced in the US Army during World War II and had three meal units: breakfast, lunch, and dinner. The special assistant to the secretary of war, Dr. Ancel Keys, developed it in 1941 for troops in combat. As a physiologist at the University of Minnesota, Dr. Ancel Keys researched likeable, nutritious, and inexpensive foods. Dr. Keys was also the man behind the Mediterranean diet and the role of cholesterol, and known for his experiments in starvation and high-altitude diet and health. When he died at the age of one hundred in 2004, he would be known as "*Monsieur* Cholesterol." For the K-ration, he collected food items from a grocery store, put them in brown paper bags, and tested them in laboratory and in the field, although only with paratroopers. His objective was to put enough calories into a small non-perishable pack. The K-ration was developed in such a way that all the components providing 2,700 calories would fit into a box that would fit into a soldier's pocket. According to the notes later published by his colleague, Dr. Keys spoke with Cracker Jack Company, which provided him with a watertight small-box concept. The result was the K-ration in sealed Cracker

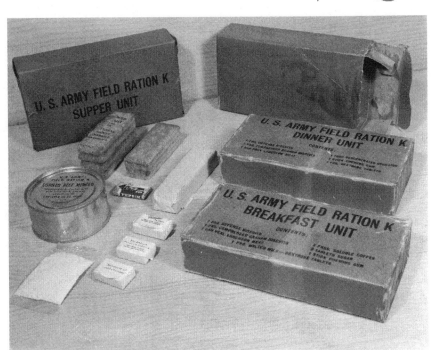

K-ration, 1943.
Library of Congress.

Jack boxes (Cracker Jack is an American brand of snack popcorn and peanuts coated with molasses and caramel).[12] Keys disregarded the need to supplement the ration with vitamins because the ration was developed as a temporary ration to be used for a maximum of fifteen consecutive meals. However, eventually this ration was used much longer throughout World War II.

In 1946, Colonel James Longino announced the good news that an E-ration would replace the C- and K-rations. Basically, it was the C-ration with some improvements. There was a comment from combat soldiers who returned from the war that they could better use a sardine-type flat can rather than in a cylindrical tall can, which was the industry standard at the time. The E-ration was designed to include this type of packaging. However, it was not possible to provide the sardine-type cans for the quantities needed for the C-rations. The bread component was so unpalatable that this ration survived only for two years.[13]

In fact, having bread in the army rations was just a dream. In real life, there was hardtack.

Hardtack—Hard Times Come Again No More

Where hardtack originates is obscure, but European armies and the US Army before the Civil War had used it. Hardtack was the bread of the standard army ration in the nineteenth century. On the march or in camp when soft bread was not available each soldier would get nine or ten hardtack.[14] Hardtack was a dried biscuit of baked dough cut into squares with holes to speed the baking process. There is a lot written and said about this hard cracker, which was practically as hard as a rock, as soon as it was baked and packed in carton boxes. Hardtack was nutritious, yet a hungry man would eat his ten and still be hungry. Hardtack came in three forms: dry and hard, wet and moldy, or infested with maggots and weevils.[15]

Hardtack was imperishable, indestructible, and practically inedible. Yet the soldiers somehow managed to find ways to eat it; they used it in stews, puddings, and in invented dishes. Hardtack and coffee was the most popular combination. Coffee was the beverage of the soldier simply because tea was not available. Only after the war has the availability of coffee increased its acceptance; coffee consumed per every pound of tea increased by more than twenty times from 1862 to 1885.[16] To soften hardtack, soldiers also dipped it in brine or any other liquid. If whiskey was available, hardtack was crumbled in it with brown sugar and hot water to make a pudding. Hardtack lasted in storage for years, but made a good host for worms. The crackers were often so full of worms that soldiers nicknamed them "worm castles" or "worm casket." A hardtack from 1862 displayed at the Wentworth museum in Pensacola, Florida, reveals not only the long endurance of this military staple but also the holes that once hosted worms as tenants.

A soldier named John Billings wrote a memoir of his life as a Union soldier in *Hardtack and Coffee* in 1887 and gave a very accurate description of what Civil War hardtack rations were like, including the following[17]:

> but hardtack was not so bad an article of food, even when traversed by insects, as may be supposed. Eaten in the dark, no one could tell the difference between it and hardtack that was untenanted.

Soldiers despised hardtack; they cursed it, they threw it away, they sang songs about it. They hated it so much that they nearly liked it. This is evident in the fact that after the war, many soldiers took it with them and kept it for many years as a war memento.[18]

To make a hardtack is not as difficult as eating it. Here is an everlasting recipe.[19]

A hardtack, also known as worm castle, from 1862, on display in Wentworth Museum.
Wentworth Museum.

Hardtack
Ingredients (for about 100 crackers):
5 cups flour
1 cup water
½ tablespoon salt

Directions:
Mix flour, water, and salt. Knead into a dough and roll out to 3/8-inch thickness. Cut into approximately three-inch squares and pierce each with a fork several times. Bake in a 400-degree Fahrenheit oven for thirty minutes, until slightly brown. Let them dry and harden out in the open before storing in a container.

Soldiers were missing soft bread the most, perhaps because they missed the bread that their mothers baked. Although they could not bake bread, they tried to turn flour into something edible, on their own, on the march, and with no ovens. They found that mixing flour, water, and a little salt and

Hardtack family photo frame, 1915.
Imperial War Museum London.

sugar made a dough that could be fried in hot lard to make fritters. The same mixture boiled in water made dumplings and if there were any eggs available, they made flapjacks.

Even if some historians such as Bell Irvin Wiley reported that the Union rations of American soldiers were more generous than those provided for the armies of other countries, this did not mean that they were fed all the time. There was suffering from hunger. There were some other recipes that demonstrate the wartime necessity of having to work with limited ingredients supplied or found. For example, ashcakes were cornmeal mixed with salt and water, wrapped in cabbage leaves, and cooked in ashes. Hardtack pudding was made with hardtack pounded into a powder, mixed with water and flour, then kneaded into a dough, rolled out like a pie crust, and filled with apples. Finally, these would be wrapped up in a cloth and boiled for an hour. Milktoast was hardtack soaked in condensed milk.[20]

Wiley himself called hardtack "white oak chips."[21] He cites some of the songs soldiers sang to express the hardship with hardtack. By parodying a song "Hard Times Come Again No More," the soldiers showed their loathing[22]:

'Tis the song of the soldier, weary, hungry, and faint,
Hardtack, hardtack, come again no more;
Many days have I chewed you and uttered no complaint,
O Greenbacks, come again once more.

In the American Civil War, food supplies were low both in the north and in the south. However, food shortages in the south were so much bigger that it is argued by some that food was a determining factor in the outcome of the war. When Robert E. Lee, the commander of the Army of Northern Virginia, surrendered, his men had been with no food for two days. William Davis claims, however, in his book A Taste of War, that the Confederacy never lost a battle because of lack of food but because it never had enough men.[23] Decisive in the outcome or not, undoubtedly the quest for food took up most of a soldier's day in camp and on the march.

Confederate soldiers were trying to get by with what was called "fire cake." Fire cake was made with flour, water, and whatever else they found. The sodden cake was described by a soldier: "Flour . . . wet with water and rolled in dirt and asked to bake . . . in a horrible manner."[24] Poor food supplies in the south led to the creation of new dishes. One was called "cush" or "slosh." It was made by putting small pieces of beef in bacon grease and pouring in water and corn bread to make a stew. Another stew was made from Irish potatoes, green apples, salt, pepper, onions, or garlic.[25]

Rations for the Union army appear to be more adequate, though recipes of desperation were developed also on that side. The Union soldiers created their own food culture, born from lack of diversity in their ration, with a bit of imagination and perhaps driven by boredom as much as necessity. One such recipe they created was called skillygalee. This Civil War recipe involved the use of hardtack. Although it cannot be recommended as a recipe to try to most of us, let us review how they made this concoction, which was also known as "hellfire stew."[26] They would soak the hardtack in hot water. This way the worms would die and float to the surface. After skimming the worms and draining the water, they would add salted pork. The stew was said to "make the hair turn."[27] The origin of skillygalee might be skilly, which is "poor broth, served to prisoners in hulks," composed of oatmeal and water in which meat has been boiled.[28]

Canned Favorites from Trenches to Kitchen Benches

A convenient, affordable, and shelf-stable canned meat product was invented in 1937 and became a perfect match for the US Army Quartermasters office. It was none other than Spam. By the time World War II ended, the US Army had bought 150 million pounds of Spam. Before it became a symbol of American processed food, Spam became the joke of soldiers. The soldiers called it "ham that didn't pass its physical," "meat loaf without basic training," and "the real reason war was hell." Spam was a recognized brand before the war. Although after the war, its sales kept increasing. England and Russia received Spam as part of the American aid package, and they were grateful for it. Nowadays, Spam is popular in parts of the world where US troops were stationed, including Hawaii.[29]

Army food was not looking much better on the other side of the Atlantic Ocean. Usually French soldiers were supplied by a squad called *corvée de soupe* (soup chore) from behind the frontline where a mobile kitchen was installed. But when resupplying was impossible because the fights were too fierce, French soldiers could eat their survival rations, which every soldier had when he moved up to the front. Usually, the survival ration consisted of one day's worth of the following: bread, 300 grams (this kind of very dry bread was called war bread); meat, 300 grams (usually corned beef); sugar, 80 grams; coffee, 36 grams; condensed soup, 50 grams; brandy, 6.25 cl.; and chocolate, 125 grams (since 1916 only).[30]

At the start of World War I, the British army soldiers had enough nourishment with 10 ounces of meat and 8 ounces of vegetables per day. By 1916, however, the meat dropped down to 6 ounces a day and later it was provided only once every nine days. In the winter of 1916, there was a shortage of flour. At this time, pea soup with horsemeat chunks was the staple of the British soldier. The widely used ration was canned soup called *Maconochie*. This was a thick and watery broth with slices of turnips and carrots. It was always cold when it reached the trenches. A soldier would state: "Warmed in a tin, machonochie is edible; cold, it is a mankiller."[31] *Maconochie* was the name of the factory that produced it. This soup was given to the British soldiers in the field during the Boer War and in World War I. After the war, *Maconochie* was one of the rations that made it from the battle front to the home front. Cans were available for the public and were advertised as being ready to cook and fuel-, labor-, and time-saving. They would be ready in twenty minutes and present an economical, delicious meal for a family. *Maconochie* was so iconic that Gordon Rottman's

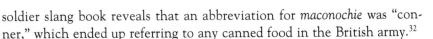

soldier slang book reveals that an abbreviation for *maconochie* was "con-ner," which ended up referring to any canned food in the British army.[32]

Rations of Other Nations

"The destiny of nations depend on how they nourish themselves," said Jean-Anthelme Brillat-Savarin, the French politician and the father of gas-tronomy.[33] For most of us, the fate of wars is history, but the contents of an army ration and how they compare in different countries is quite a mystery.

In 2014, *The Guardian* published an article comparing the current-day rations of Spain, the United States, Norway, Italy, Australia, the United Kingdom, Estonia, Canada, Germany, and France, with accompanying images and tasting results. All country rations displayed a wide range of packaging of different sizes and materials, cups, sachets, bags, spoons, mini bottles, cans, bars, and tubes. Some came with a camping stove like the Italian ration or a disposable heater as in French and Spanish rations. Oth-ers had the American self-heating bags called flameless heaters, like the Norwegian rations. The Italian ration had biscuits, cappuccino, and pasta, whereas the French ration had a sophisticated selection of *paté* and *confit de canard*. The German ration had liver-sausage spread, rye bread, and gou-lash with potatoes, and the British pack had plenty of tea, chicken tikka masala, and pork and beans for breakfast. The Australian ration had the love-it-or-hate-it Vegemite, cheddar cheese, and many little sweets. The American ration had all things American: poppy seed pound cake, cranber-ries, spiced apple cider, peanut butter, and crackers. Surprisingly enough, the Canadian box did not contain any maple syrup and the Spanish ration did not offer any paella.[34] This work gave a snapshot of today's rations and demonstrated that all nations try to offer rations likeable by their soldiers growing up in that country. It is important not to forget that they are designed under no shortage of food and with the help of new lightweight packs and equipment.

For example, the British Army revamped their army ration to a gourmet version only in 2014, after forty years of battle with dishes like Lancashire hotpot, treacle pudding, and fruit dumplings in custard. In the 1990s, boil-in-the-bag sachets replaced tins; however, the food offer had not changed. With this modernization, freeze-dried or ready-to-boil meals are swapped for minced meat bases that can be flavored with curry, chili, or Bolognese sachets for more variety. New ration packs needed to reflect the changing trends as it was recognized that food has an incredible effect on morale. As

British soldiers eating hot rations in the Ancre Valley during the Battle of the Somme, October 1916.
Imperial War Museum London.

Brigadier Jeff Little, the director of the British Defense catering group, admitted the need for a change: "We need to give them food that they recognize and is a comfort in testing times—such as curry and chocolate."[35]

German Kommissbrot

Also in the German army, bread was the foundation of nutrition but its availability and shelf life were an important problem. Since the sixteenth century, *Kommiß* had been used as a word for a military troop, and so *Kommissbrot* was used for the type of bread provided for the military. *Kommissbrot* was a dark bread made from rye and wheat flours as a sourdough. It had a firm crust, and it was baked in a loaf pan. It is noted for its long shelf life.[36] *Kommissbrot* was used as military provision in World War I when it was said to be mixed with sawdust to compensate for the shortage of flour. Following World War I, it became available in civilian bakeries, and the recipe was changed to produce a softer bread.

During World War I, when German soldiers were displaying signs of vitamin C deficiency (such as gingivitis and scurvy) and had nervous attacks and psychosis, a German scientist analyzed the army rations and deficiencies and made recommendations. In order to stimulate a desire to eat an early breakfast, especially when traveling, he recommended a cold shower in the early morning. This should be followed by a good and abundant breakfast consisting of strong coffee with sugar and buttered sandwiches with sausages and eggs. He also recommended a vegetarian diet as a defense against diseases. He analyzed the *kommissbrot* and concluded that it provided the daily requirements of vitamin B1. With hard work and increased metabolism the soldiers needed more vitamin B than normal. After this study it was decided to retain the old-fashioned *kommissbrot* for the army, which was made of coarse whole rye, containing all parts of the grain except the outer hull, and a liberal consumption of it was recommended.[37]

In World War II, German rations that were used in the desert could not contain the German staples of bread, butter, and potatoes and had to be adjusted. Legumes were introduced to replace potatoes and olive oil instead of butter. German soldiers never liked olive oil or the Italian rations they received with cheese, marmalade, and preserved meat. They were often rancid and loathed by both German and Italian soldiers. The tins were stamped with the initials A.M., which stood for *"Administrazione Militare"* (military administration) but the Germans referred to them as Alter man (the old man) and the Italians, less forgivingly, *Asinus Mussolini* (Mussolini's Arse). German soldiers instead preferred the British ration whenever they found a supply dump. They would then dine on corned beef, white bread, jam, tea, hardtack, and tinned fruit. These were considered luxurious compared to the bland German rations.[38] This is surprising, considering that the British rations were much despised by the British soldiers. One man's ration trash was another's trench treasure.

Pervitin—Beyond a Little Energy Boost

Army rations had to include enough calories and therefore always had a room for a snack. Chocolate was a common snack that was likeable by all, mostly in an energy bar format. For example, in World War II, German rations had a special chocolate called ShoKaKola. This was a caffeine-enhanced "energy chocolate" introduced at the 1936 Summer Olympics in Berlin by Hildebrand as a "sport chocolate." Later it was used during the war, especially by German pilots. Four pieces of this chocolate contained about as much caffeine as a strong espresso and six pieces contained about as much caffeine as a cup of coffee. This would surely have been a great wakeup, especially for troops that were in combat. Today this chocolate is still made in Berlin.

The wish to boost up combat energy, however, did not have chemical limits. Pervitin, a methamphetamine-based drug, was manufactured from 1937 onwards by the Nazis and distributed among the armed forces. Methamphetamine was fashionable in Nazi Germany, especially in the trenches of World War II. A drug that kept you awake and exhilarated for hours was helpful. Hitler's armies carried out their "Blitzkrieg" invasions of Poland and France while high on a version of crystal meth that kept them wide awake, feeling euphoric and invincible. It is said that the Nazis rejected recreational drugs such as cocaine, opium, and morphine, which were readily available in Germany during the 1930s, and condemned them as "Jewish." The Third Reich's chemists were instead encouraged to find an alternative stimulant "more suited to an Aryan Master Race." The Nazi chemist Fritz Hauschild came up with Pervitin after seeing the effects of benzedrine on American athletes in Berlin in 1936 for the Olympics. Pervitin spread quickly. It was taken by athletes, singers, and students. The factory that produced Pervitin even invented "the chocolate to cheer housewives."

It was the head of doctors of the Reich, Otto Ranke, who saw Pervitin as a drug valuable for military use. When Germany invaded France, Ranke convinced the generals, including Erwin Rommel, who led the attack, to distribute Pervitin among the soldiers. Wehrmacht attacked and forged ahead through the Ardennes without ever stopping, night and day, in four days grinding hundreds of kilometers. In mid-May 1940, they reached and razed the French military camp at Avesnes into the ground. The French soldiers were devastated. Their enemy was unstoppable. It was the blitzkrieg, the lightning war. German journalist Ohler was convinced that this is in part attributable to drugs.[39]

It was not only army rations; Pervitin was also taken to the mountains. In 1953, Hermann Buhl took Pervitin, the superdrug, to his solo first ascent of Pakistan's Nanga Parbat. In his report of the ascent, he wrote the struggle he had with taking it. On the summit Buhl's climbing partner, Otto Kempter, was too slow in joining the ascent, so Buhl struck off alone. He took with him a rucksack filled with a warm jacket, his crampons, camera, and food to eat, dextro, Ovosport, a few cuts of Neopolitan, coca tea from Bolivia, a packet of dried fruit, a few tablets of Paludin (a drug that stimulates circulation and prevents frostbite), and a few pills of Pervitin. Below the summit, he fell on the snow exhausted and thought about the little pill he was carrying in his pocket in case of extreme necessity. He fought with himself about taking it.

His mind didn't want it, but his body did. Eventually he gave in and took the pill. Doubtfully, he swallowed two tablets. He went on walking, unsure if Pervitin helped him or not. "Nothing seemed to happen and I felt no benefit. Or was it that they had already done their work and without them I would never been able to get up again?" Before his successful Nanga Parbat expedition, thirty-one people had died trying to make the first ascent. Buhl returned forty-one hours later, having barely survived the arduous climb to the summit, perhaps thanks to the two little pills.[40]

Ten years later, during his historic 1963 traverse of Everest, American climber Tom Hornbein gave two teammates, Lute Jerstad and Barry Bishop, dexedrine to aid their descent. "My impression is it didn't do a damn bit of good," said Hornbein. Steroids hit the scene shortly after. In the late 1960s, the Indian army began giving soldiers a corticosteroid called betamethasone, similar to dexamethasone, as a way to treat severe mountain sickness.[41] The International Mountaineering and Climbing Federation, which governs competitive sport climbing and strives to preserve the "spirit and traditions" of alpinism, is strongly against the use of drugs. However, the organization has no regulatory power and doesn't enforce any regulations in mountaineering.[42]

CHAPTER 8

Street Food

"The surprises, liberations, and clarifications of travel can sometimes be garnered by going around the block as well as going around the world, and walking travels both near and far." —Rebecca Solnit, *Wanderlust*[1]

Walking on the street is freedom. Walking in the city can be likened to walking in nature in that we are in transit looking for something while we experience our environment on a human scale at a human speed. Urbanization and the city life offer variety, anonymity, and possibilities in walking distance. There is danger and magic. Whether we walk with a purpose or just stroll in the city, we grab food on our feet more often than not.

Eighteenth-century philosopher Voltaire believed that the only way to see a place was by walking. In his magnum opus *Candide*, where he portrayed the human condition with wit and satire, the protagonist voices his belief that "it is a privilege of the human race to make use of their legs as they pleased."[2]

In nineteenth-century Paris, a man of leisure was exploring the streets. He was the *flâneur*, the stroller in French. From the late 1950s, as Paris was rebuilt by architect Haussmann, the *flâneur* could go from arcades to boulevards. This idle, literary stroller who was not wasting his time but actively experiencing the urban scenery became the symbol of modern urban walking. It was Charles Baudelaire who first described the *flâneur* as "the lover of life" and "the passionate spectator."[3] The work of Walter Benjamin instead made it a widely recognized interest in the twentieth century. His *flâneur* absorbed the outside world and this way became an active participant of the city. He was also the symbol of the alienation of man due to standardization of work in the society. He was looking for a new individuality by being deliberately aimless and spending this time savoring the city. Honoré de Balzac generously mixed the metaphors: "Oh! Wander in Paris! Sweet and delicious life! Strolling is a science, it is the gastronomy of the eye."[4] And of course there is no aimless savoring and gastronomy without eating. It is no coincidence that the contemporary *flâneur* enjoys food as much as the sights of city streets.

In nearly any country, one can find food on the street. Street food is not just eating on foot. It is an eating culture outdoors all over the world that is older than the history of restaurants. It has its own economy, politics, dishes, and etiquette. Rice and beans, corn on the cob, hot dogs, tacos, *arepas*, *oliebollen*, fries, chestnuts, cotton candy, ice cream, *kurtoskacas* . . .

Food on the street has a history as diverse as the personalities and histories of cities. In cities where pedestrian movement is limited, there cannot be talk of a street food. For example, in the Arabian peninsula, street food as a commercial channel was unthinkable before the region modernized. Instead, people had the habit of offering food freely to everyone that passed. And in Europe, cities only became clean and safe as the cities were illuminated in the nineteenth century, with sidewalks, street names, and streetlights. Eating on the street did not always represent the same sense of comfort; however, it was also a place to find exotic food adventures. Especially before the restaurant era, tea, coffee, chocolate, and spiced drinks would be sold on the streets of Europe to the enjoyment of street-walking bourjois as well as to the working class. In one form or another, street food has always been there since streets connected people through a public space.

Hot and Round—Early Street Foods

In the seventeenth and eighteenth centuries, a new exotic drink was to be had on the streets of London, not tea, not coffee, but *salep*. *Salep* was a popular beverage in the Ottoman Empire. It spread to England and Germany before the spread of coffee and tea. It was most popular when these were not available, as an alternative warm drink. In England, the drink was known as *saloop*. Its preparation required that the *salep* powder be added to water until thickened. After this, it would be sweetened and flavored with orange flower or rose water. Substitution of British orchid roots, known as "dogstones," was acceptable. *Sahlab* was made with hot milk instead of water. From *salep* flour, which is the flour of wild orchids, pudding and ice cream were also made. In the early 1800s, *salep* stalls in London were visited at night by workers. These stalls were later replaced by coffee stalls. The drink in London might have been thickened with sassafras plant instead. Nonetheless, this plant and its bark were considered to be more than a good drink. It was thought to be good against syphilis, a public concern on the streets at that time.[5]

There was some confusion between *salep* and other drinks; they were different recipes, evolved from *salep*, or were completely different drinks. One such drink was Early Purl, sold on High Street in London at the end of the nineteenth century:

> Suddenly we came upon a stall, whence arose the steam of Early Purl, or Salop, flattering our senses. Ye Gods ! what a breakfast ! In vain a cautious scepticism suggests that the liquid was one which my palate would *now* shudderingly reject; perhaps so; I did not reject it *then*; and in memory the flavour is beatified. I feel its diffusive warmth stealing through me. I taste its unaccustomed and exquisite flavour. Tea is great, coffee greater; chocolate, properly made, is for epicures; but these are thin and characterless compared with the salop swallowed in 1826. That *was* nectar, and the Hebe who poured it out was *not* a blear-eyed old woman, though to vulgar vision she may have presented some such aspect.[6]

The real *Salep* was made by boiling the pulverized dried roots of an orchid species, *Orchis mascula*, which grew in the mountains of Anatolia. The ancient Romans used ground orchid bulbs to make drinks, which they called by a number of names, especially *satyrion* and *priapiscus*. These names indicated that the drink was considered a powerful aphrodisiac because these were the names of the horse-like fertility god in Greek mythology. Satyrion takes a clear role as an aphrodisiac in the satirical novel *Satyricon* by Petronius, identifying its place in the Roman Empire. In addition, Paracelsus, the Swiss philosopher physician of the Middle Ages, wrote: "behold the Satyrion root, is it not formed like the male privy parts? No one can deny this. Accordingly magic discovered it and revealed that it can restore a man's virility and passion."[7]

In the Ottoman capital of Istanbul, street vendors sold pilaf, fried liver, meatballs, roasted chickpeas, coffee, and *salepi*. These were often Greek and Armenian vendors. In Greece, *salepi* was sold until the 1930s.

When the wild orchids were becoming extinct, the export of *salep* was stopped and the availability has decreased. Today, *sahleb* mixes are made with artificial flavoring and are still sold in Turkey and in Greece by street vendors during the cold months of the year. This drink is rarely made at home. The tradition is to buy it from street vendors who sell it from brass urns. It is made by adding *salep* powder and sugar to milk, served hot with cinnamon sprinkled on top.

Salep vendor in Istanbul. Anonymous, 1896.
Engin Özendes Collection.

In the streets of Ottoman, Istanbul vendors also sold *simit*, a circular bread encrusted with sesame seeds. These are still sold by street vendors in Turkey today, who either have a cart or carry the *simit* in a tray on their head. *Simit* is made slightly differently in various cities in Turkey and in the Balkans, and is called different names. In Izmir, it is *gevrek*; in the Balkans, *gjevrek* or *djevrek*; in Greece, *kuluri*; and in Romania, *covrigi*.[8]

Other breads resemble *simit*: the bagel of Askenazi Jews and *girdeh* of Uygur Turks. The name *simit* comes from the Arabic word *samīd*, which means pure white flour. *Simit* was first mentioned on the food price list in the Ottoman Empire in 1525, because its price was regulated. It was not only a street food but also the food of the poor. Evliya Celebi, who was an Ottoman Turk who traveled through the territory of the Ottoman Empire and neighboring lands over a period of forty years, recorded *simit* in great detail in his travelogue called *Seyâhatnâme* in the seventeenth century. He wrote that there were two types of *simit*: one was called *hurda* (scrap) *simit* and the other was big as a wheel. Considering that cars had not yet been invented then, he was most likely referring to the wheel of a horse-drawn carriage. Perhaps this large version was sold for customers to take home, but it has not survived the test of time; the smaller *simit* remained a favorite street

Simit vendor. Street scene, Istanbul, Turkey, 1903.
Brooklyn Museum Archives, Goodyear Archival Collection. Visual materials [6.1.003]: 1903 survey expedition photographs.

food at every corner. Evliya Celebi also recounted *simit* of Belgrade, yet we don't know if this is the same *simit* as in Istanbul, as he also mentioned one made with chickpea flour in Serbia and in Albania. He praised the white Albanian *simit*, which might be the *gjevrek* of today: sweet, boiled, and then baked, much like a bagel.[9]

The fact that people of Izmir call *simit gevrek* possibly indicates the fact that this street food traveled with migrants from the Balkans to Izmir. This shows how sometimes food travels on foot, too, and stays where it is welcomed.

Eating on Foot in the Urban Wilderness

Eating on foot in city culture is eating during movement and transition, and therefore it is packed and designed for the urban jungle, much like in the wilderness. We can nearly call big cities of the world the new wilderness, where one needs to survive against a different element, not against cold, heat, or altitude, but against time and passing through a man-made structure of buildings, with interwoven expectations of work and leisure. In this new environment, people are challenged much like in the wilderness, under pressure of surviving and performing, against time and sometimes against others. In this transitional state of mind, then, it is not incredible that people often look for comfort in food. It is not as much about calories and energy as it is about taking along what comforts us, what gives us a familiar support or a new flavor along the way.

There are as many types of street food as there are cities. In Ukraine, dumplings are sold on the street, in train stations, often made by older women called *babtia* (grandmothers). They are filled with mashed potatoes, onions, ground meats, cabbage, and mushrooms, and they are served with sour cream and dill. Egyptians take roasted mixed nuts, peanuts, pumpkin or melon seeds, and lupine beans when they walk along the Nile, while drinking freshly squeezed sugarcane. In England, sandwiches have been the street food since the late eighteenth century, and coffee, soft drinks, and pastries are served to take away. In Greece, corn on the cob is sold by street vendors who sell roasted chestnuts in the winter. In Austria, chestnuts are sold on street corners in the winter and ice cream in the summer. In Budapest, street vendors sell *kürtőskalács* (chimney cake), which is made from sweet, yeast dough that is spun in strips around a thick metal spit and then rolled in granulated sugar. It is roasted over charcoal while basted with melted butter until its surface cooks to a golden-brown color. While baking, the sugar caramelizes and forms a shiny, crispy crust. The surface of the cake can then be topped with ground walnuts or powdered cinnamon.

Sugar blowing (*chui teng*) is a street spectacle in China. Street vendors who blow thick malt sugar syrup into animal shapes, much like Venetian glass artists. In a more two-dimensional version, in Chengdu peddlers make a picture by drizzling molten caramel onto a board and picking up the flat image on a wooden stick as a lollipop. Also in Chengdu, *ding ding* malt sugar toffee (*ding ding tang*) takes its name from the sound of their metal clappers signaling their presence. Dragon's beard toffee (*long xu tang*) is another marvel, a miniature and sweet version of hand-pulled noodles made of toffee.[10]

American Classics

Street food is about experience, pleasure, joy, color, and taste. Sweet, savory, fizzy, greasy, it entertains and stimulates, is often quick and almost always unhealthy. It can become routine and familiar, but it is certainly different than food at home that is separated by a front door. The streets allow us to eat differently. These foods have hit those points of convenience, taste, and appeal, and bring us the sense of danger, discovery, and routine all together. For this they have become iconic, some of them not only in their home countries but also all over the world.

In New York City in the twentieth century, street food was pretzels, coffee, soda, ice cream, popsicles, and sandwiches. As waves of immigrants arrived, street vendors introduced new foods like gyros, burritos, tacos, Italian ice, and nuts. Homemade pretzels were one of the first snacks that street vendors sold in New York even before commercial pretzel machines started making pretzels in 1861, by Julius Sturgis in Lititz, Pennsylvania. These glazed, salted biscuits twisted into knots are said to have been introduced by Dutch immigrants to America.[11] Most accounts credit the invention of the pretzel in 610 CE to a monk in northern Italy who twisted leftover bread dough into crossed praying arms to be given as a little reward to children who learned their prayers. *Pretioli* means little rewards in Italian. The world pretzel can be a corruption of this word or the Old German *brezitella*, from the Latin word for arm, *brachium*. While the *pretiolas* soon became popular in Austria and Germany, where they were known as *bretzels*, it was not until ten-plus centuries later that they made their way to the United States in the hands of the Pennsylvania Dutch. Soft, chewy, and often topped off with mustard, pretzels became a quick breakfast while on the go. Their metal carts can still be seen on street corners in Philadelphia and New York.

Another street favorite was the hot dog. Eaten out of the hand in a bun garnished often with pickle relish, sometimes with sauerkraut and mustard, hot dogs seemed to have it all. A fatty juicy warm sausage with crispy and tangy toppings contained in a soft bread that fits in the palm. Hot dogs became a street staple in many big American cities. Known as frankfurter in Germany and wiener in Austria, the hot dog likely came to the United States with German immigrants in the late nineteenth century. The Germans called it *dachshund*, probably the origin of the name of the dog breed. New York hot dogs were cooked in hot water on Sabrett carts. In Chicago, they were served with sport peppers, onions, pickle, relish, yellow mustard, and sliced tomatoes. The hot dog is said to have been invented by businessman Charles Feltman in Coney Island, New York, in 1860. Early in the twentieth century, when Coney Island was a wonderland of lights and amusement, people strolled on the boardwalk and felt like children again, eating their frozen custard or hot dog against a background of the screams from the roller coaster and the smells of french fries from food stalls.[12]

The hot dog was a cultural food, an iconic food on the go. It came on the street food scene at a time when transportation was picking up and urban

Coney island hot dog, between c. 1910 and c. 1915.
Library of Congress.

living was increasing. It was portioned, cheap, and comforting. The colors and textures were festive. It offered comfort in post-industrialized America. It was an escape and a homecoming at the same time. Soon it spread to the west coast and to the south of the United States, and the rest of the world. Nowadays, variations of hot dogs are plentiful: they can be boiled, grilled, or fried, and served with any sauce imaginable.

Some of these street vendors were also able to launch successful businesses. Cracker Jack was one of them.[13] Cracker Jack was a snack of the late nineteenth century. It contained the element of surprise with a trivial prize inside along with the sweet and salty caramel-coated peanuts and popcorn. It started as a street food by a German immigrant (Frederick William Rueckheim) sold at 113 Fourth Avenue, now known as Federal Street, in Chicago in 1871, before it became a popular food at baseball games.

American poet Frank O'Hara, strolling along the streets of New York, wrote[14]:

Who dropped that empty carton
Of cracker jacks I wonder I find the favor
That's a good sign

Street vendors were selling ice cream for pennies by the end of the nineteenth century. Peddlers sold ice cream in small glass containers called penny licks. The customer would lick the ice cream off the glass and give it back to the vendor to clean the glass with a rag and serve the next customer with it. After the end of the Civil War, American ice cream boomed. Soon more hygenic ice creams were available, in paper-wrapped bricks called hokey-pockeys, ice cream sandwiches, eskimo pies, good humor bars, popsicles, and many others.[15] Italian imigrants sold Italian ice, which included sorbetto, granita, and slush. A coffee- or lemon-flavored granita was a mixture of sugar syrup and a flavored liquid. Slush was frozen water ice with a slushy consistency. Sorbetto was churned and frozen to a more compact consistency.[16] Lemonade salesmen sold ice pops on wooden sticks, which were first called epsicles and then became popsicles.

There were also other more exotic street foods. For example, in New Orleans, the capital of the oldest sugarcane-producing state of the United States, street vendors sold many sweet treats such as *tac-tac* (popcorn balls covered with cane sugar), sugared pecans, flat ginger cakes called stage planks, and *la colle*, a cake of molasses and roasted peanuts and pecans. Street vendors also sold pralines and calas ladies sold *calas*, ancient rice cakes originally from West Africa.[17]

One of the most common street foods around the world today is coffee. After it left its birthplace of Abyssinia (today's Ethiopia), it reached Yemen, from there it found its way to the Middle East, Turkey, North Africa, Balkans, Italy, and the rest of Europe, and then to America. By the fifteenth century, coffee was roasted and brewed as we recognize it. It was also a street food in the Middle East, but the vendor was mobile, while the drinker would be seated.

It is in America centuries later that coffee became a street food people took around. Where breakfast was a takeaway occasion, food stalls started selling bagels and coffee. Coffee shops started selling coffee in to-go cups, and soon it became custom to see drinkers walking around with store-bought or home-brewed coffee on streets, campuses, and parks.

From Chuck Wagon to Food Trucks

Food trucks are the ultimate expression of food on foot in cities. It is a particular way of serving and eating food that appeals to the citizens of today. It is an American phenomenon, which in fact has a long-standing tradition. Before hot dog stands and ice cream carts were visible on the streets of big American cities like New York, Washington, District of Columbia, and Philadelphia, a truck was set up by a rancher to feed cattle herdsmen from Texas to New Mexico. Charles Goodnight had invented the "chuck wagon" in 1866. He converted a Studebaker wagon carried by a horse into a shop that sold beans, biscuits, salted meat, and coffee. He used firewood to cook when they stopped and found fresh meat and vegetables. Although this was far away from current food trucks, it was the first "food wagon."

After motorization of wagons, the mobility of kitchens improved. During World War I, German soldiers used *die Gulaschkanone* (goulash cannon) for mobile kitchens that had a resemblance to an artillery piece with their long chimney. They cooked soups with vegetables, legumes, and whatever they could find. During the Second World War, field kitchens were carried on wagons; British civilians drove mobile canteens to bring food and tea to troops in isolated posts to boost their morale. After the war, the 1950s brought ice cream trucks, which were very similar to current food trucks. After the 1960s, hamburger and taco food trucks took to the streets.

It was only after the 2000s, after the economic crisis in the United States, when chefs started offering high-quality fare on wheels (such as seafood tacos and lobster rolls), that eating on foot became a gourmet activity, and the food truck phenomenon started. The association of food trucks with greasy and unhygienic foods changed to gourmet and innovative foods. These

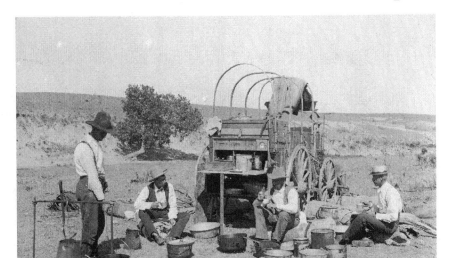

The camp wagon on a Texas roundup.
Library of Congress.

trucks were also not stuck on fairgrounds or street markets, but they were designed, painted, and dressed to look good in major public spaces.

Food trucks are no longer only American. At first, food trucks across the world were only selling classics such as hot dogs, hamburgers, and fries. Nowadays, local fast dishes are also brought onto the street with this new culinary vehicle, such as *crêpes* in France and *farinata* (chickpea pancakes) in Italy (called *socca* in France). In this, food trucks are not only a global food-on-foot phenomenon but they are instrumental in rebranding local food culture. They represent the new urban experience while eating on foot: inexpensive and fast, but foremost innovative and fun.

Food on the street connects our body, mind, and the place to experience the world through our body and our body through the world. While we walk, our mind engages with our body and the place. We know the place through our body. While we eat, the engagement is strengthened. Food creates memorable experiences, also in the wilderness of the cities, perhaps not as in survival stories in historic expeditions or spiritual scarifies as in pilgrimage trails, but it marks nonetheless our personal geography. It draws a map of where we walk, where we eat, and ultimately who we become.

Afterword

A sense of curiosity and taste for adventure launches us on our feet. Whether it is a walk in nature, a hike, a pilgrimage, or an expedition, a departure on foot has a personal promise. It also has rules on preparation, planning, and rules on what to do and how to do them. Eating and food planning is an important part of any walk and outdoor activity.

As we have seen, the food histories of expeditions on different geographies have developed in parallel to each other: army, mountain, and polar expeditions all rely on the human capacity to plan, organize, and carry food. Advances in technology help explorers achieve this goal, but explorers can never truly control nature. They could at best resist it or work with it. What made expeditions heroic was the fact of going into an adventure with some plan but no guarantee of its success.

How voyagers talked and wrote about food tells us a lot about their intentions, motivations, and worldviews. The explorer, the adventurer, the naturalist, and all other travelers on foot can be viewed through the lens of their relationship with food in their journeys. This relationship is interesting to observe, as it is a strong reflection of their relationship with the environment and with other people.

Army food was often about control and domination, mainly of the enemy, but also the environment in which they had to survive. It was desirable for soldiers to eat well and reduce the stresses of combat, even if taste was not always up to high standards. Army food affected the language of food in other expeditions.

In polar journeys food was "ration," "tin," and "supply." Food was also hunted, skinned, collected, and foraged. Polar food memories in diaries, letters, and journals are of cravings and starvation. At the edge of survival, food was a supply that must be portioned, rationed, weighed, and calculated to last.

Mountaineering was no exception. As an invention of the Victorian middle class, mountaineering was masculine in its goals for dominance over nature and militaristic in its approach to planning. For this reason in the early days of mountaineering, we see the word "assault" often being used, for the last part of the journey to the summit, or "attack" or "charge." The food for the summit day was also called "assault ration."

In the records of Victorian female mountaineers, we instead see gentle words for their achievements. The mountain was "attained by a lady," we would read, or the "lady ascends the summit." Their reason for travel might have been writing, painting, mission work, or photographing. In any case, it reflected the Victorian middle-class passion to improve oneself. The food of the ladies was described in the details, the cutlery, the eccentric cake, and the champagne they took along on mountain trips, next to how they wore impractical dresses that sometimes flipped with the wind and made it impossible to move forward.

As climbing became an activity accessible to more people of other classes after the 1960s, it lost its nationalistic character and became more of a personal sport. Now mountaineers come from all classes, and this means that the activity has become more athletic and more about problem solving rather than nationalist achievements in militaristic ways. This naturally changed the approach for food. Now, mountain food is more technical than ever but also very personalized. It is part of the toolset for better performance.

Pilgrims and desert travelers were similar in that they did not seek control and performance in their journeys. This is reflected by their acceptance of what comes their way to learn and to eat. And because of this, pilgrim destinations as well as deserts were places where food was shared with others more willingly.

Another fact that emerged from historic expeditions is how locals and explorers approached their environment completely differently. The approach of adventure and hardship of the explorers creates a survivalist view on food. Stories of food range from worry to enjoyment, from starvation to hallucination, from being in control to being in awe of how locals dealt with little food available. Nomads see their relationship with the environment long term. The traveler is in this transition, the local endures. Nomads create a year-round culture to cope with geographical difficulties. They gather food when they can, preserve it when there is enough, and eat something when there is nothing to gather or hunt. They seem to be eating on the go but this is how they are settled. Explorers instead could not always cope with the local nature immediately, and they remain observers. Nonetheless, within this group there are those who take their limits to the far edge and prove that we humans are capable of coping with extreme environments and achieve the rewards that we set for ourselves.

We all see comfort in our own view of the world, of what we think is normal. We bring ourselves wherever we go. Early explorers had to be exposed to more adventure, as technology in food and equipment had not allowed them to bring as much control to their expeditions. Nonetheless, even when the objectives were militaristic, a sense of adventure was part of the equation. Nowadays, when we go on a hike in Nepal, we can find energy bars and pizza along hiking routes; no matter how remote, a villager carries these to sell to the tourist who has the expectation to find familiar food far from home. Even for recreation and adventure when we head to a new environment, sometimes we make it so convenient with our food and equipment, that no walk is too adventurous.

In our daily lives, we might have lost the vulnerability of being in a place and not knowing where we will end up. Still, we all seek the sense of adventure out of our doorsteps, no matter how far we go. When we step outside and are confronted with street stalls and food trucks with familiar or exotic foods, we are allowing ourselves to enter an unknown world. Any step on our feet is a possible adventure. Food on foot enables us to have small adventures all the time, in small steps and in small bites. While walking in cities, which are getting more crowded and alienating each day, through food we share, we define what it means to be part of a city culture.

When being "the first, fastest, or the most" seem to be titles reserved for historic expeditions, what is there to experience for the rest of us? We all can certainly have our own heroic personal experiences on trails and in the wilderness. We can do this by connecting to our environment not only as who we already are but also as who we can become, with genuine curiosity, humble respect, and a selfless wish to conserve and share, with food as our companion.

Notes

Introduction

1. Marvin Harris, *Our Kind: Who We Are, Where We Came From, Where We Are Going* (New York: Harper Perennial, 1990), 2.

Chapter 1

1. Raey Tannahill, *Food in History* (New York: Three Rivers Press, 1988), 229.

2. Ibid., 257–58.

3. M. F. K. Fisher, "The Pleasures of Picnics (1957)," in *A Stew or a Story: An Assortment of Short Works by M. F. K. Fisher*, ed. Joan Reardon (Emeryville: Shoemaker & Hoard, 2006), 198–207.

4. Walter Levy, *The Picnic: A History. The Meals Series* (Lanham: Alta Mira Press, 2014), 6.

5. Kenneth Grahame, *The Wind in the Willows* (New York: Scribner, 1913), 11, https://archive.org/details/windinwillows00grah (accessed January 26, 2016).

6. Samuel Johnson, *A Journey to the Western Isles of Scotland* (Project Gutenberg ebook, 2005), http://www.gutenberg.org/files/2064/2064-h/2064-h.htm (accessed on July 12, 2016).

7. Ibid., chapter: Coriatachan in Sky.

8. James Boswell, *Boswell's Life of Johnson* (Project Gutenberg ebook, Charles Grosvenor Osgood, ed., 2006), http://www.gutenberg.org/files/1564/1564-h/1564-h.htm (accessed on July 12, 2016).

9. Michael Pollan, *The Botany of Desire: A Plant's-Eye View of the World* (London: Bloomsbury, 2003), 39.

10. George William Hill and Williams Bros, *History of Ashland County, Ohio* (Philadelphia: J. B. Lippincott, 1863), 30.

11. Howard Means, *Johnny Appleseed: The Man, the Myth, the American Story* (New York: Simon & Schuster, 2012), 168.

12. W. D. Haley, "Johnny Appleseed: A Pioneer Hero," *Harper's New Monthly Magazine*, 43 (1871): 830–36, https://archive.org/stream/harpersnew43various#page/836/mode/2up (accessed on July 15, 2016).

13. John Tallmadge, *Meeting the Tree of Life: A Teacher's Path* (Salt Lake City, UT: University of Utah Press, 1997), 52.

14. John Muir, *My First Summer in the Sierra* (Boston: Houghton Mifflin Company, 1911), 99.

15. Ibid., 104–05.

16. Sally M. Miller and Daryl Morrison, *John Muir: Family, Friends, and Adventures* (Albuquerque: University of New Mexico Press, 2005), 74.

17. Ibid., 154.

18. Muir, *My First Summer in the Sierra*, 237.

19. James R. Hare, *Hiking the Appalachian Trail* (Emmaus, PA: Rodale Press, 1975), 1406.

20. Trademark ORIGINAL TRAIL MIX. Retrieved from http://www.tmfile.com/mark/?q=763459399 (accessed October 8, 2015).

21. John F. Mariani, *Encyclopedia of American Food and Drink* (New York: Lebhar Friedman, 1999), 142.

22. "Definition of gorp," *Oxford English Dictionary*, http://www.oed.com/view/Entry/249107?redirectedFrom=gorp#eid (accessed October 8, 2015).

23. "Scroggin," *Ozwords* 12 (2005): 5, http://andc.anu.edu.au/sites/default/files/ozwords_april05.pdf (accessed October 8, 2015).

24. "Adapted from Scroggin recipe," http://allrecipes.com.au/recipe/22564/scroggin.aspx (accessed October 8, 2015).

25. John M. Gould, *How to Camp Out* (1877), ebook edition (2006), 44, http://archive.org/stream/howtocampout17575gut/17575.txt (accessed January 25, 2015).

26. Ibid., 46–47.

27. "Definition of S'more," *Merriam-Webster*, www.merriamwebster.com (accessed January 25, 2016).

28. *Tramping and Trailing with the Girl Scouts, Compiled and Published by Girl Scouts, Inc., 1927* (New York: Girls Scouts of the United States of America, 1930 revision), 71–72.

Chapter 2

1. Adin Baber, "Food Plants of the De Soto Expedition, 1539–1543," *Tequesta*, 2 (1942), 34–40, Tequesta online, http://digitalcollections.fiu.edu/tequesta/ (accessed July 19, 2016).

2. C. F. McGlashan, *History of the Donner Party* (1879, ebook, 2009), Chapter VIII, http://www.gutenberg.org/files/6077/6077-h/6077-h.htm (accessed on July 16, 2016).

3. Ibid., Chapter XIX.

4. Dana Goodyear, "What happened at Alder Creek?" *The New Yorker*, April 24, (2006), 140–51.

5. Melissa Harper, *The Ways of the Bushwalker: On Foot in Australia* (Sydney: University of New South Wales Press, 2007), 3.

6. Ernest Favenc, *The Explorers of Australia and Their Life-work* (Forgotten Books edition, 2012, original, Christchurch: Whitcombe & Tombs, 1908), 134–44.

7. "Financial Records of the Royal Society of Victoria's Exploration Committee," *Royal Society of Victoria Exploration Committee account book 1858–1873* (State Library of Victoria, SLV MS13071, Box 2088B/2, 1–13). List of articles and services supplied by [Richard Nash] the Government Storekeeper. http://www.burkeandwills.net.au/ Stores/provisions.htm#thumb (accessed March 30, 2016).

8. "John King's Narrative as told to Howitt at the Cooper Depot, September 1861," *Diary of Victorian Contingent Party, 13 August–7 October 1861*. State Library of Victoria, SLV MS13071, Box FB33, Item #255110. Victorian Relief Expedition Records, Alfred William Howitt's expedition diaries and notebooks. http://www .burkeandwills.net.au/Journals/King/Kings_Narrative.htm (accessed March 30, 2016).

9. "WOMEN 'SWAGGIES,'" *The Register*, April 6, 1926, http://nla.gov.au/nla .news-article55030263 (accessed February 9, 2016).

10. "A Popular Bush Song," *The Capricornian*, December 14, 1901, http://nla.gov .au/nla.news-article68258559 (accessed February 3, 2016).

11. Andrew Barton Paterson, *The Old Bush Songs*, 1906 (Charleston, SC: BiblioBazaar, 2008), 28–32.

12. "Homemade 'Swaggie' doll, 1933," Sydney: Powerhouse Museum Collection, http://www.powerhousemuseum.com/collection/database/?irn=39144#ixzz3zZTbj88b (accessed on February 9, 2016).

13. "Mountain Trails Club Outfit List for one man," *Letter from Myles Dunphy to Johaness Clement Charles Marie de Mol. 1916*, Colony Foundation for Wilderness, Sydney, Australia (received in an e-mail message to author, February 5, 2016).

14. Drew Hutton and Libby Connors, *History of the Australian Environment Movement* (Cambridge: Cambridge University Press, 1999), 64–70.

15. "FEMALE SWAGGIES," *Northern Standard*, April 7, 1922, http://nla.gov.au/ nla.news-article48005334 (accessed February 9, 2016).

16. Harper. 2007, *The Ways of the Bushwalker: On Foot in Australia*, 285.

17. Ibid., 272–305.

18. Michael Symons, *One Continuous Picnic: A History of Australian Eating* (Victoria: Melbourne University Publishing, 1984).

Chapter 3

1. Anthony Dalton, *Sir John Franklin. Expeditions to Destiny* (Victoria: Heritage House Publishing, 2012), 351.

2. Ibid., 341.

3. Ibid., 358.

4. Ibid., 49–58.

5. N. G. Ilbäch and S. Källman, "The Lichen Rock Tripe (*Lasallia pustulata*) as Survival Food: Effects on Growth, Metabolism, and Immune Function in Balb/c Mice," *Natural Toxins* 7(6) (1999): 321–29.

6. Charles L. Cutler, *Tracks that Speak: The Legacy of Native American Words in North American Culture* (Boston: Houghton Mifflin Company, 2002), 101.

7. Mark Morton, *Cupboard Love: A Dictionary of Culinary Curiosities* (London: Insomniac Press, 2000), 222; Charles L. Cutler, *Tracks that Speak*, 99.

8. Alexander Mackenzie, *Voyages from Montreal Through the Continent of North America to the Frozen and Pacific Oceans in 1789 and 1793, Vol. I.* (New York: A. S. Barnes and Company, 1903), 191, http://www.gutenberg.org/files/35658/35658-h/35658-h.htm (accessed on April 1, 2016).

9. Francis Parkman, *The Oregon Trail. Sketches of Prairie and Rocky Mountain Life* (Boston: Little, Brown, and Company, 1900), 213.

10. Ken Albala, *Food Cultures of the World Encyclopedia, Volume 1* (Santa Barbara, CA: ABC-CLIO, LLC, 2011), 235.

11. Robert E. Peary, *Secrets of Polar Travel* (New York: The Century Co., 1917), 77–83. https://archive.org/details/secretspolartra00peargoog (accessed on April 1, 2016).

12. Eivind Astrup, *With Peary near the Pole* (London: C. A. Pearson, limited, 1898), 192.

13. Robert E. Peary, *The North Pole: Its Discovery in 1909 Under the Auspices of Peary Arctic Club* (New York: Greenwood Press Publishers, 2006, First published in 1910), 23–24.

14. Ibid., 139–40.

15. Ibid., 209–10.

16. Tom Avery, *To the End of the Earth: Our Epic Journey to the North Pole and the Legend of Peary and Henson* (New York: St. Martin's Press, 2010), 47.

17. "Interview with Tom Avery," *Vanity Fair,* http://www.vanityfair.com/news/2009/04/explorer-tom-avery-you-spend-forever-trekking-to-the-south-pole-you-get (accessed on May 13, 2016).

18. Roald Amundsen, *The South Pole (Volume I)* (London: John Murray, 1912), http://gutenberg.net.au/ebooks/e00111a.html (accessed on July 13, 2015).

19. Ibid.

20. Roald Amundsen, *My Life as an Explorer* (London: Heineman, 1927), 265, https://archive.org/details/roaldamundsenmyl00amun_0 (accessed on July 13, 2015).

21. Ibid., 265–66.

22. Fergus Fleming, *Ninety Degrees North: The Quest for the North Pole* (London: Granta Books, 2011), 424–26.

23. Kenneth J. Carpenter, *The History of Scurvy and Vitamin C* (Cambridge: Cambridge University Press, 1986), 90–96, 240.

24. Benjamin Alvord, "Importance of Lime-juice in the Pemmican for Arctic Expeditions," *Science* 35 (1883): 471.

25. Ernest Lockhart, "Antarctic Trail Diet. Reports on Scientific Results of the United States Antarctic Service Expedition, 1939–1941," *Proceedings of the American Philosophical Society,* 89 (1945): 235–48.

26. Ibid.

27. Autumn Stanley, *Mothers and Daughters of Invention: Invention Notes for a Revised History of Technology* (New Brunswick, NJ: Rutgers University Press, 1995), 72.

28. Winifred Helmes, *Notable Maryland Women* (Centreville, MD: Tidewater Publishers, 1977), 334.

29. Frank Worsley, *Shackleton's Boat Journey* (Cork: The Collins Press: original printed in 1940, reprinted in 2005), 34.

30. *Photocopy of a Diary of Thomas Orde Lees, on Elephant Island* (Original held at Scott Polar Research Institute, 1916, Royal Geographical Society 1978-79, EHS/9).

31. A.G.E. Jones, "Frankie Wild's Hut," *Journal of the Royal Naval Medical Service*, 64 (1978): 51–58.

32. "Shackleton's Men Kept Hope of Rescue High," *New York Times*, September 11, 1916, www.nytimes.com (accessed on February 1, 2106).

33. *Photocopy of a Diary of Thomas Orde Lees, on Elephant Island.*

34. "Shackleton's Men Kept Hope of Rescue High."

35. *Pemmican brochure. A Christmas present from the Manitoba Free Press* (Winnipeg, Canada: Manitoba Free Press, 1902) (retrieved from the National Library of Canada by the Canadian Institute for Historical Microreproductions in 1996).

Chapter 4

1. Ernest Hamilton Stevens, "Dr. Paccard's narrative. An attempted Reconstitution," *Alpine Club Journal*, May 1929, 94–96.

2. Eric Shipton, *Mountain Conquests* (ebook, New Word City, 2015).

3. John Auldjo, *Narrative of an Ascent to the Summit of Mont Blanc Made in July, 1819* (CreateSpace Independent Publishing Platform, 2015, first published in 1821).

4. Albert Smith, *The Story of Mont Blanc* (New York: G. P. Putnam, 1853), 154–55.

5. Henriette d'Angeville, *My Ascent of Mont Blanc* (Paris: Harper Collins, 1987), 30–33.

6. Cicely Williams, *Women on the Rope. The Feminine Share in Mountain Adventure* (London: George Allen & Unwin Ltd., 1973), 22.

7. The Alpine Club, *Mountaineers. Great Tales of Bravery and Conquest* (London: DK Publishing, 2011), 100.

8. Henriette d'Angeville, *My Ascent of Mont Blanc* (Paris: Harper Collins, 1987), 77–82.

9. Williams, *Women on the Rope*, 31–33.

10. Ibid., 40–41.

11. F. Gardiner and C. Pilkington, "In Memoriam: Miss Lucy Walker," *Alpine Journal*, 31 (1917): 97–102.

12. Adam Smith, "Walker, Lucy (1836–1916)," *Oxford Dictionary of National Biography* (Oxford: Oxford University Press, 2004), www.oxforddnb.com/view/articles/52561 (accessed on January 25, 2016).

13. "A climbing girl," *Punch*, 61 (1871): 86.

14. Dana Francis, "Elders of the Tribe: 7 Fanny Bullock Workman," *Backpackers-7*, 2 (3) (1974): 84.

15. Williams, *Women on the Rope*, 50–53.

16. George Band, *Summit: 150 Years of the Alpine Club* (London: HarperCollins UK, 2007), 36.

17. Clare Roche, "Women Climbers 1850–1900: A Challenge to Male Hegemony?" *Sport in History*, 33(2013), 1–24.

18. Williams, *Women on the Rope*, 60.

19. Sara Mills, *Discourses of Difference: An Analysis of Women's Travel Writing and Colonialism* (London: Routledge, 1991), 40–42.

20. Ibid., 67.

21. Ibid., 97.

22. Aubrey Le Bond, "Then and now," *Ladies' Alpine Club Yearbook* (1932): 7–8.

23. Ibid., 158–59.

24. C. G. Bruce, *The Assault on Mount Everest 1922* (London: Edward Arnold & Co., 1923), 177–78.

25. Geoffrey Winthrop Young, *Mountain Craft* (New York: Charles Scribner's Sons, 1920).

26. Bruce, *The Assault on Mount Everest 1922*, 177–78.

27. "'Why climb Mount Everest?' 'Because it's there' said Mallory," *New York Times*, March 18, 1923, www.nytimes.com (accessed on October 7, 2015).

28. Reinhold Messner, *Everest: Expedition to the Ultimate* (Seattle, WA: The Mountaineers, 2014), 16, 22.

29. Harriet Tuckey, *Everest. The First Ascent. The Untold Story of Griffith Pugh the Man Who Made it Possible* (London: Random House, 2013), 11.

30. Ernst Gellhorn, *Physiological Foundations of Neurology and Psychiatry* (Minneapolis: The University of Minnesota Press, 1953), 46.

31. Michael Ward, *First Ascent of Everest 1953: Medical and Scientific Aspects. By Griffith Pugh* (London: Alpine Club Archives, 1998).

32. Mick Conefrey, *Everest 1953. The Epic Story of the First Ascent* (London: Oneworld Publications, 2012), 99.

33. Wilfrid Noyce, *Expedition report. 1953 Personnel – Personal*, Archives of the Royal Geographical Society, 2.

34. John Hunt, *The Ascent of Everest 1953* (London: Hodder & Stoughton, 1993), 247.

35. L. G. C. E. Pugh, "Scientific Aspects of the Expedition to Mount Everest, 1953," *The Geographical Journal*, 120, Part 2 (1954), 186–89.

36. L. G. C. Pugh and M.P. Ward, "Some Effects of High Altitude on Man," *The Lancet*, December 1 (1956), 1115–21.

37. Noyce, *Expedition report. 1953 Personnel – Personal*, 5.

38. "Hillary of New Zealand and Tenzing reach the top," *The Guardian*, June 2, 1953, www.guardian.com (accessed on October 7, 2015).

39. Maurice Herzog, "Earth's Third Pole—Everest; The assaults on the 29,002-foot summit of the world symbolize man's eternal drive to conquer the unconquerable," *New York Times*, May 31, 1953, www.nyt.com (accessed on January 27, 2016).

40. L. G. C. E. Pugh, *Scientific Aspects of the Expedition to Mount Everest, 1953*, 186–89.

41. Monica Jackson and Elizabeth Stark, *Tents in the Clouds. The First Women's Himalayan Expedition* (original published in 1956, Seal Press, US edition 2000), 30–31.

42. Jackson and Stark, *Tents in the Clouds*, 163.

43. Noyce, *Expedition report. 1953 Personnel – Personal*, 5.

44. Jackson and Stark, *Tents in the Clouds*, 191.

45. Antonia Deacock, *No Purdah in Padam. The Story of the Women's Overland Himalayan Expedition in 1958* (London: George G. Harrap & Co., 1960), 205–06.

46. Bill Birkett and Bill Peascod, *Women Climbing. 200 Years of Achievement* (London: A&C Black Publishers, 1989), 104–06.

47. John B. West, Robert B. Schoene, Andrew M. Luks, and James S. Milledge, *High Altitude Medicine And Physiology*, fifth edition (Boca Raton: CRC Press, 2013), 251.

48. Guanghao Shen, Kangning Xie, Yili Yan, Da Jing, Chi Tang, Xiaoming Wu, Juan Liu, Tao Sun, Jianbao Zhang, and Erping Luo, "The Role of Oxygen-increased Respirator in Humans Ascending to High Altitude," *BioMedical Engineering OnLine* 11, 49 (2012): 1–8, http://www.biomedical-engineering-online.com/content/11/1/49 (accessed on January 15, 2016).

49. John B. West, *High Life: A History of High-Altitude Physiology and Medicine* (Oxford: Oxford University Press, 1998), 304.

50. Ibid., 227–29.

51. P. G. Firth, H. Zheng, J. S. Windsor, A. I. Sutherland, C. H. Imray, G. W. K. Moore, J. L. Semple, R. C. Roach, and R. A. Salisbury, "Mortality on Mount Everest, 1921–2006: descriptive study," *BMJ*, 337 (2008), 1–6, www.bmj.com (accessed on January 15, 2016).

52. Charles Houston, *Going Higher: Oxygen, Man and Mountains*, fourth edition (Seattle, WA: Mountaineers Books, 1998), 94.

53. "What To Eat When You're High (up): Why Not Caviar? And Plenty Of H2O," http://blogs.scientificamerican.com/food-matters/what-to-eat-when-you-8217-re-high-up-why-not-caviar-and-plenty-of-h2o/ (accessed on November 11, 2015).

54. Reinhold Messner, *My Life at the Limit (Legends & Lore)* (Seattle, WA: Mountaineers Books, 2014), 171.

55. Houchang Esfandiar Chehabi, "How Caviar Turned Out to Be Halal," *Gastronomica* 7:2 (Spring 2007): 17–23.

56. King's Fine Food, "King's and the Community," http://www.kingsfinefood.co.uk/articles/king_s_and_the_community (accessed on November 11, 2015).

57. Reinhold Messner, *Everest: Expedition to the Ultimate* (Seattle, WA: Mountaineers Books, 2014), 155.

58. Kenneth Koh, e-mail message to author, May 14, 2016.

59. West et al., *High Altitude Medicine and Physiology*, 298.

60. Mark Twight and James Martin, *Extreme Alpinism: Climbing Light, Fast & High* (Seattle, WA: Mountaineers Books, 1999), 71–72.

61. N. Morihara, T. Nishihama, M. Ushijima, N. Ide, H. Takeda, and M. Hayama, "Garlic as an Anti-fatigue Agent," *Mol Nutrition Food Research*, 51 (2007): 1329–34.

62. M. B. Fallon, G. A. Abrahams, T. T. Abdel-Razek, J. Dai, S. J. Chen, Y. F. Chen, B. Luo, S. Oparil, and D. D. Ku. "Garlic Prevents Hypoxic Pulmonary Hypertension in Rats." *American Journal of Physiology*, 275 (1998): 283–87.

63. Gelbu Pemba, e-mail message to author, May 17, 2016.

64. Messner, *My Life at the Limit (Legends & Lore)*, 60–61.

65. Ibid., 95.

66. Ibid., 121.

67. Ibid., 186.

Chapter 5

1. Marco Polo, Ernst Rhys, ed., *The Travels of Marco Polo the Venetian* (London: J. M. Dent, 1908, ebook), 100, https://archive.org/stream/marcopolo00polouoft/marcopolo00polouoft_djvu.txt (accessed on July 20, 2016).

2. Milton Rugoff, *Marco Polo* (New Word City, ebook, 2015).

3. Marco Polo, *The Travels of Marco Polo the Venetian*, 1908, 68.

4. John Masefield, foreword to *The Travels of Marco Polo the Venetian* by Marco Polo, Ernst Rhys, ed. (London: J. M. Dent, 1908, ebook), xi. https://archive.org/stream/marcopolo00polouoft/marcopolo00polouoft_djvu.txt (accessed on July 20, 2016).

5. Royal Geographical Society, *Explorers. Great Tales of Adventure and Endurance* (New York: DK Publishing, 2010), 246–47.

6. Ibid., 249.

7. H. St. J. B. Philby, *The Empty Quarter* (London: Constable & Company Ltd., 1933), 42.

8. Ibid., 11–12.

9. Ibid., 280–81.

10. Ibid., 343.

11. Ibid., 278.

12. Ibid., 315.

13. Ibid., 238.

14. Ibid., 280–81.

15. Ibid., 278.

16. Ibid., 361.

17. Ibid., 357.

18. Ibid., 334.

19. Ibid., 340.

20. Royal Geographical Society, *Explorers*, 248.

21. Wilfred Thesiger, "Heart of a Nomad. In Conversation with David Attenborough," Interview Transcript (Channel 4 Television, London, 1994), 10–11.

22. Wilfred Thesiger, "A New Journey in Southern Arabia," *Geographical Journal*, 108 (1946): 17.

23. Wilfred Thesiger, *Private Notes*, RGS Thesiger Collection, archives of the Royal Geographical Society, London.

24. Wilfred Thesiger, "A New Journey in Southern Arabia," 17.

25. Ibid., 6–7.

26. Wilfred Thesiger, *Arabian Sands* (Original in 1959, London: Penguin Books, 2007), 154.

27. Said Hamdun and Noel King, *Ibn Battuta in Black Africa* (Princeton, NJ: Markus Wiener Publications, 1995), 78.

28. Mohamed Hassan Mohamed, *Between Caravan and Sultan: The Bayruk of Southern Morocco* (Leiden: Koninklijke Brill, 2012), 160.

29. Geoffrey Moorhouse, *The Fearful Void* (Kindle Version, Faber & Faber, 2012).

30. Michael Asher, e-mail conversations with the author, June 11, 18, 2016.

31. Ibid.

32. Ibid.

33. Ibid.

34. A. G. Hopkins, *An Economic History of West Africa* (New York: Routledge, 1973).

35. Mungo Park, *Travels in the Interior Districts of Africa: Performed in the years 1795, 1796, and 1797. With an Account of a Subsequent Mission to that Country in 1805* (London: Printed for John Murray, by William Bulmer and Co., 1816), 273, https://archive.org/details/travelsininterio01park (accessed on April 5, 2016).

36. C. A. Brebbia, *Patagonia, a Forgotten Land: From Magellan to Perón* (Southhampton: WIT Press, 2008), 24–28.

37. Charles Darwin, *A Naturalist's Voyage Round the World. The Voyage of the Beagle* (First edition 1860, 1913 edition), 534–35, http://www.gutenberg.org/cache/epub/3704/pg3704.txt (accessed on April 5, 2016).

38. Ibid., 345.

39. Ibid., 254.

40. Robert FitzRoy, *Narrative of the Surveying Voyages of His Majesty's Ships Adventure and Beagle between the Years 1826 and 1836, Describing Their Examination of the Southern Shores of South America, and the Beagle's Circumnavigation of the Globe. Proceedings of the Second Expedition, 1831–36, under the Command of Captain Robert FitzRoy, R.N. Volume II.* (London: Henry Colburn, 1838), 183, http://darwin-online.org.uk/content/frameset?itemID=F10.2&viewtype=text&pageseq=1 (accessed on April 18, 2016).

41. Darwin, *A Naturalist's Voyage Round the World*, 115.

42. Sir John Richardson, *Fauna Boreali-Americana or, The Zoology of the Northern Parts of British America: Containing Descriptions of the Objects of Natural History Collected on the Late Northern Land Expeditions, under Command of Captain Sir John*

Franklin, R.N. volume 1. (London: John Murray, 1829), 35, https://archive.org/details/faunaborealiamer01rich (accessed on April 15, 2016).

43. "Ultramarathoners Lahcen and Mohamad Ahansal: 'What's the Best Post-run Indulgence? Sleep!'" *Guardian online*, February 20, 2015, http://www.theguardian.com/lifeandstyle/the-running-blog/2015/feb/20/lahcen-mohamad-ahansal-marathon-des-sables-trans-atlas-marathon (accessed on May 16, 2016).

44. Raffaele Brattoli, personal conversation with the author, May 11, 2016.

45. Ibid.

46. Ibid.

47. Alberto Tagliabue, personal conversation with the author, May 12, 2016.

Chapter 6

1. Jonathan Sumption, *The Age of Pilgrimage: The Medieval Journey to God* (Mahwah, NJ: Hidden Spring, 2003), 244–46.

2. Ibid., 234–35.

3. Sir Walter Raleigh, *The Pilgrimage* (1618), http://quod.lib.umich.edu/e/eebo/A57518.0001.001/1:1?rgn=div1;view=fulltext (accessed on May 17, 2016).

4. Fabrizio Vanni, "*Certaldo, le sue cipolle, lo zafferano e i caci di Lucardo,*" *De Strata Frācigena* XIV/2 (2008): 39–60.

5. Alison Raju, *The Via Francigena Canterbury to Rome – Part 2: The Great St Bernard Pass to Rome* (Milnthorpe, UK: Cicerone Press, 2014), 16–23.

6. R. C. Wilson, "Kailas Parbat and Two Passes of the Kumaon Himalaya," *Alpine Journal*, 40 (1928): 23–26.

7. John Baptist Lucius Noel, *The Story of Everest* (New York: Blue Ribbon Books, 1931), 108.

8. Mikkel Aaland, *Pilgrimage to Kailash* (ebook, Blurb Publishing, 2013).

9. David C. Moreton, "The History of Charitable Giving Along the Shikoku Pilgrimage Route" (M.A. Thesis, The University of British Columbia, 1995).

10. Teigo Yoshida, "Strangers and pilgrimage in village Japan," in *Pilgrimages and Spiritual Quest in Japan*, ed. Maria Rodrigues del Alisal, Peter Ackerman, and Dolores P. Martinez (New York: Routledge, 2007), 50–53.

11. Paul L. Swanson, "Shugendō and the Yoshino-Kumano Pilgrimage. An Example of a Mountain Pilgrimage," *Monumenta Nipponica*, 36 (1982): 55–84.

12. H. Byron Earhart, "Mount and Shugendō," *Japanese Journal of Religious Studies*, 16 (1989): 205–26.

13. Andrea K. Gill, "Shugendō: Pilgrimage and Ritual in a Japanese Folk Religion," *Pursuit: The Journal of Undergraduate Research at the University of Tennessee*, 3 (2012): 49–65.

14. Peter V. N. Henderson, *The Course of Andean History* (Albuquerque: The University of New Mexico Press, 2013), 38–39.

15. Alan L. Kolata, *Ancient Inca, Case Studies in Early Societies* (New York: Cambridge University Press, 2013), 112.

16. Linda Kay Davidson and David M. Gitlitz, *Pilgrimage. From the Ganges to Graceland. An Encyclopedia* (Santa Barbara, CA: ABC-Clio, 2002), 123–25.

17. Andrew S. Wilson, Emma L. Brown, Chiara Villa, Niels Lynnerup, Andrew Healey, Maria Constanza Ceruti, Johan Reinhard, Carlos H. Previgliano, Facundo Arias Araoz, Josefina Gonzalez Diez, and Timothy Taylor, "Archaeological, radiological, and biological evidence offer insight into Inca child sacrifice," *PNAS*, 110 (2013): 13322–27, http://www.pnas.org/content/110/33/13322 (accessed on April 26, 2016).

18. Giulio Magli, "At the other end of the sun's path. A new interpretation of Machu Picchu," *Nexus Network Journal*, 12 (2010): 321–41.

19. Maritza Chacacanta, PEAK Destination Management Company in Cusco Peru, e-mail message to author, May 24 and 30, 2016.

20. Josephie Brefeld, *A Guidebook for the Jerusalem Pilgrimage in the Late Middle Ages* (Hilversum, Netherlands: Verloren, 1994), 17–19.

21. Albrecht Classen, *Urban Space in the Middle Ages and the Early Modern Age* (Berlin: Walter de Gruyter, 2009), 220.

22. Elkan Nathan Adler, ed., *Jewish Travellers in the Middle Ages. 19 Firsthand Accounts* (New York: Dover Publications, 2011), 194–95.

23. John Cooper, *Eat and Be Satisfied. A Social History of Jewish Food* (Northvale, NY: Jason Aronson Inc., 1993), 94.

24. Nicole Chareyron and Donald W. Wilson, *Pilgrims to Jerusalem in the Middle Ages* (New York: Columbia University Press, 2005), 39.

25. Jane Elisabeth Archer, Richard Marggraf Turley, and Howard Thomas, *Food and the Literary Imagination* (London: Palgrave MacMillan, 2014).

26. Geoffrey Chaucer, Ronald L. Ecker, and Eugen Crook, *The Canterbury Tales. A Complete Translation into Modern English* (Palatka, FL: Hodge & Braddock, 1993), 9–10.

27. Constance B. Hieatt, "A Cook of 14th-Century London: Chaucer's Hogge of Ware, in Cooks & Other People," *Proceedings of the Oxford Symposium on Food and Cookery*, Harlan Walker, ed. (Devon, UK: Prospect Books, 1996), 138.

28. Talal Itani, tr, "Quran 22:27, The Pilgrimage (al-Hajj)," *Quran in English: Clear and Easy to Understand. Modern English Translation* (CreateSpace Independent Publishing Platform, 2014), 142.

29. F. E. Peters, *The Hajj. The Muslim Pilgrimage to Mecca and the Holy Places* (Princeton, NJ: Princeton University Press, 1994), 71–96.

30. Amy Singer, *Constructing Ottoman Beneficence: An Imperial Soup Kitchen in Jerusalem* (Albany: State University of New York Press, 2002), 142.

31. Murat Ozyuksel, *The Hejaz Railway and the Ottoman Empire* (London: I. B. Tauris, 2014), 205.

32. Marie Dhumieres, "The Bosnian Who Made the Pilgrimage to Mecca—On Foot," *The Independent*, October 24, 2012, independent.co.uk (accessed on July 5, 2015).

33. Christopher S. Bowron and Salahudin M. Maalim, "Saudi Arabia: Hajj Pilgrimage," in *CDC Health Information for International Travel 2016* (Oxford: Oxford

University Press, 2016), http://wwwnc.cdc.gov/travel/yellowbook/2016/select-destinations/saudi-arabia-hajj-pilgrimage (accessed on 5 July 2016).

34. Esma Sayin, *Haccin kalbine Yolculuk* (Journey to the Heart of Hajj) (Istanbul: Nesil, 2012, digital edition).

Chapter 7

1. Robert Flacelière, *Daily Life in Greece at the Time of Pericles* (London: Macmillan, 1965), 170–71.

2. Vindolanda Tablets Online, http://vindolanda.csad.ox.ac.uk/about.shtml (accessed on July 17, 2016).

3. Adrian Keith Goldsworthy, *The Roman Army at War: 100 BC–AD 200* (Oxford: Clarendon, 1998), 291–92.

4. R.W. Davies, "The Roman Military Diet," *Britannia*, 2 (1971): 122–42.

5. Gordon L. Robertson, *Food Packaging Principles and Practice* (New York: Marcel Dekker, 1993), 174–75.

6. Richard Briggs, *The New Art of Cookery According to Present Practice* (Kansas City, MO: Andrews MacMeel, 2013), 52–53.

7. Charles L. Cutler, *Tracks that Speak. The Legacy of Native American Words in North American Culture* (Boston: Houghton Mifflin Company, 2002), 101.

8. Alexis Soyer, *Culinary Campaign. Being Historical Reminiscences of the Late War with The Plain Art of Cookery for Military and Civil Institutions, the Army, Navy, Public, etc.etc.* (London: G. Routledge & Co.: 1857), ebook: Chapter XXVII, http://www.gutenberg.org/files/42544/42544-h/42544-h.htm (accessed on July 16, 2016).

9. William Phillips Thompson, *Handbook of Patent Law of All Countries* (London: Stevens, 1920), 42.

10. Bovril advert featuring Chris Bonington from 1979, https://www.youtube.com/watch?v=LH3PHL6vTJw (accessed on February 1, 2016).

11. Erna Risch, *The Technical Services, the Quartermaster Corps: Organization, Supply and Services, Volume 1* (Washington, DC: Center of Military History, United States Army, 1995), 206.

12. Elsworth R. Buskirk, "From Harvard to Minnesota: Keys to Our History," *Exercise & Sport Sciences Reviews*, 20 (1992): 1–26.

13. James C. Longino (Col.), "Rations in Review," *The Quartermaster Review* May–June (1946), http://www.qmmuseum.lee.army.mil/WWII/rations_in_review.htm (accessed on January 13, 2016).

14. William C. Davis, *A Taste of War. The Culinary History of the Blue and the Gray* (Mechanicsburg, PA: Stackpole Books, 2003), 40–44.

15. John Davis Billings, *Hardtack and Coffee: or, the Unwritten Story of Army Life* (Ithaca, NY: Cornell University Press, 2009), 113–15.

16. Lily Mary Spalding and John Spalding, *Civil War Recipes: Receipts from the Pages of Godey's Lady's Book* (Lexington: The University of Kentucky Press, 1999), 16.

17. Billings, *Hardtack and Coffee*, 115–16.

18. Davis, *A Taste of War*, 40–44.

19. Adapted from Ibid., 130.

20. Spalding and Spalding, *Civil War Recipes*, 15–16.

21. Bell Irvin Wiley, *The Life of Billy Yank: The Common Soldier of the Union* (Baton Rouge: Louisiana State University Press, 2008 edition, first published in 1952), 34.

22. Ibid., 164.

23. Davis, *A Taste of War*, 126.

24. Andrew F. Smith, *Oxford Encyclopedia of Food and Drink in America* (New York: Oxford University Press, 2013), 199.

25. Spalding and Spalding, *Civil War Recipes*, 11–16.

26. Davis, *A Taste of War*, 44.

27. Billings, *Hardtack and Coffee*, 117.

28. Anna Chotzinoff Grossman and Lisa Grossman Thomas, *Lobscouse and Spotted Days: Which It's a Gastronomic Companion to the Aubrey/Maturin Novels* (New York: W. W. Norton & Co Inc., 2000), 5.

29. Andrew F. Smith, *The Oxford Companion to American Food and Drink* (Oxford: Oxford University Press, 2007), 559.

30. Silvano Serventi, Food historian, the author of *La cuisine des tranchées*, personal conversation with the author, February 8, 2016.

31. Victor Breedon, *Best Regards Freddie* (Pittsburgh, PA: Dorrance Publishing, 2014).

32. Gordon L. Rottman, *SNAFU Sailor, Airman, and Soldier Slang of the World War II* (Oxford: Osprey Publishing, 2013).

33. Jean Anthelme Brillat-Savarin, *The Physiology of Taste: Or Meditations on Transcendental Gastronomy* (New York: Vintage Classics, 2011), 15.

34. "The Eat of Battle—How the World's Armies get Fed," *The Guardian*, February 18, 2014, www.theguardian.com (accessed on January 19, 2016).

35. "The Gourmet Army," *Daily Mail*, April 9, 2004, www.dailymail.co.uk (accessed on January 20, 2016).

36. "Kommissbrot," *Kleines Brotlexikon* (Museum der Brotkultur, Ulm), http://www.museum-brotkultur.de/pdf/06Brotformen%20und%20Brotsorten.pdf (accessed on February 2, 2016).

37. Max Gerson, "Feeding the German Army," *New York State Journal of Medicine*, 41, 13 (July 15, 1941): 1471–76, http://www.cancer-research.net/ (accessed February 2, 2016).

38. Timothy C. Dowling, *Personal Perspectives: World War II* (Santa Barbara, CA: ABC-Clio, 2005), 67.

39. Norman Ohler, *Der totale Rausch. Drogen im Dritten Reich* (Koln: Kiepenheier & Witshc Verlag, 2015).

40. Herman Buhl, *Nanga Parbat Pilgrimage: The Lonely Challenge* (Seattle, WA: Mountaineers Books, 1998), 325, 329.

41. "Climbing's Little Helper," *Outside Magazine*, March 14, 2013, www.outsideonline.com (accessed on January 21, 2016).

42. D. Hillebrandt, T. Kupper, E. Donegani, U. Hefti, J. Milledge, V. Schoffl, N. Dikic, J. Arnold, and G. Dubowitz, "Drug Use and Misuse in Mountaineering," *Official Standards of the UIAA Medical Commission*, 22 (2014).

Chapter 8

1. Rebecca Solnit, *Wanderlust: A History of Walking* (London: Verso, 2001).

2. Voltaire, *Candide* (Ballingslöv, Sweden: Wisehouse Classics, 2015), 9.

3. Charles Baudelaire, *The Painter of Modern Life and Other Essays* (London: Phaidon, 1970), 9.

4. Honoré de Balzac, *Physiologie du marriage* (ebook: Bibebook, 32), http://www.bibebook.com/files/ebook/libre/V2/balzac_honore_de_-_physiologie_du_mariage.pdf, (accessed on July 12, 2016).

5. Holly Chase, "Suspect Salep," in *Look & Feel. Proceedings of the Oxford Symposium on Food and Cookery 1993*, Harlan Walker, ed. (London: Prospect Books, 1994), 44–47.

6. George Smith, William Makepeace Thackeray, and Elder Smith, "Unctuous Memories," *The Cornhill Magazine*, 8 (1863): 613–17.

7. Jolanda Jacobi, ed., *Paracelsus: Selected Writings* (Princeton, NJ: Princeton University Press, 1995), 722.

8. Alan Davidson and Tom Jaine, *The Oxford Companion to Food* (New York: Oxford University Press, 2014), 53.

9. Fahri Dikkaya, "*Evliya Celebi Seyahatnamesinde Simit ve Simitciler* (Simit and Simit Sellers in the Book of Travels of Evliya Celebi)," *Millî Folklor*, 92 (2011): 72–76.

10. Darra Goldstein, *The Oxford Companion to Sugar and Sweets* (New York: Oxford University Press, 2015), 141.

11. Andrew F. Smith, *Food and Drink in American History* (Santa Barbara, CA: ABC-Clio, 2013), 716.

12. Jim Lilliefors, *America's Boardwalks: From Coney Island to California* (New Brunswick, NJ: Rutgers University Press, 2006), 23–43.

13. Ibid., 871.

14. Frank O'Hara, "Excerpt from F. (Missive & Walk) I. #53," *The Collected Poems of Frank O'Hara* (Berkeley: University of California Press, 1995), 420.

15. Goldstein, *The Oxford Companion to Sugar and Sweets*, 348.

16. Ibid., 365.

17. Ibid., 478.

Bibliography

Books

Aaland, Mikkel. *Pilgrimage to Kailash*. ebook. Blurb Publishing, 2013.

Adler, Elkan Nathan, ed., *Jewish Travellers in the Middle Ages. 19 Firsthand Accounts*. New York: Dover Publications, 2011.

Albala, Ken. *Food Cultures of the World Encyclopedia, Volume 1*. Santa Barbara, CA: ABC-CLIO, LLC, 2011.

Amundsen, Roald. *The South Pole (Volume I)*. London: John Murray, 1912. http://gutenberg.net.au/ebooks/e00111a.html. Accessed on July 13, 2015.

Amundsen, Roald. *My Life as an Explorer*. London: Heineman, 1927. https://archive.org/details/roaldamundsenmyl00amun_0. Accessed on July 13, 2015.

d'Angeville, Henriette. *My Ascent of Mont Blanc*. Paris: Harper Collins, 1987.

Archer, Jane Elisabeth, Richard Marggraf Turley, and Howard Thomas. *Food and the Literary Imagination*. London: Palgrave MacMillan, 2014.

Asher, Michael. *Impossible Journey: Two Against the Sahara*. London: Viking, 1988.

Astrup, Eivind. *With Peary near the Pole*. London: C. A. Pearson, limited, 1898.

Auldjo, John. *Narrative of an Ascent to the Summit of Mont Blanc Made in July, 1819*. CreateSpace Independent Publishing Platform, 2015. First published in 1821.

Avery, Tom. *To the End of the Earth: Our Epic Journey to the North Pole and the Legend of Peary and Henson*. New York: St. Martin's Press, 2010.

Balzac, Honoré de. *Physiologie du marriage*. ebook. Bibebook. http://www.bibebook.com/files/ebook/libre/V2/balzac_honore_de_-_physiologie_du_mariage.pdf. Accessed on July 12, 2016.

Band, George. *Summit: 150 Years of the Alpine Club*. London: HarperCollins UK, 2007.

Baudelaire, Charles. *The Painter of Modern Life and Other Essays*. London: Phaidon, 1970).

Billings, John Davis. *Hardtack and Coffee: or, the Unwritten Story of Army Life*. Ithaca, NY: Cornell University Press, 2009. First published in 1887.

Birkett, Bill, and Bill Peascod. *Women Climbing. 200 Years of Achievement*. London: A&C Black Publishers, 1989.

Boswell, James. *Boswell's Life of Johnson*. Project Gutenberg ebook, Charles Grosvenor Osgood, ed., 2006. http://www.gutenberg.org/files/1564/1564-h/1564-h.htm. Accessed on July 12, 2016.

Bowron, Christopher S., and Salahudin M. Maalim. "Saudi Arabia: Hajj Pilgrimage," in *CDC Health Information for International Travel 2016*. Oxford: Oxford University Press, 2016. http://wwwnc.cdc.gov/travel/yellowbook/2016/select-destinations/saudi -arabia-hajj-pilgrimage. Accessed on 5 July 2016.

Brebbia, C. A. *Patagonia, a Forgotten Land: From Magellan to Perón*. Southampton: WIT Press, 2008.

Breedon, Victor. *Best Regards Freddie*. Pittsburgh, PA: Dorrance Publishing, 2014.

Brefeld, Josephie. *A Guidebook for the Jerusalem Pilgrimage in the Late Middle Ages*. Hilversum, Netherlands: Verloren, 1994.

Briggs, Richard. *The New Art of Cookery According to Present Practice*. Kansas City, MO: Andrews MacMeel, 2013.

Brillat-Savarin, Jean Anthelme. *The Physiology of Taste: Or Meditations on Transcendental Gastronomy*. New York: Vintage Classics, 2011.

Bruce, C. G. *The Assault on Mount Everest 1922*. London: Edward Arnold & Co., 1923.

Buhl, Herman. *Nanga Parbat Pilgrimage: The Lonely Challenge*. Seattle, WA: Mountaineers Books, 1998.

Carpenter, Kenneth J. *The History of Scurvy and Vitamin C*. Cambridge: Cambridge University Press, 1986.

Chareyron, Nicole, and Donald W. Wilson. *Pilgrims to Jerusalem in the Middle Ages*. New York: Columbia University Press, 2005.

Chaucer, Geoffrey, Ronald L. Ecker, and Eugen Crook. *The Canterbury Tales. A Complete Translation into Modern English*. Palatka, FL: Hodge & Braddock, 1993.

Classen, Albrecht. *Urban Space in the Middle Ages and the Early Modern Age*. Berlin: Walter de Gruyter, 2009.

Conefrey, Mick. *Everest 1953. The Epic Story of the First Ascent*. London: Oneworld Publications, 2012.

Cooper, John. *Eat and Be Satisfied. A Social History of Jewish Food*. Northvale, NY: Jason Aronson Inc., 1993.

Cutler, Charles L. *Tracks that Speak. The Legacy of Native American Words in North American Culture*. Boston: Houghton Mifflin Company, 2002.

Dalton, Anthony. *Sir John Franklin. Expeditions to Destiny*. Victoria: Heritage House Publishing, 2012.

Darwin, Charles. *A Naturalist's Voyage Round the World. The Voyage of the Beagle*. 1913 edition. First edition printed in 1860. http://www.gutenberg.org/cache/epub/3704/pg3704.txt. Accessed on April 5, 2016.

Davidson, Alan, and Tom Jaine. *The Oxford Companion to Food*. New York, Oxford University Press, 2014.

Davidson, Linda Kay, and David M. Gitlitz. *Pilgrimage. From the Ganges to Graceland. An Encyclopedia*. Santa Barbara, CA: ABC-Clio, 2002.

Davis, William C. *A Taste of War. The Culinary History of the Blue and the Gray*. Mechanicsburg, PA: Stackpole Books, 2003.

Deacock, Antonia. *No Purdah in Padam. The Story of the Women's Overland Himalayan Expedition in 1958*. London: George G. Harrap & Co., 1960.

Dowling, Timothy C. *Personal Perspectives: World War II*. Santa Barbara, CA: ABC-Clio, 2005.

Favenc, Ernest. *The Explorers of Australia and Their Life-work*. Forgotten Books edition, 2012 (original, Christchurch: Whitcombe & Tombs, 1908).

Fisher, M. F. K. "The Pleasures of Picnics (1957)," in *A Stew or a Story: An Assortment of Short Works by M. F. K. Fisher*, edited by Joan Reardon, 198–207. Emeryville: Shoemaker & Hoard, 2006.

FitzRoy, Robert. *Narrative of the Surveying Voyages of His Majesty's Ships* Adventure *and* Beagle *between the Years 1826 and 1836, Describing Their Examination of the Southern Shores of South America, and the* Beagle's *Circumnavigation of the Globe. Proceedings of the Second Expedition, 1831–36, under the Command of Captain Robert Fitz-Roy, R.N.* Volume II. London: Henry Colburn, 1838. http://darwin-online .org.uk/content/frameset?itemID=F10.2&viewtype=text&pageseq=1. Accessed on April 18, 2016.

Flacelière, Robert. *Daily Life in Greece at the Time of Pericles*. London: Macmillan, 1965.

Fleming, Fergus. *Ninety Degrees North: The Quest for the North Pole*. London: Granta Books, 2011.

Gellhorn, Ernst. *Physiological Foundations of Neurology and Psychiatry*. Minneapolis: The University of Minnesota Press, 1953.

Girl Scouts, Inc. *Tramping and Trailing with the Girl Scouts, 1927*. New York: Girls Scouts of the United States of America, 1930 revision.

Goldstein, Darra. *The Oxford Companion to Sugar and Sweets*. New York: Oxford University Press, 2015.

Goldsworthy, Adrian Keith. *The Roman Army at War: 100 BC–AD 200*. Oxford: Clarendon, 1998.

Gould, John M. *How to Camp Out*. Ebook edition, 2006 (First edition 1877). http:// archive.org/stream/howtocampout17575gut/17575.txt. Accessed January 25, 2015.

Grahame, Kenneth. *The Wind in the Willows*. New York: Scribner, 1913. https:// archive.org/details/windinwillows00grah. Accessed January 26, 2016.

Grossman, Anna Chotzinoff, and Lisa Grossman Thomas. *Lobscouse and Spotted Days: Which it's a Gastronomic Companion to the Aubrey/Maturin Novels*. New York: W. W. Norton & Co Inc., 2000.

Hamdun, Said, and Noel King. *Ibn Battuta in Black Africa*. Princeton, NJ: Markus Wiener Publications, 1995.

Hare, James R. *Hiking the Appalachian Trail*. Emmaus, PA: Rodale Press, 1975.

Harper, Melissa. *The Ways of the Bushwalker: On Foot in Australia.* Sydney: University of New South Wales Press, 2007.

Harris, Marvin. *Our Kind: Who We Are, Where We Came From, Where We Are Going.* New York: Harper Perennial, 1990.

Helmes, Winifred. *Notable Maryland Women.* Centreville, MD: Tidewater Publishers, 1977.

Henderson, Peter V. N. *The Course of Andean History.* Albuquerque: The University of New Mexico Press, 2013.

Hill, George William, and Williams Bros. *History of Ashland County, Ohio.* Philadelphia: J. B. Lippincott, 1863.

Hopkins, A. G. *An Economic History of West Africa.* New York: Routledge, 1973.

Houston, Charles. *Going Higher: Oxygen, Man and Mountains,* fourth edition. Seattle, WA: Mountaineers Books, 1998.

Hunt, John. *The Ascent of Everest 1953.* London: Hodder & Stoughton, 1993.

Hutton, Drew, and Libby Connors. *History of the Australian Environment Movement.* Cambridge: Cambridge University Press, 1999.

Itani, Talal, tr., "Quran 22:27, The Pilgrimage (al-Hajj)," *Quran in English: Clear and Easy to Understand. Modern English Translation.* CreateSpace Independent Publishing Platform, 2014.

Jackson, Monica, and Elizabeth Stark. *Tents in the Clouds. The First Women's Himalayan Expedition.* Seal Press, US edition 2000. First published in 1956.

Jacobi, Jolande, ed. *Paracelsus: Selected Writings.* Princeton, NJ: Princeton University Press, 1995.

Johnson, Samuel. *A Journey to the Western Isles of Scotland.* Project Gutenberg ebook, 2005. http://www.gutenberg.org/files/2064/2064-h/2064-h.htm Accessed on July 12, 2016.

Kolata, Alan L. *Ancient Inca, Case Studies in Early Societies.* New York: Cambridge University Press, 2013.

Lees, Thomas Orde. *Photocopy of a Diary of Thomas Orde Lees, on Elephant Island.* Original held at Scott Polar Research Institute, 1916, Royal Geographical Society London, 1978–1979, EHS/9.

Levy, Walter. *The Picnic: A History. The Meals Series.* Lanham, MD: Alta Mira Press, 2014.

Lilliefors, Jim. *America's Boardwalks: From Coney Island to California.* New Brunswick, NJ: Rutgers University Press, 2006.

Mackenzie, Alexander. *Voyages from Montreal Through the Continent of North America to the Frozen and Pacific Oceans in 1789 and 1793, Vol. I.* New York: A. S. Barnes and Company, 1903. http://www.gutenberg.org/files/35658/35658-h/35658-h.htm. Accessed on April 1, 2016.

Mariani, John F. *Encyclopedia of American Food and Drink.* New York: Lebhar Friedman, 1999.

Masefield, John. Foreword to *The Travels of Marco Polo the Venetian* by Marco Polo, Ernst Rhys, ed. London: J. M. Dent, 1908, ebook. https://archive.org/stream/marcopolo00polouoft/marcopolo00polouoft_djvu.txt. Accessed on July 20, 2016.

McGlashan, C. F. *History of the Donner Party*. Ebook, 2009 (first published in 1879). http://www.gutenberg.org/files/6077/6077-h/6077-h.htm. Accessed on July 16, 2016.

Means, Howard. *Johnny Appleseed: The Man, the Myth, the American Story*. New York: Simon & Schuster, 2012.

Messner, Reinhold. *Everest: Expedition to the Ultimate*. Seattle, WA: The Mountaineers, 2014.

Messner, Reinhold. *My Life at the Limit (Legends & Lore)*. Seattle, WA: Mountaineers Books, 2014.

Miller, Sally M., and Daryl Morrison. *John Muir: Family, Friends, and Adventures*. Albuquerque: University of New Mexico Press, 2005.

Mills, Sara. *Discourses of Difference: An Analysis of Women's Travel Writing and Colonialism*. London: Routledge, 1991.

Mohamed, Mohamed Hassan. *Between Caravan and Sultan: The Bayruk of Southern Morocco*. Leiden: Koninklijke Brill, 2012.

Moorhouse, Geoffre. *The Fearful Void*. Kindle Version, Faber & Faber, 2012.

Moreton, David C. "The History of Charitable Giving Along the Shikoku Pilgrimage Route." M.A. Thesis, The University of British Columbia, 1995.

Morton, Mark. *Cupboard Love: A Dictionary of Culinary Curiosities*. London, Ontario: Insomniac Press, 2000.

Muir, John. *My First Summer in the Sierra*. Boston: Houghton Mifflin Company, 1911.

Noel, John Baptist Lucius. *The Story of Everest*. New York: Blue Ribbon Books, 1931.

Noyce, Wilfrid. *Expedition report. 1953 Personnel – Personal*. Archives of the Royal Geographical Society. London.

O'Hara, Frank. "Excerpt from F. (Missive & Walk) I. #53," *The Collected Poems of Frank O'Hara*. Berkeley: University of California Press, 1995.

Ohler, Norman. *Der totale Rausch. Drogen im Dritten Reich*. Koln: Kiepenheier & Witsch Verlag, 2015.

Ozyuksel, Murat. *The Hejaz Railway and the Ottoman Empire*. London: I. B. Tauris, 2014.

Park, Mungo. *Travels in the Interior Districts of Africa: Performed in the years 1795, 1796, and 1797. With an Account of a Subsequent Mission to that Country in 1805*. London: Printed for John Murray, by William Bulmer and Co., 1816. https://archive.org/details/travelsininterio01park. Accessed on April 5, 2016.

Parkman, Francis. *The Oregon Trail. Sketches of Prairie and Rocky Mountain Life*. Boston: Little, Brown, and Company, 1900.

Paterson, Andrew Barton. *The Old Bush Songs, 1906*. Charleston, SC: BiblioBazaar, 2008.

Peary, Robert E. *The North Pole: Its Discovery in 1909 Under the Auspices of Peary Arctic Club*. New York: Greenwood Press Publishers, 2006. First published in 1910.

Peary, Robert E. *Secrets of Polar Travel*. New York: The Century Co., 1917. https://archive.org/details/secretspolartra00peargoog. Accessed on April 1, 2016.

Peters, F. E. *The Hajj. The Muslim Pilgrimage to Mecca and the Holy Places*. Princeton, NJ: Princeton University Press, 1994.

Philby, H. St. J. B. *The Empty Quarter*. London: Constable & Company Ltd., 1933.

Pollan, Michael. *The Botany of Desire: A Plant's-Eye View of the World.* London: Bloomsbury, 2003.

Polo, Marco. Ernst Rhys, ed. *The Travels of Marco Polo the Venetian.* London: J. M. Dent, 1908, ebook. https://archive.org/stream/marcopolo00polouoft/marcopolo00 polouoft_djvu.txt. Accessed on July 20, 2016.

Raju, Alison. *The Via Francigena Canterbury to Rome – Part 2: The Great St Bernard Pass to Rome.* Milnthorpe, UK: Cicerone Press, 2014.

Richardson, Sir John. *Fauna Boreali-Americana or, The Zoology of the Northern Parts of British America: Containing Descriptions of the Objects of Natural History Collected on the Late Northern Land Expeditions, under Command of Captain Sir John Franklin, R.N. volume 1.* London: John Murray, 1829. https://archive.org/details/faunaborealiamer01 rich. Accessed on April 15, 2016.

Risch, Erna. *The Technical Services, the Quartermaster Corps: Organization, Supply and Services, Volume 1.* Washington, DC: Center of Military History, US Army, 1995.

Robertson, Gordon L. *Food Packaging Principles and Practice.* New York: Marcel Dekker, 1993.

Rottman, Gordon L. *SNAFU Sailor, Airman, and Soldier Slang of the World War II.* Oxford: Osprey Publishing, 2013.

Royal Geographical Society, *Explorers. Great Tales of Adventure and Endurance.* New York: DK Publishing, 2010.

Rugoff, Milton. *Marco Polo.* New Word City, ebook edition, 2015.

Sayin, Esma. *Haccin kalbine Yolculuk* (Journey to the Heart of Hajj). Digital edition. Istanbul: Nesil, 2012.

Shipton, Eric. *Mountain Conquests.* ebook. New Word City, 2015.

Singer, Amy. *Constructing Ottoman Beneficence: An Imperial Soup Kitchen in Jerusalem.* Albany: State University of New York Press, 2002.

Smith, Albert. *The Story of Mont Blanc.* New York: G. P. Putnam, 1853.

Smith, Andrew F. *Food and Drink in American History.* Santa Barbara, CA: ABC-Clio, 2013.

Smith, Andrew F. *Oxford Encyclopedia of Food and Drink in America.* New York: Oxford University Press, 2013.

Smith, Andrew F. *The Oxford Companion to American Food and Drink.* Oxford: Oxford University Press 2007.

Solnit, Rebecca. *Wanderlust: A History of Walking.* London: Verso, 2001.

Soyer, Alexis. *Culinary Campaign. Being Historical Reminiscences of the Late War with The Plain Art of Cookery for Military and Civil Institutions, the Army, Navy, Public, etc.etc.* London: G. Routledge & Co.: 1857, ebook. http://www.gutenberg.org/files/ 42544/42544-h/42544-h.htm. Accessed on July 16, 2016.

Spalding, Lily Mary, and John Spalding. *Civil War Recipes: Receipts from the Pages of Godey's Lady's Book.* Lexington: The University of Kentucky Press, 1999.

Stanley, Autumn. *Mothers and Daughters of Invention: Invention Notes for a Revised History of Technology.* New Brunswick, NJ: Rutgers University Press, 1995.

Sumption, Jonathan. *The Age of Pilgrimage: The Medieval Journey to God.* Mahwah, NJ: Hidden Spring, 2003.

Symons, Michael. *One Continuous Picnic: A History of Australian Eating.* Victoria: Melbourne University Publishing, 1984.

Tallmadge, John. *Meeting the Tree of Life: A Teacher's Path.* Salt Lake City: University of Utah Press, 1997.

Tannahill, Raey. *Food in History.* New York: Three Rivers Press, 1988.

The Alpine Club. *Mountaineers. Great Tales of Bravery and Conquest.* London: DK Publishing, 2011.

Thesiger, Wilfred. "Heart of a Nomad. In conversation with David Attenborough," *Interview transcript.* Channel 4 Television, London, 1994.

Thesiger, Wilfred. *Arabian Sands.* London: Penguin Books, 2007. First published in 1959.

Thesiger, Wilfred. *Private Notes.* RGS Thesiger Collection. Archives of the Royal Geographical Society, London.

Thompson, William Phillips. *Handbook of Patent Law of All Countries.* London: Stevens, 1920.

Tuckey, Harriet. *Everest. The First Ascent. The Untold Story of Griffith Pugh the Man Who Made it Possible.* London: Random House, 2013.

Twight, Mark, and James Martin. *Extreme Alpinism: Climbing Light, Fast & High.* Seattle, WA: Mountaineers Books, 1999.

Voltaire. *Candide.* Ballingslöv, Sweden: Wisehouse Classics, 2015.

Ward, Michael. *First Ascent of Everest 1953: Medical and Scientific Aspects.* By Griffith Pugh. London: Alpine Club Archives, 1998.

West, John B. *High Life: A History of High-Altitude Physiology and Medicine.* Oxford: Oxford University Press, 1998.

West, John B., Robert B. Schoene, Andrew M. Luks, and James S. Milledge. *High Altitude Medicine and Physiology.* Fifth edition. Boca Raton, FL: CRC Press, 2013.

Wiley, Bell Irvin. *The Life of Billy Yank: The Common Soldier of the Union.* Baton Rouge: Louisiana State University Press, 2008 edition. First published in 1952.

Williams, Cicely. *Women on the Rope. The Feminine Share in Mountain Adventure.* London: George Allen & Unwin Ltd., 1973.

Worsley, Frank. *Shackleton's Boat Journey.* Cork: The Collins Press: original printed in 1940, reprinted in 2005.

Yoshida, Teigo. "Strangers and pilgrimage in village Japan," in *Pilgrimages and Spiritual Quest in Japan,* ed. Maria Rodrigues del Alisal, Peter Ackerman, and Dolores P. Martinez. New York: Routledge, 2007.

Young, Geoffrey Winthrop. *Mountain Craft.* New York: Charles Scribner's Sons, 1920.

Periodicals

Alvord, Benjamin. "Importance of Lime-juice in the Pemmican for Arctic Expeditions," *Science,* 35 (1883): 471.

Baber, Adin. "Food Plants of the De Soto Expedition, 1539–1543," *Tequesta,* 2 (1942), 34–40, Tequesta online, http://digitalcollections.fiu.edu/tequesta/, accessed July 19, 2016.

Buskirk, Elsworth R. "From Harvard to Minnesota: Keys to Our History," *Exercise & Sport Sciences Reviews*, 20 (1992): 1–26.

Chase, Holly. "Suspect Salep," in *Look & Feel. Proceedings of the Oxford Symposium on Food and Cookery 1993*, Harlan Walker, ed. London: Prospect Books, 1994, 44–47.

Chehabi, Houchang Esfandiar. "How Caviar Turned Out to Be Halal," *Gastronomica* 7:2 (Spring 2007): 17–23.

Daily Mail. "The Gourmet Army," April 9, 2004, www.dailymail.co.uk, accessed January 20, 2016.

Davies, R. W. "The Roman Military Diet." *Britannia*, 2 (1971): 122–42.

Dhumieres, Marie. "The Bosnian Who Made the Pilgrimage to Mecca—on Foot," *The Independent*, October 24, 2012, independent.co.uk, accessed July 5, 2015.

Dikkaya, Fahri. "*Evliya Celebi Seyahatnamesinde Simit ve Simitciler* (Simit and Simit Sellers in the Book of Travels of Evliya Celebi)," *Millî Folklor*, 92 (2011): 72–76.

Earhart, H. Byron. "Mount and Shugendo," *Japanese Journal of Religious Studies*, 16 (1989): 205–26.

Fallon, M. B., G. A. Abrahams, T. T. Abdel-Razek, J. Dai, S. J. Chen, Y. F. Chen, B. Luo, S. Oparil, and D. D. Ku. "Garlic Prevents Hypoxic Pulmonary Hypertension in Rats." *American Journal of Physiology*, 275 (1998): 283–87.

Firth, P. G., H. Zheng, J. S. Windsor, A. I. Sutherland, C. H. Imray, G. W. K. Moore, J. L. Semple, R. C. Roach, and R. A. Salisbury. "Mortality on Mount Everest, 1921–2006: descriptive study." *BMJ*, 337 (2008): 1–6, www.bmj.com, accessed January 15, 2016.

Francis, Dana. "Elders of the Tribe: 7 Fanny Bullock Workman," *Backpackers-7*, 2: 3 (1974): 84.

Gardiner, F., and C. Pilkington. "In Memoriam: Miss Lucy Walker." *Alpine Journal*, 31 (1917): 97–102.

Gerson. Max. "Feeding the German Army." *New York State Journal of Medicine*, 41:13 (July 15, 1941): 1471–76, http://www.cancer-research.net/, accessed February 2, 2016.

Gill, Andrea K. "Shugendō: Pilgrimage and Ritual in a Japanese Folk Religion." *Pursuit: The Journal of Undergraduate Research at the University of Tennessee*, 3 (2012): 49–65.

Goodyear, Dana. "What happened at Alder Creek?" *The New Yorker* (April 24, 2006): 140–51.

Haley, W. D. "Johnny Appleseed: A Pioneer Hero," *Harper's New Monthly Magazine*, 43 (1871): 830–36, https://archive.org/stream/harpersnew43various#page/836/mode/2up, accessed July 15, 2016.

Herzog, Maurice. "Earth's Third Pole—Everest; The assaults on the 29,002-foot summit of the world symbolize man's eternal drive to conquer the unconquerable." *New York Times* (May 31, 1953), www.nyt.com, accessed January 27, 2016.

Hieatt, Constance B. "A Cook of 14th-Century London: Chaucer's Hogge of Ware, in Cooks & Other People." *Proceedings of the Oxford Symposium on Food and Cookery*, Harlan Walker, ed. (Devon, UK: Prospect Books, 1996), 138.

Hillebrandt, D., T. Kupper, E. Donegani, U. Hefti, J. Milledge, V. Schoffl, N. Dikic, J. Arnold, and G. Dubowitz. "Drug Use and Misuse in Mountaineering." *Official Standards of the UIAA Medical Commission*, 22 (2014).

Ilbäch, N. G. and S. Källman. "The Lichen Rock Tripe (*Lasallia pustulata*) as Survival Food: Effects on Growth, Metabolism, and Immune Function in Balb/c Mice," *Natural Toxins* 7(6) (1999): 321–29.

Jones, A. G. E. "Frankie Wild's Hut." *Journal of the Royal Naval Medical Service*, 64 (1978): 51–58.

Le Bond, Aubrey. "Then and now." *Ladies' Alpine Club Yearbook* (1932): 7–8.

Lockhart, Ernest. "Antarctic Trail Diet. Reports on Scientific Results of the United States Antarctic Service Expedition, 1939–1941." *Proceedings of the American Philosophical Society*, 89 (1945): 235–48.

Longino (Col.), James C. "Rations in Review." *The Quartermaster Review*, May–June (1946), http://www.qmmuseum.lee.army.mil/WWII/rations_in_review.htm, accessed January 13, 2016.

Magli, Giulio. "At the other end of the sun's path. A new interpretation of Machu Picchu." *Nexus Network Journal*, 12 (2010): 321–41.

Morihara, N., T. Nishihama, M. Ushijima, N. Ide, H. Takeda, and M. Hayama. "Garlic as an anti-fatigue agent." *Mol Nutrition Food Research*, 51 (2007): 1329–34.

Northern Standard. "FEMALE SWAGGIES." April 7, 1922, http://nla.gov.au/nla.news-article48005334, accessed February 9, 2016.

Outside Magazine. "Climbing's Little Helper." March 14, 2013, www.outsideonline.com, accessed on January 21, 2016.

Ozwords. "Scroggin." 12 (2005): 5, http://andc.anu.edu.au/sites/default/files/ozwords_april05.pdf, accessed October 8, 2015.

Pugh, L. G. C. E. "Scientific Aspects of the Expedition to Mount Everest, 1953." *The Geographical Journal*, 120:Part 2 (1954): 186–89.

Pugh L. G. C., and M. P. Ward, "Some Effects of High Altitude on Man." *The Lancet* (December 1, 1956): 1115–21.

Punch. "A climbing girl." 61 (1871): 86.

Roche, Clare. "Women Climbers 1850–1900: A Challenge to Male Hegemony?" *Sport in History*, 33 (2013): 1–24.

Shen, Guanghao, Kangning Xie, Yili Yan, Da Jing, Chi Tang, Xiaoming Wu, Juan Liu, Tao Sun, Jianbao Zhang, and Erping Luo. "The role of oxygen-increased respirator in humans ascending to high altitude." *BioMedical Engineering OnLine*, 11:49 (2012): 1–8. http://www.biomedical-engineering-online.com/content/11/1/49, accessed January 15, 2016.

Smith, George, William Makepeace Thackeray, and Elder Smith. "Unctuous Memories." *The Cornhill Magazine*, 8 (1863): 613–17.

Stevens, Ernest Hamilton. "Dr. Paccard's Narrative. An Attempted Reconstitution," *Alpine Club Journal* (May 1929): 94–96.

Swanson, Paul L. "Shugendō and the Yoshino-Kumano Pilgrimage. An Example of a Mountain Pilgrimage." *Monumenta Nipponica*, 36 (1982): 55–84.

The Capricornian. "A Popular Bush Song." December 14, 1901, http://nla.gov.au/nla.news-article68258559, accessed February 3, 2016.

The Guardian. "Hillary of New Zealand and Tenzing reach the top." June 2, 1953, www.guardian.com, accessed October 7, 2015.

The Guardian. "Ultramarathoners Lahcen and Mohamad Ahansal: 'What's the best post-run indulgence? Sleep!'" February 20, 2015, http://www.theguardian.com/lifeandstyle/the-running-blog/2015/feb/20/lahcen-mohamad-ahansal-marathon-des-sables-trans-atlas-marathon, accessed May 16, 2016.

The Guardian. "The Eat of Battle—How the World's Armies get Fed." February 18, 2014, www.theguardian.com, accessed January 19, 2016.

The New York Times. "Shackleton's Men Kept Hope of Rescue High." September 11, 1916, www.nytimes.com, accessed February 1, 2106.

The New York Times. "'Why climb Mount Everest?' 'Because it's there' said Mallory." March 18, 1923, www.nytimes.com, accessed October 7, 2015.

The Register. "WOMEN 'SWAGGIES.'" April 6, 1926, http://nla.gov.au/nla.news-article55030263, accessed February 9, 2016.

Thesiger, Wilfred. "A New Journey in Southern Arabia." *Geographical Journal,* 108 (1946): 17.

Vanity Fair. "Interview with Tom Avery." http://www.vanityfair.com/news/2009/04/explorer-tom-avery-you-spend-forever-trekking-to-the-south-pole-you-get, accessed May 13, 2016.

Vanni, Fabrizio. *"Certaldo, le sue cipolle, lo zafferano e i caci di Lucardo."* De Strata Frācigena, XIV/2 (2008): 39–60.

Wilson, Andrew S., Emma L. Brown, Chiara Villa, Niels Lynnerup, Andrew Healey, Maria Constanza Ceruti, Johan Reinhard, Carlos H. Previgliano, Facundo Arias Araoz, Josefina Gonzalez Diez, and Timothy Taylor. "Archaeological, radiological, and biological evidence offer insight into Inca child sacrifice." *PNAS,* 110 (2013): 13322–27, http://www.pnas.org/content/110/33/13322, accessed April 26, 2016.

Wilson, R. C. "Kailas Parbat and Two Passes of the Kumaon Himalaya." *Alpine Journal,* 40 (1928): 23–26.

Websites

Allrecipes Australia. "Scroggin recipe." http://allrecipes.com.au/recipe/22564/scroggin.aspx. Accessed October 8, 2015.

Burke & Wills Web Digital Research Archive. "Financial Records of the Royal Society of Victoria's Exploration Committee." *Royal Society of Victoria Exploration Committee account book 1858–1873* (State Library of Victoria, SLV MS13071, Box 2088B/2, 1–13). List of articles and services supplied by [Richard Nash] the Government Storekeeper. http://www.burkeandwills.net.au/Stores/provisions.htm#thumb. Accessed March 30, 2016.

Burke & Wills Web Digital Research Archive. "John King's Narrative as told to Howitt at the Cooper Depot, September 1861." *Diary of Victorian Contingent Party, 13 August–7 October 1861*. State Library of Victoria, SLV MS13071, Box FB33, Item #255110. Victorian Relief Expedition Records, Alfred William Howitt's expedition diaries and notebooks. http://www.burkeandwills.net.au/Journals/King/Kings_Narrative.htm. Accessed March 30, 2016.

King's Fine Food. "King's and the Community." http://www.kingsfinefood.co.uk/articles/king_s_and_the_community. Accessed November 11, 2015.

Merriam-Webster. "Definition of S'more." www.merriamwebster.com. Accessed January 25, 2016.

Museum der Brotkultur, Ulm. "Kommissbrot," *Kleines Brotlexikon*. http://www.museum-brotkultur.de/pdf/06Brotformen%20und%20Brotsorten.pdf. Accessed February 2, 2016.

Oxford English Dictionary. "Definition of Gorp." http://www.oed.com/view/Entry/249107?redirectedFrom=gorp#eid. Accessed October 8, 2015.

Powerhouse Museum Collection Sydney. "Homemade 'Swaggie' doll, 1933." http://www.powerhousemuseum.com/collection/database/?irn=39144#ixzz3zZTbj88b. Accessed February 9, 2016.

Raleigh, Sir Walter. *The Pilgrimage*. 1618. http://quod.lib.umich.edu/e/eebo/A57518.0001.001/1:1?rgn=div1;view=fulltext. Accessed May 17, 2016.

Scientific American Blog. "What To Eat When You're High (up): Why Not Caviar? And Plenty of H2O." http://blogs.scientificamerican.com/food-matters/what-to-eat-when-you-8217-re-high-up-why-not-caviar-and-plenty-of-h2o/. Accessed November 11, 2015.

Smith, Adam. "Walker, Lucy (1836–1916)," *Oxford Dictionary of National Biography*. Oxford University Press, 2004. www.oxforddnb.com/view/article/52561. Accessed January 25, 2016.

Trademark ORIGINAL TRAIL MIX. http://www.tmfile.com/mark/?q=763459399. Accessed October 8, 2015.

University of Alberta Libraries. *Pemmican Brochure. A Christmas Present from the Manitoba Free Press*. Winnipeg, Canada: Manitoba Free Press, 1902. http://peel.library.ualberta.ca/bibliography/2635.html. Accessed July 31, 2016.

Vindolanda Tablets Online. http://vindolanda.csad.ox.ac.uk/about.shtml. Accessed July 17, 2016.

Youtube. Bovril advert featuring Chris Bonington from 1979. https://www.youtube.com/watch?v=LH3PHL6vTJw. Accessed February 1, 2016.

Index

About the Author

Demet Güzey is a freelance food and wine writer with a PhD in food science and a passion for trekking in high mountains. She has published numerous articles in academic journals and magazines, ranging from *Food Biophysics* to *Gastronomica*, and climbed some grand mountains, such as Mont Blanc and Mount Ararat.